PASTORAL POWER, CLERICAL STATE

CONTENDING MODERNITIES

Series editors: Ebrahim Moosa, Atalia Omer, and Scott Appleby

As a collaboration between the Contending Modernities initiative and the University of Notre Dame Press, the Contending Modernities series seeks, through publications engaging multiple disciplines, to generate new knowledge and greater understanding of the ways in which religious traditions and secular actors encounter and engage each other in the modern world. Books in this series may include monographs, co-authored volumes, and tightly themed edited collections.

The series will include works that frame such encounters through the lens of "modernity." The range of themes treated in the series might include war, peace, human rights, nationalism, refugees and migrants, development practice, pluralism, religious literacy, political theology, ethics, multi- and intercultural dynamics, sexual politics, gender justice, and postcolonial and decolonial studies.

Pastoral Power, Clerical State

PENTECOSTALISM, GENDER,
AND SEXUALITY IN NIGERIA

Ebenezer Obadare
FOREWORD BY JACOB K. OLUPONA

University of Notre Dame Press
Notre Dame, Indiana

Copyright © 2022 by the University of Notre Dame
Notre Dame, Indiana 46556
undpress.nd.edu
All Rights Reserved

Published in the United States of America

Library of Congress Control Number: 2022935741

ISBN: 978-0-268-20313-9 (Hardback)
ISBN: 978-0-268-20314-6 (Paperback)
ISBN: 978-0-268-20315-3 (WebPDF)
ISBN: 978-0-268-20312-2 (Epub)

To Kunle Ajibade, the unelected Guardian of Culture, for random acts of generosity too numerous to total, too prohibitive to reimburse

To Jimmy Lai and all the journalists at *Apple Daily* and to the Uyghurs, for various reasons — and for the same reason

In sweet memory of Pius Adesanmi, who exited too soon. Rest in peace, *iwọ boy jáku jàku yii*!

In societies in which religious beliefs are strong and ministers of the faith form a special class a priestly aristocracy almost always arises and gains possession of a more or less important share of the wealth and the political power.
— Gaetano Mosca, *The Ruling Class*

The frequent, and often wonderful, success of the most ignorant quacks and impostors, both civil and religious, sufficiently demonstrate how easily the multitude are imposed upon by the most extravagant and groundless pretensions. But when those pretensions are supported by a very high degree of real and solid merit, when they are displayed with all the splendour which ostentation can bestow upon them, when they are supported by high rank and great power, when they have often been successfully exerted, and are upon that account attended by the loud acclamations of the multitude, even the man of sober judgment often abandons himself to the general admiration. The very noise of those foolish acclamations often contributes to confound his understanding; and while he sees those great men only at a certain distance, he is often disposed to worship them with a sincere admiration, superior even to that with which they appear to worship themselves.
— Adam Smith, *The Theory of Moral Sentiments*

I cannot imagine what life would have been in Nigeria without our men of God, the pastors like Apostle Suleman, who leads millions like you to continuously pray for this country.... I am very, very supportive of the work of the churches, because, when governments fail, the church carries the burden of the state.
— Godwin Obaseki, Edo State Governor

CONTENTS

Foreword, by Jacob K. Olupona — xi
Preface — xvii
Acknowledgments — xxi

Introduction: Apprehending a Ubiquitous Subject — 1

ONE The Social Origins of Clerical Power in Nigeria — 23

TWO The Pastor as Political Entrepreneur — 57

THREE Erotic Pentecostalism: The Pastor as Sexual Object — 81

FOUR When Women Rebel — 97

Conclusion: Rule by Prodigy — 115

Notes — 123
Bibliography — 164
Index — 186

FOREWORD

Intense scholarly and popular discussions on the critical place of Pentecostal churches in African societies, particularly Nigeria, have grown significantly, especially since the erosion of state institutions in the 1980s. Professor Ebenezer Obadare's acclaimed book *Pentecostal Republic: Religion and the Struggle for State Power in Nigeria* has established a rigorous analytical framework for interrogating these enigmatic church movements in Nigerian politics and society. Following on the heels of *Pentecostal Republic*, Obadare's new book, *Pastoral Power, Clerical State: Pentecostalism, Gender, and Sexuality in Nigeria*, engages in depth the critical subjects of gender and sexuality in Nigeria's powerful Pentecostal churches.

Pastoral Power, Clerical State is a compelling, timely, and intellectually stimulating book. In this book Obadare enlightens us on the phenomenon of Pentecostal pastors serving as prominent national figures and celebrities in Nigerian society. Given the growing central role of charismatic Pentecostal pastors in the public sphere, Obadare is interested in answering these pertinent questions for his readers: What is responsible for the rise of Pentecostal pastors to national prominence in Nigerian society? And why are talented and charismatic young Nigerians embarking on the vocation of pastoring?

Unlike in the early period of Nigerian Christianity, when pastoring and ministerial professions were intimately connected to the struggle of the masses of the people, pastoring in many Pentecostal churches, especially those in major cities such as Lagos, Abuja, Ibadan, and Port Harcourt, is a manifestation of affluence and influence. Obadare's book deeply reflects changes in the fortunes of churchgoers against the mirror of the Pentecostal clergy. He backs his claims up with rigorous and insightful theories, ideas, and ethnographic narratives to paint a candid picture of Nigeria's society.

A critical social theorist, Obadare suggests that the popularity of these Pentecostal pastors is connected to the decline of the social status of the Nigerian intellectual class—itself an offshoot of the rapid erosion of Nigerian state institutions. Indeed, many well-educated Nigerians see the Pentecostal pastor as a miracle worker whose power transcends the rational and temporal spaces of human existence. Through the use of anecdotes, Obadare illustrates the degree to which the Pentecostal pastor exhibits this supernatural power as healer and diviner. To illustrate his argument, Obadare recounts the stories of two of his now-deceased friends. Upon their deaths, the wives of both gentlemen insisted that their dead bodies be laid out before their pastors so that they might miraculously be brought back from the dead. Here the probing sociological interpretation Obadare raises with his questions sets out squarely the rationale for his interpreting these anecdotes the way he does in order to draw from them some explanation as to why the Pentecostal pastor is given the final word as regards matters of mortality, especially when medical professionals have established the finality of such matters.

Obadare's approach establishes the norm and criteria for a sociological instead of a theological, even phenomenological, inquiry. Nevertheless, the wives of his two friends believed that the "miracles" for which the Pentecostal pastors are famed could make their dead husbands rise and walk, just as Jesus of Nazareth himself did for many during his ministry.

Obadare further answers his probing questions and addresses his bewilderment over how Nigerian intellectuals took a back seat in the nation's developmental project. He then chronicles the height of social dominance of Nigeria's intellectual elite and its eventual demise at the hands of a dictatorial government. He rightly posits that this tyrannical military government demystified the intellectual class, thereby accelerating its eventual unraveling in the eyes of the broader society. Numerous Nigerian academics in the days of military rule compromised on the side of the politics of relevance that many naïvely embraced. During this period, several announced in the hearing of their colleagues with fanfare that they had been invited to visit Dodan Barracks and Aso Rock, the seats of government, for consultation, indications that they were close to the seats of power in the country.

A master of Nigerian storytelling, Obadare utilizes major national events to elaborate on his subject. In telling about one interesting case, he recalls the consequences of the execution of Major General Mamman Jiya Vatsa, the soldier-poet—a prolific writer in his own right, who had published many works of verse and served as a patron of the Association of Nigerian Authors. The latter position cemented Vatsa's identity as a friend to members of the intellectual class, crystallizing his position as more than just an ordinary army man. The secrecy surrounding his execution and the drama accompanying the violent death he suffered traumatized many Nigerians, including the literati who had hoped to save his life through their intervention. Nigerians who witnessed the era of military dictatorship in their lifetimes will never forget the brutality of Nigerian military leaders like Ibrahim Babangida, for example. Babangida ordered the execution of his childhood friend Mamman Vatsa after his conviction by a kangaroo military court on March 5, 1986. While literary giants were still meeting on how best to intervene and save Vatsa's life, it was announced on national television that Vatsa had been executed by firing squad for plotting an alleged coup.

Beaming his scholarly searchlight on fascinating case studies like the one above, Obadare investigates the reasons for the intelligentsia's forfeiture of social space, which has been all but offered up to the Pentecostal pastors to occupy and dominate. He highlights the liaisons between the Pentecostal pastors and the players within the country's political system, who together wield immense control over the affairs of the intelligentsia, which has further weakened the influence and authority commanded by the intellectual elites of Nigeria.

Obadare investigates the manner in which the political class courts members of the intellectual class, frequently co-opting them into the political system. He establishes that the intention behind this courting may not always be straightforward, but it may be inferred that a form of legitimacy is what those making such moves are seeking. One recalls, for example, how even highly respected nationalists and intellectuals such as Samuel Aluko and Ikenna Nzimiro, distinguished professors and nationalists, along with others, served under such an authoritarian state.

Given the growing literature and research on Pentecostalism, one can argue that Obadare's unique contribution to this field is the uncommon scholarship provided in his insightful analysis of the shifting definition of "professional." In this analysis, he makes use of two lenses and archetypes: that of the "Man of Letters" (referring to both Nigeria's intelligentsia and the national nostalgia associated with this class) and the "Man of God" (referring to the male Pentecostal pastor, whose modes of authority include prayer, preaching, prophecy, healing, his attire, and making general lifestyle recommendations). Second, Obadare interrogates legal and socioanthropological work on juridical and extra-juridical power and authority. More specifically, he is concerned with the tenuous relationship between the facticity of law and regular assertions of power in the country. Reflecting on the push and pull of secularism and religion within the public sphere and, given the burgeoning liberal democratic rule and past military misrule, Obadare's work highlights Pentecostalism—and, more specifically, the leadership of the Pentecostal pastor—as filling a type of sociopolitical void.

It is also crucial to emphasize that Obadare does not describe Nigeria as a classic theocracy, nor does he identity Pentecostal pastors as a homogenous group. Additionally, his use of the pronoun "he" is intentional in this study because gender is critical in his analysis of the pastor as a social patriarch and—in some cases—as an erotic subject. What is of interest to Obadare is the overarching social veneration of Pentecostal clergy members.

The empirical approach with which Obadare begins the narrative of *Pastoral Power, Clerical State* is compelling, though in its sad opening pages he records the unfortunate deaths of his dear colleagues. The book is also essential for the methodological, multidisciplinary approach he uses to solicit valuable data for analysis. While the data is primarily ethnographical, he utilizes archival sources, including newspapers, church manuals and bulletins, and others.

While pursuing the central thesis of this evocative work, Obadare also raises pertinent topical issues that may ultimately lead to independent works on their own. Among these are how the national upheaval of the 1980s, caused by the IMF World Bank loans and conditionality, plunged Nigeria into deep poverty from which it has never recovered. While he rightly identifies this pivotal period as the "social origin of clerical power" and the current decline of the Man of Letters and the ascendancy of the Man of God. Obadare rightly contends that the decline of the university was the fulcrum of the archetype of the Pentecostal preacher. However, in the previous era, between 1960 and

1980, when Protestant Christian denominations such as the Anglican, Methodist, and Presbyterian mainly held sway as state churches in many regions of the country, theological literacy and the so-called Men of Letters were central to the functioning of the state. The universities were where pockets of enlightened society emerged, grew, and flowered, and Men of God emerging from this clerical class played a significant role in modernizing Nigerian society.

I must remark that in the era of mission churches, influential clerics such as the Anglican bishops Solomon Odutola and Seth Kale; Bolaji Idowu, the patriarch of the Methodist Church; and Edmund Ilogu, a professor of religion and highly placed cleric in the Anglican Church, were both Men of Letters and Men of God. This further points to the contrast Obadare shows in the contemporary period, when clerics have been solely Men of God. In another context, the case of President Kagame in Rwanda may teach us a lesson. Kagame ordered that every pastor was to have a theological degree to be licensed to found and run a church. In reaction, the country must push back on the mushrooming of Pentecostal churches in Rwanda. The Pentecostal pastors today *are acting not only as political entrepreneurs but also as religious entrepreneurs*. The most visible signs are the security details that accompany a pastor's entourage, which at times outclass those assigned to protect state political actors such as state governors.

The presence of clergy involvement in politics triggers questions about clerical limits in a secular society. Perhaps the chapter titled "Erotic Pentecostalism: The Pastor as Sexual Object," which advances the idea of the pastor as an erotic object, will draw both amusing and sober comments. In yet another chapter, titled "When Women Rebel," the book documents the rebellions of four women in their interactions with different pastors, a reflection of a circumscribed agency and gender. Rather than seeing women as passively succumbing to pastors' male dominance and authority, Obadare whets our appetites by showing how women have displayed both passive and active *resistance* to male authority in some Pentecostal churches. I say it whets our appetites because here Obadare throws down a gauntlet regarding a subject that deserves separate treatment in its own right. Until we see a full-blown work on the status and scope of women's authority and participation in Nigerian Pentecostalism, the scholarship on this topic, particularly in its gender context, will be incomplete. I also believe that Obadare is well poised to do subsequent work on Pentecostal women clergy in Nigeria.

Overall, this book is a fascinating read, one that should be essential reading in ministerial studies as well as studies of religion and society and global Pentecostalism. Without question, this work forwards the study of Christianity in Africa. Unlike most books available on African religion, Obadare's demonstrates the usefulness of transdisciplinary work that fuses empirical, theoretical, and ethnographic analysis to produce a robust interpretive work on the state of religion and society in contemporary Nigeria. However, and, most importantly, *Pastoral Power, Clerical State* helps to articulate what the West struggles with, a general epochal shift from the intelligentsia to clerics, particularly televangelists. While it may be too much to ask Professor Ebenezer Obadare to shine further research light on the situation of the African diaspora, since Black evangelists seem to be acting out similar scripts in the Americas to those seen in Nigeria, an interdisciplinary, cross-cultural work on Black evangelicals may be needed to add to the vast contributions of this work.

Jacob K. Olupona
Harvard University
August 2021

PREFACE

That Pentecostal pastors enjoy an unprecedented prominence in contemporary Nigerian society can hardly be disputed. In tandem with the ascendance of Pentecostalism as the most popular Christian denomination, they have captured politics, public policy, popular culture, and, crucially, the moral imagination. Without any prejudice as to how such elections are made, pastoring has become one of the most sought-after professions in a job market that has always labored for options. What accounts for the sudden rise to social visibility of Pentecostal pastors and—a related question—the attraction of pastoring for young Nigerians?

In *Pastoral Power, Clerical State* I propose that the ascent of the Pentecostal pastor is a function of the loss of social prestige by the Nigerian intelligentsia (primarily, though not exclusively, based in the universities) and that the star of the former is on the rise because, among other things, the latter's is on the wane. There is no suggestion that both the intellectual and the priestly classes cannot coexist and be concurrently dominant; what I am arguing is that, in the Nigerian context, it was the evacuation of one that prepared the ground for the emergence of the other. Such, as a matter of fact, is the social power and prestige of today's Pentecostal pastor that, judging by current trends, members of the Nigerian intelligentsia do not so much wish to compete with the pastor as desire to be like him. If the pastor secures an honorary degree to boost his renown *as a pastor*, the university professor desires the honorific "pastor" (or some such cognomen) as a way to overcome his comparative social anonymity.

The second installment of a projected trilogy on the politics of religion in the Nigerian Fourth Republic (1999–), *Pastoral Power, Clerical*

State is an account of how this mutual substitution took place. In *Pentecostal Republic*, the first installment, I argued that the inauguration of the Fourth Republic coincided with the emergence of Pentecostalism as the most assertive expression of Christianity in Nigeria and that such is Pentecostalism's influence on politics and society at large that the Republic is more appropriately described as a Pentecostal republic. Extending this argument, I advance the idea that none of the demonstrable influence of Pentecostalism can be fully understood without attention to the agency of the Pentecostal pastor. If, as I maintain, the Fourth Republic is inexplicable without recourse to the power of Pentecostalism, Pentecostalism itself gains special illumination when viewed through the lens of its ubiquitous pastorate.

The mutual substitution in question goes beyond a mere replacement of professors by pastors. At root it is, as I go on to demonstrate, a profound transition in the basis of authority from reason, on the one hand, to revelation, on the other. I call this new mode of authority rule by prodigy. Because of this, one of the big themes—arguably not the biggest, but definitely the most consequential—in the book is the degradation of the Nigerian intelligentsia, itself a product of the radical vitiation of the Nigerian academy. Whatever else it may be, the Fourth Republic is not the Republic of Letters. I do not so much attempt a comprehensive treatment of this transition as highlight and analyze things that help bolster my analysis. If anything, I hope that some of the claims I have made in relation to that epochal collapse, particularly as regards the ideological composition of the academic elite at one historical juncture, will spur further reflections on the impetus behind its deterioration. In discussing intellectuals, or, specifically, in lamenting their capitulation to the ascendant quasi-hierocracy, I am under no illusions about intellectuals, and I impute no essential or timeless virtues to them as a class. My grievance is the wholesale concession of their role, as captured by Ralf Dahrendorf: "to doubt everything that is obvious, to make relative all authority, to ask all those questions that no one else dares to ask." The ethos of rule by prodigy is the exact opposite.

When dealing with Pentecostal pastors, one cannot hope to avoid the topic of sex, or, for that matter, women. Across the Nigerian news media, salacious tales of extracurricular copulation by pastors jostle for space with incredulous reports of their miraculous performances and prophetic proclamations. Accordingly, I have analyzed the pastor not just in relation to his impact on the political space, the scale of which is all too evident, but also as a masculine object of erotic fascination able to generate sexual frisson in his female congregants. Yet, and as the book shows, the agency of women in relation to powerful pastors is not uncomplicated, with seeming sexual surrender on the one hand being leavened by stirring examples of calculated insubordination on the other.

In *Pastoral Power, Clerical State* I focus on the contemporary Nigerian Pentecostal pastor, the social antecedents of his emergence, and his expanding influence on the country's conjoined political, sexual, and cultural topography. Therefore, the historical backdrop and illustrations I have summoned are primarily Nigerian. Nonetheless, this is also a book about a social actor that is not unknown in other African countries, particularly those—Ghana, Zimbabwe, Kenya, Uganda, and South Africa immediately come to mind—where Pentecostal churches have more or less established a theological monopoly. For every pastor casually resurrecting a dead body in Zimbabwe, there is another in Ghana valiantly restoring "power" to the deflated members of male congregants.

The Pentecostal pastor, at any rate, is a transnational actor, active in the commercial, political, and cultural lives of neighboring countries and distant regions. Thus, even as I have been guided by Nigerian examples, I have also, necessarily, linked up to personnel and parallel events in other parts of the region. More to the point, my analysis is firmly planted in the relevant socioanthropological discourses and perspectives on power, authority, legitimacy, gender, and sexuality, both in Africa and globally. Whether in Zimbabwe, Ghana, Kenya, or Uganda, we witness the same crisis of intellectual authority and elite reproduction, helped along, among other things, by the capitulation of the gown to the town, as seen in the former's wholesale assumption of the latter's mores and fetishes and, truth be told, its pettinesses and indulgences. Amid this tumult, the pertinent question, it seems to me, is not why anyone would want to become a pastor but rather why any right-thinking person would pass up the opportunity. Straddling the divide between the spiritual and the temporal spheres and wielding spiritual authority in a context in which the power of invisible forces over daily reality is axiomatic, the Pentecostal pastor, in seeming confirmation that religious matters are invariably a critical nexus for matters that transcend "mere" belief, provides a path to broader sociological questions around rule, legitimacy, class, and status in Africa—and beyond.

While I build on and extend the argument in *Pentecostal Republic*, claiming that the ground for the emergence of the pastor was prepared by the debasement of the intelligentsia necessitates that my historical compass be widened to include the period prior to the inauguration of the Fourth Republic. As a result, and owing largely to the need to demonstrate how the intellectual class surrendered its former glory, parts of *Pastoral Power, Clerical State* are, in effect, a prequel to the account in *Pentecostal Republic*. No one doubts that the Nigerian academy is in stasis or that the pastor is regnant. In *Pastoral Power, Clerical State* I posit a direct causal relationship between the two.

ACKNOWLEDGMENTS

Several people have helped in bringing this book to completion. Although I cannot hope to name them all, I do thank them all with all my heart.

I undertook field research for the book with financial support from the Contending Modernities Program of the Kroc Institute for International Peace Studies, University of Notre Dame. I wish to extend my sincere gratitude to the two coordinators, Emmanuel Katongole and Scott Appleby, and to my fellow Contending Modernities grantees: Cecelia Lynch, Elias Bongmba, and Ludovic Lado. Both Emmanuel and Scott read the first draft of the complete manuscript and gave me plenty to chew on. I am in their debt. Cecelia, Elias, and Ludovic have heard and critiqued various parts of the book over the years and have favored me with their time and intelligence. I am humbled by their generosity. Dania Straughn, James Adams, Paola Bernardini, and staff of the Contending Modernities program treated me with unbelievable courtesy. I owe them all a ton of gratitude. Stephen Little worked with me to organize my data and read and commented on individual chapters as I wrote them. I thank him for his kindness and encouragement.

I am lucky to be surrounded by mentors, colleagues, and friends with a genuine interest in my work. Among this cohort, I am especially indebted to Professor "Malam" Olufemi Taiwo, Wale Adebanwi, Tade Ipadeola, Kunle Ajibade, Akin Adesokan, James Yeku, and Omolade Adunbi for conversations that offered me guidance, alerted me to errors, and helped untie many a difficult knot. Malam and Wale took time off their own writing to read the original draft of the manuscript and offer thoughtful critiques. I thank them for making me look good.

In Nigeria, Wale Fatade, Gbemisola Animasawun, Oluwaseun Saibu, and Ben Ezeamalu helped in various ways with data collection. Gbenga Osinaike, editor-in-chief of *Church Times Nigeria*, made his publication's archive available to me and provided unique insights and perspectives. All were selfless with their time and resources, and I cannot thank them enough.

I am profoundly grateful for the support of my colleagues in the University of Kansas Department of Sociology, most especially Bob Antonio, Joane Nagel, and David N. Smith. I couldn't have hoped for a more wonderful set of colleagues, and I thank them from the bottom of my heart for genuinely caring about me, my family, and my work.

Against all odds, and under tremendous personal pressure, Sam Kendrick came through with the consolidated bibliography. I am in debt to her, not just for that, but for having come to my rescue time and again over the past few years. Sam is the person I call whenever I am at sea, which is all the time, and without her becalming composure under fire, and her utter and totally frightening competence in all things technology, my life would be poorer.

Marilyn Martin was one hell of a copyeditor, a genuine linguistic detective with an uncanny ability to smoke out rogue constructions. Her rigor and pertinacity helped procure freedom for many an idea that would have perished in the prison of my singular muddleheadedness. My debt to her is incalculable.

Over the past several years, I have presented different parts of the book as works in progress at academic conferences and invited seminars in various African, European, and American institutions. These include the Institute for Religion, Culture and Public Life (IRCPL), Columbia University; the Conference on Evangelical Christianity and the Transformation of Africa, Radcliffe Institute for Advanced Study, Harvard University; the African Interdisciplinary Studies Hub, University of Missouri; the Workshop on Pentecostalism and Sexual Citizenship in Africa, hosted by the Center for Religion and Public Life, School of Philosophy, Religion and History of Science, University of Leeds, United Kingdom; the Leeds University Centre for African Studies (LUCAS) Seminar; the Conference on Religion, Governance and Humanitarianism in Africa, organized by the Ujamaa Centre at the University of KwaZulu-Natal and hosted by the Seth Mokitimi Methodist Seminary, Pietermaritzburg, South Africa; the Kansas African Studies Center (KASC) Faculty Seminar series; and the Department of Geography and Atmospheric Science Colloquium, University of Kansas. I thank the organizers of these events for the opportunity to present my work and the various audiences for their patient listening and engagement.

I wrote the first draft of the manuscript amid the uncertainty of the Covid-19 lockdown between March and September 2020. It goes without saying that I could not have hoped to pull it off without the support of the ever-indulgent staff of Obadare Homeland Security. As ever, my most important gratitude is to Kemi, my compact model of matriarchal metronomy. Like Nemanja Matić in his pomp, vigilantly screening the defense, it is Kemi who, constantly in motion, ensures that everything is ticking along on the domestic front, all the while keeping two barbarous teenagers in check. Without her, I—and they—would be lost.

An earlier version of chapter 3 appeared in *Citizenship Studies* 22, no. 6: 603–17 (2018) as "The Charismatic Porn-Star: Social Citizenship and the West African Pentecostal Erotic." This version has been substantially revised.

Introduction

Apprehending a Ubiquitous Subject

Between July 2014 and June 2015, I lost two close friends. One was a successful Lagos-based human rights lawyer, the other a social scientist of international renown who had taught with distinction at one of the first-generation (as they are called) Nigerian universities in the western part of the country. Since I was not aware that either of them had been indisposed before their quite unexpected passing, I sorrowfully reached out to close family friends to inquire as to the circumstances leading to their deaths. Although both had died months apart in different locations, I was struck by a certain regularity in the accounts of what had transpired in the hours immediately following their apparent biological deaths.

DEPARTURES

On the day he breathed his last, the lawyer had been scheduled to take a work-related trip out of Lagos, only for his health to deteriorate rapidly. It was clear that he needed urgent medical attention, and it took his wife, a senior physiotherapist, pulling all the stops at the nearby Lagos State University Teaching Hospital (LASUTH), Ikeja, for a couple of doctors to agree to break a Nigerian Medical Association (NMA) strike then in force in order to attend to him. However, by the time they arrived at the hospital it was too late, and he was declared dead on arrival.

The story should have ended there but for the insistence of his wife, a member of the Redeemed Christian Church of God (RCCG), Nigeria's most popular Pentecostal group, on taking her husband's body to the RCCG's Redemption Camp on the Lagos-Ibadan Expressway, some 10 kilometers away. On getting to the Redemption Camp, the lawyer's lifeless body was laid out inside the main auditorium while an urgent message was sent to the general overseer, Pastor Enoch Adeboye. Daddy G.O., as he is affectionately called, was apparently engaged elsewhere, but he sent, through a personal assistant, a white handkerchief and a bottle of "anointing oil" with instructions that the handkerchief should be soaked with the oil, which should then be used to wipe down my friend's lifeless body. His wife and a handful of family members gathered at the scene eagerly complied, all the while praying at the top of their voices and speaking in tongues.[1]

With dusk approaching and chances of resurrection looking more and more unlikely, a decision was taken to take the dead body back to Lagos, where it was deposited at a mortuary.

Something similar had happened in the case of the social scientist. A professor at one of the church-owned private universities in Ogun State, he had suddenly taken ill in the middle of the night and had given up the ghost even as his wife was seeking to rally medical assistance. But just like the dead lawyer's wife, his wife immediately reached out to a well-known Nigerian pastor, who also happens to be the owner of the university where the professor taught. Fortunately, he was available and drove down to meet the distressed wife and other family members. He then prayed over the dead body, assuring the small gathering that the dead professor would rise up of his own accord "within twelve hours." He did not.

Obviously, there is a moral in the foregoing anecdotes regarding the poverty of physical infrastructure in Nigeria, particularly the perennial problem of reliable access to healthcare. However, while not impertinent to the narrative of this book (problems of infrastructure remain, after all, the warp and woof of the broader social crisis that the book posits), they are not my primary objects of inquiry.[2] I am interested, rather, in the denial of the apparent finality of biomedical death by the respective wives and families of the deceased lawyer and professor and their decisions, individually, to approach their respective pastors as the final arbiters on such grave matters. The fact that the bereaved, understandably, will lean on anything for succor, especially where the normal structures of mourning for family groups no longer avail or are no longer the substructure of emotional support for many, does not detract from my emphasis.

It matters, of course, that in both cases the families were, in Pentecostal parlance, desperate for "divine intervention." Yet it is worth noting that it is not just, quite literally, in such matters of life and death as the foregoing that a cross section of Nigerians right up and down the social hierarchy often actively seek such divine intervention through the instrumentality of a "Man of God." A special report published in June 2019 by *Punch* reveals the reality of an inverted hierarchy in which Nigerians either second-guess medical advice by seeking a second opinion from a Man of God or totally set aside medical opinion whenever it clashes with the opinion of a "prayer warrior," as some pastors are called. According to the report, in cases involving the death of a loved one, it is not unusual for the deceased's relatives to wait for a few days before agreeing to release the body to a morgue. This is because "the doctor can never convince the deceased's relatives that this person can no longer be revived, so they will say he is alive, until the man of God says otherwise."[3] In lieu of additional evidence, it suffices to say at this point in our analysis that the foregoing is consistent with the argument in *Pentecostal Republic* regarding how, among Nigerians, religion has displaced other systems as the framework for living and relating to the world and that this has meant a reordering of explanatory regimes for social and other phenomena in the country.

I ask: How is it that in contemporary Nigeria (and indeed in many other African countries where Pentecostal Christianity exercises an outsize influence) the pastor has come to occupy such a central place in the social imaginary, to such an extent that medical and other forms of professional judgment must defer to him? What does it mean for scientific-medical expertise to be subordinated to or *dependent on* the validation of a pastor?[4] What becomes of institutions in state and civil society when a large number of people in a community put their faith in the figure of the pastor? What specific transformations in social trust, state-society relations, politics, the economy, legitimacy, and authority are evoked by the recent ascendance and continued visibility of the contemporary Pentecostal pastor?

THE ARGUMENT

In my quest to adduce answers to these critical questions, I have written *Pastoral Power, Clerical State* to make a specific contribution to the extensive and growing literature on Pentecostalism, primarily within an African context,[5] but with global ramifications always on the radar. While this body of work is particularly perceptive about the unique power of Pentecostalism to upset and reimagine existing sociopolitical and sexual relations and hierarchies, it remains, with some significant exceptions,[6] more or less silent on the figure of the pastor. This omission is critical because, as I go on to demonstrate, not only is the pastor an essential cog in the elaboration of Pentecostal culture, wielding a tremendous influence on congregants and the society at large, but also the figure of the pastor can be a point of entry into broader topics not usually discussed in relation to pastors whose discussion their recent visibility mandates. Therefore, and in an advance on the body of work just mentioned, I am not interested in the contemporary Pentecostal pastor only as a religious figure or authority. Instead, I portray and analyze him as the logical consummation of a many-threaded social process originating in the sociopolitical and economic discombobulation of the 1980s in Nigeria, if not indeed across Africa. In the process, I outline the passage (some might argue a declension) of authority from yesterday's "Man of Letters" to today's "Man of God." Parenthetically—and I will have more to say about this later on—I should declare right away that in this book I use "Man of Letters" more out of nostalgic affection than out of sociological precision. What I really have in mind is "the intellectual elite," primarily, though not exclusively, based in the universities. As Thomas Heyck has reminded us, the social class—nay, the era (early and mid-Victorian)—that "men of letters" appropriated is now extinct.[7] Whenever I say "Man of Letters" therefore, I have in mind more or less what Samuel Taylor Coleridge captured as "the clerisy of a nation, that is, its learned men, whether poets, or philosophers, or scholars."[8] In the Nigerian context, one might, with understandable nervousness, add journalists. The cause of my nervousness is simple: the crisis that has sapped the Nigerian academy of its old vigor has produced a commensurate stagnation across the media.

While this is not the place for an elaborate discussion of the idea of the intellectual,[9] it seems necessary nonetheless to indicate how I view intellectuals—and why their substitution by the figure of the pastor is of such moment. William Ellery Channing's definition of an intellectual as "whoever seeks truth with an earnest mind, no matter when or how"[10] appeals both because it emphasizes the centrality of the pursuit of truth and, in my judgment, disposes of the debate over who qualifies to be regarded as an intellectual. "Everyone harbors the gene" would be Channing's answer. That being said, although I am partial to this elastic understanding of the intellectual, the interest of the book, as earlier indicated, is in a narrow band of "professional" intellectuals. When I refer to intellectuals, I am thinking of a class of people for whom, in the words of Lewis Coser, ideas "have far more than mere instrumental value: they have terminal value. Intellectuals may not be more curious than other men, but theirs is what Thorstein Veblen has aptly called *idle* curiosity."[11] My basic intuition about intellectuals is that, precisely because of their commitment to ideas beyond their instrumental value, every society needs them; accordingly, says Syed Hussein Alatas, "A society without a functioning group of intellectuals is deprived of a certain level of consciousness and insight into vital problems."[12] Because, for various reasons, that need for "insight into vital problems" is arguably more acute across postcolonial societies, the poverty is more achingly felt. Hence, if the reader detects a whiff of an impatient anti-clericalism within these pages, it is at bottom a yearning for some sort of intellectual restoration, which I happily admit is one of the founding impulses behind the book.

A second body of work with which this book is in conversation is the socioanthropological and legal literature on power and authority in Africa,[13] particularly in its emphasis on the elusive question of rule and legitimacy. I am interested, for one thing, in the legal understanding of power, particularly where what exists in reality coincides with the mandates and requirements of law. For another, I am intrigued by departures from such coincidences, insofar as they enable a deeper understanding of how power is composed and operates *as a matter of fact*, and what the tension between what the law specifies and what brute facticity demands means for the everyday performance of authority in Nigeria. Third, given the common assumption among the public that secular authority is permanently shadowed by and in fact is impotent sans some form of spiritual enabling, an assumption that many holders of secular office give teeth to with their actions, I am interested in what those transactions—overt and covert—between secular and religious agents say about the exercise of power within a notionally democratic matrix. For Nigeria and other African countries now finally beginning to see military rule in their rearview mirrors, that this is an important consideration goes without saying, especially as, for many of them, the key political question about liberal democracy is that of the locus of rule. This was the reason why, in the heyday of resistance to military rule in the late 1980s, sundry social movements and civil society groups rallied under the banner of "people power," under the assumption that liberal democracy is the regime best equipped to underwrite it. Thus, my postulation of Pentecostal pastors as a new axis of authority is a specific nod at the problems and contradictions of power and authority in a context in which democratic rule, emergent from the ruins of yesterday's martial despotism, is yet to fully assert itself. In other words, the collapse of military (mis)rule, the nascent nature of liberal democratic rule, the escape into religion to relieve the existential consequences of economic collapse and moral failures on all fronts, not least in the spheres of governance and social relations—all this created a vacuum that Pentecostal pastors have filled.

With these bodies of work as interlocutors, in *Pastoral Power, Clerical State* I advance two related arguments, as follows: First, I suggest that the emergence of the contemporary Pentecostal pastor on the social scene in many African countries reflects a fundamental rupture—and realignment—in the basis, formation, and mobilization of authority in these societies. If, as I go on to expound, the contemporary Pentecostal pastor has become an existential micromanager, a blend of spiritual guide, political consultant, statesman without portfolio, financial coach, prophet, seer, general overseer, marriage counselor, matchmaker, social influencer, peddler of aphrodisiacs, author, fashion icon, playboy, travel advisor, all-around celebrity, and, last but not least, a hypermasculine object of erotic fascination, it is, I argue, because conventional poles of authority have waned, opening up a crack in the social fabric that the figure of the pastor has happily stepped into. One key contribution of this book is my tracing of the historical sociology of this process of decomposition and reconfiguring of authority.

Second, I claim that the pastor's newfangled authority is the upshot of Pentecostalism's infiltration of politics, economic life, and cultural production in much of Africa, a process I elaborated in my last book.[14] Accordingly, while this book is, on the one hand, a critical examination of how pastors have annexed considerable social power, effectively establishing an aristocracy of wonderment, on the other hand, it is an analysis of the social crucible in which this annexation has taken place. For precisely this reason, my interest in the book is not *just* in political authority, but, given the contention that the pastor's influence spills over across a variety of social domains, authority in a much more capacious sense.

DISCLAIMERS

To be sure, in *Pastoral Power, Clerical State* I do not claim that Nigeria is run by the clerical or theocratic class or that it is a theocracy. As a matter of fact, the country's perennial struggle to "clearly articulate the relationship between religion and the state," in the words of Isaac Terwase Sampson,[15] by and large rules out that possibility. What I affirm is that, owing to a combination of factors that I shall elaborate, the outsize visibility and influence of the Pentecostal pastorate in contemporary Nigeria is such that the country is more or less a clerical state. Writing this book is my way of trying to capture the reality that, today, it is the pastor who is aggressively courted and feted, not just by the corporate and political classes but also, crucially, by the underclass. He may not have a constitutionally defined role, at least not yet; in the meantime, the pastor is the supreme authority appealed to by various segments of the society. In this regard, there is more than mere symbolism in the two opening anecdotes, where, as we saw, the final determination of the fate of two authentic members of the intelligentsia—a lawyer and a professor—was entrusted to two leading Pentecostal pastors.

To argue in this way is to beg some antecedent questions about the character of the (Nigerian) state. For instance: If there is a clerical state, where does that leave the real state? Whither, for instance, its conceit as the ultimate depository of legitimate authority? Part of what my analysis aims to draw out is the profound transformation in the character of the state, especially the logic of its recession into what

Jean and John Comaroff call "governance-by-franchise and into an institutional nexus for the distribution of public assets into private hands."[16] Occupying territories surrendered by a state in retreat and seemingly vanquishing other competitors within the civic space, pastors, headlining a revitalized and appropriative Pentecostalism, are, I claim, among the foremost beneficiaries of this logic of organized dereliction. As bona fide members of an expanded power elite and seemingly set apart by the halo of spiritual capital, they alert us to critical apertures and weaknesses in both the state and civil society.

The Pentecostal pastorate may be collectively influential, but it is by no means homogeneous. All pastors may be equal; but some are more equal than others. There are, for instance, important differences between, say, Pastor Adeboye of the Redeemed Church (Daddy G.O.) and Pastor Tunde Bakare of the Latter Rain Assembly, just as there are important differences between them and T. B. Joshua of the Synagogue, Church of All Nations (SCOAN). Ibadan-based *Paito Wa* (Gbade Ogunlana) and Francis Madojemu of The Bridge Network seem set apart by the social thrust of their apostleship, while Femi Aribisala of Healing Wings, Victoria Island, Lagos, is a one-man ecclesiastical mutiny. (I say more about him in the next chapter.) Yet these important differences—of class, education, aspiration, political preference, primary audience, and personal temperament, not to mention theology, differences I will address throughout the book—while underlining the need to be attentive to critical cleavages that undercut the appearance of homogeneity, do not vitiate my basic contention regarding the authority and power of the Pentecostal pastorate *as a social cohort*. The pastors may differ in outlook and personae; as a matter of fact, some pastors, albeit within a larger struggle for validation and prestige, go out of their way to separate themselves from the rest by cultivating markers of distinction in their mannerisms, dress, coiffures, and automobiles. Nonetheless, those differences pale into relative insignificance in an economy in which pastors drive social discourse and enjoy almost unqualified social veneration.

ON AUTHORITY

Wedged between parallel normative and descriptive uses, the idea of authority is perennially elusive. In the analysis that follows, it is understood as the right to rule or command, the "commanders" in this case being the clerical elite and the "commanded" those who submit to their authority of fall under their spell. Classically, and contra power, authority requires a moment of consent, some modicum of morality, and a sense that it is *right*, prima facie, to obey or concede to it that is not motivated by fear or consequences. What does clerical authority in Nigeria derive from, what is its content, and what explains obedience to it? In the first place, and as I go on to explain in the next chapter, it is born of social and intellectual dislocation and turbulence; in other words, it is a product of concrete sociopolitical and economic factors that combined to undermine the authority of the intelligentsia. Furthermore, insofar as it is grounded in claims to supernatural "intelligence" that can be accessed by only a few, it is sustained by an agreement among the commanded (whether members of the political elite or ordinary citizens) as to the reality of that intelligence, the ways to access it, and its potency. Clerical authority exists in tension with the authority of the state, the latter of which is, at least in principle, superior. This raises fundamental questions about the implications of clerical authority as to what goes on inside the political arena. Since, for instance, reconciliation of any potential conflict between the two must rest on some overarching tenets, what are those tenets, and what normative traditions do they derive from? In reality, potential conflicts tend to be obviated by the deference of members of the political elite to clerical authority (it is not the same without some form of collective awe), which explains why power frequently shows up in places or agents either not recognized by, or totally unknown to, the law.

Now, there are two sides to my argument on the newfangled authority of the pastor—how he came to acquire it and how he exercises it. The first, as already indicated, relates to the social upheaval that simultaneously eroded the authority of the Man of Letters and led to the enthronement of the Man of God. Being neither completely "traditional" nor "modern," but in fact, as I shall argue, a remarkable fusion of both, the authority of the pastor is mobilized via, among other things, prophecy, prayer, official visitation, and the force of charisma. Prophecy and prayer essentially possess the same ideological utility as technologies of social control, allowing the pastorate to more or less take possession of and shape the national narrative. By praying for the country for relief from travails vouchsafed only to him and by forecasting tribulations whose occurrence the state can guard against only through prayer, the pastor channels a mode of authority through revelation. Through visitation—to Aso Rock, seat of presidential power; state governors; local government authorities (LGAs); sundry state parastatals; and media houses—the pastor, operating essentially as a statesman without portfolio, legitimizes his social standing as a person of eminence.

In these performances, and in ways that bring to mind Patrick Chabal and Jean-Pascal Daloz's argument regarding the ostensible "re-traditionalization" of African society,[17] the ancestral ghosts of "traditional" authority unfailingly follow in the pastor's wake. This is what I mean by saying that the contemporary pastor represents a fusion of the modern and "pre-modern" forms of authority. In his contemporary incarnation, implied in my reference to him as an existential micromanager, the Pentecostal pastor harks back to the African traditional ruler, whose authority spanned both spiritual and temporal zones of life.

Nor is that all. There is also, as I shall demonstrate, a real sense in which this recession into traditional authority is also an embrace of the masculinity that one often sees enfolded into it. For example, it is clear that when members of the Redeemed Church, and with evident ardor, refer to Pastor Adeboye as "Daddy," it goes beyond the culturally sanctioned respect for someone of his age—or status. Central to the authority of Daddy G.O., as a representative of the new Pentecostal pastorate, is a form of masculinity that, I will argue, is not without an erotic dimension. For every "Daddy," there is a "Mummy." Nevertheless, at the risk of being reductionist about the complex interplay of gender and sexual dynamics in many Pentecostal churches, it seems to me that, in more than a few instances, Mummy's role is to reinforce the status of Daddy as a symbol of patriarchy.

Joseph Raz has reminded us that "not everyone who has authority can make something authoritative, not everyone can make something bind."[18] In applying this insight to the nature of pastoral authority in Nigeria, we perceive, first, that pastoral authority carries significant fractures and punctuations. What I mean by this is that, although, as I contend, the contemporary Pentecostal pastor is imbued with all the attributes of an uberauthority—one whose word sometimes carries the weight, if not force, of law—that does not mean that he always gets his way. As I have shown with the example of the 2015 presidential election,[19] the fact that the Pentecostal pastoral elite is influential and presides over large congregations does not *necessarily* mean that its political preferences, for instance, always prevail. Hence, it matters, as I demonstrate, that the pastor in reality splits his *spiritual* authority with a constellation of "divines," ranging from seers to palm readers, mediums, psychics, shamans, Muslim clerics, witch doctors, astrologers, and other spiritual practitioners normally categorized as "traditional." Indeed, one of the more fascinating aspects of contemporary African spirituality is the open and persistent traffic between the traditional world of the diviner, and the modern world of the pastor, recalling J.D.Y. Peel's insight, specifically in regard to Yoruba spirituality, of "the epistemological priority of interaction."[20]

WHY PASTORS?

I am often asked why anyone would want to pursue pastoring as a career. I think the answer is simple. In a social milieu in which the opportunity for upward social mobility is drastically limited, pastoring, as Karen Lauterbach's study on Ghana confirms and as I shall demonstrate, offers the young African agent perhaps the best opportunity of becoming "somebody." The more interesting question, in my opinion, and as I go on to show, is this: Why wouldn't anyone want to become a pastor, considering, inter alia, the relative ease of becoming one (barriers to entry ranging from low to nonexistent), the social prestige that accrues to the contemporary pastor, and the ethical indulgence granted to him based on the perception of his "anointing"? In *Pastoral Power, Clerical State* I argue that, given an environment in which anonymity is the equivalent of social death, pastoring is the ultimate repudiation of social invisibility. It is the ultimate prize in that unique social struggle that Adéléke Adéèkó describes as the "pursuit of eminence,"[21] the eminent receiving not only attention and certain social advantages but, most important, the ability to bypass the law to the point of practically becoming an exception to it.

That is why, even for many ordinarily successful professionals, it is no longer enough to secure excellence or renown in one's chosen field. For example, in a growing number of cases a university professor, perhaps in his own case tacitly admitting a real degradation in status as a professor, *still* aspires to be a pastor, not just because of the awe that spiritual authority commands, as he rightly calculates, but precisely because of the tremendous social capital that redounds to the pastor. He rightly recognizes the social logic according to which doors otherwise closed to other experts, including members of the intelligentsia, are flung open for the pastor; how the pastor, contra other kinds of "experts," tends to be given the benefit of the doubt; and how, in general, the pastor is crowned with a kind of spiritual and secular halo. In a status-conscious Nigerian society, being a pastor, it would seem, offers the *ultimate* status—a place, ostensibly, beyond scrutiny or censure. Novelist Elnathan John has it right: "Being a pastor is one of the most rewarding things you can do as a Nigerian."[22] The "reward" here, as I go on to show, is not just financial but includes a variety of social allowances and indulgences that technically place the pastor in a state of ecclesiastical exception.

Partly due to the aforementioned social regard accruing to the person of the pastor, and partly due to the opportunities for self-fashioning, not to mention accumulation, that the position licenses, the number of people claiming to be pastors has increased exponentially, leading to interesting public conversations on how to separate "genuine" from "fake" pastors. Other than placing this controversy in the broader Nigerian moral economy in which the ersatz permanently exists in tension—and contention—with the real,[23] I have no interest in whether a pastor is genuine or fake. What interests me is the category—its appeal, its enchantments, and, staying with the theme of enchantment, why it casts such a powerful spell on the popular imagination.

Although I use "pastor," "the pastorate," and "the cleric" almost interchangeably, I am for the most part referring to pastors of the Pentecostal variant. They are the focus of my analysis, and, minus one or two exceptions, I distinguish between them and the bulk of the Protestant or Catholic clergy, which, in its heyday, was a significant player in the sociopolitical process, specifically, as Wale Adebanwi has shown, in the arbitration of political conflicts.[24] That the latter has ceded ground, if not prestige or social standing, to the former, is inarguable. This process of elite substitution, as I advanced in *Pentecostal Republic*, is inseparable from the broader dynamic of Pentecostal Christianity's hijack and continued domination of the religious space over the course of the Nigerian Fourth Republic. The distinction between the Pentecostal elite and the old Christian clergy could not be more stark, and continued tensions between them reflect genuine struggles over social power and resources (more of which appear to have accrued to the Pentecostal elite), legitimate differences on the role of Christianity and Christian leaders in democratic politics in particular, and in the public sphere as a whole.

Introduction 13

How crucial is the figure of the Pentecostal pastor in the contemporary constellation of divines? Numerical growth and sheer ubiquity capture something of that salience. Yet appearances can be deceiving, and, at any rate, there is a category of social fact to which statistics cannot do justice. At such times, it helps to look for other indications in the social economy, for instance, jokes and caricatures, which, as I have argued elsewhere,[25] constitute a unique barometer for measuring the cultural mood. A few years ago, a parody of a classic Yoruba poem, *"Ise l'oogun ishe"* (translation: "Work Is the Cure for Poverty"), by the late J. F. Odunjo, started circulating in the Nigerian blogosphere. Contra the spirit of the original poem, which celebrates the virtues of industry and persistence, the parody preaches the opposite. For instance, instead of counseling diligence and application, it exhorts young people to go into politics as a means of getting rich in short order. Should that fail, it enjoins, young people should consider becoming pastors, for, apparently, this has no equal as the quickest route to untold riches in contemporary Nigeria. The portion of the parody regarding the figure of the contemporary pastor is worth quoting in full:

Iṣẹ́ Pastor sì tún ń sọni d'ọ̀gá
Also, sweating as Pastor sets you up in life

Múra kí o kọ́ ọ dáradára
Apply yourself to learn exactly how

Kí o wá 'Olúgbohùn'; 'Ohun-awí-f'Ọgbọ́-l'Ọgbọ́-gbọ́'
The modulated voice can hold thousands in thrall

Kí ìdámẹ̀wá, ẹ̀bùn àti ọọrẹ máa wọlé bọ̀ lókù
So tithes and offerings can berth and breathe with you

Private jets á wá fi ilé rẹ sopo
So private jets can hug within your hangars

Big mansions á wá fọ̀dẹ̀dẹ̀ rẹ sọ̀nà
And your plush mansions can reach across the globe

Taa ló ńjẹ́ Jésù, Kínni wọ́n ńpè ní Bíbélì
Who is the Christ—what on earth are scriptures?

Lójú owó burúkú, owó ibi?
When satanic money is busy speaking?

Ọ̀rẹ́, bí o rí ọ̀pọ̀ ènìyàn Tí ó ńfi pastor sẹ̀rínrín
My friend, when you see them mocking Pastors

Sọ́ra kí o má fara wé wọn
Look out, do not as much as humor them

Torí owó ńlá, owó burúkú ni ńbẹ lọ́wọ́ wọn
There is Godless wealth beyond belief with Pastors

Sùgbọ́n asoroiyanro
Yet, a caveat has its place as I exhort or else an ancient error repeats itself

Lo pa Elempe akoko nijosi
Of Elenpe's generic claim that the calabash

Tó ní igbá wúwo lọ́pọ̀, ó jàwo lọ
Weighs heavier than ceramics—for which he paid

Kìí kúku ṣe gbogbo pastor ayé là ńbáwí
These robes of words won't fit every Shepherd

Sùgbọ́n òjò ló kéyẹlé pọ̀ mádìẹ
Though doves and chickens must co-habit when rainstorms cart their kind together

Ẹni burúkú bá ẹni rere jẹ pọ̀ọ̀!
Some scoundrels make monsters of men

Ṣé ẹgbẹ́ ẹyẹ lẹyẹ́ ń wọ́ tọ̀ lókè
Birds follow their own in the skies

Ẹgbẹ́ ẹja lẹja ń wọ́ tọ̀ lódò
As fish follow their kind in the seas

Àwọn pastor irú èyí níí folè joyè
The clerics we castigate enthrone thieves

Àwọn á torí owó wọn a gbọlá fún ẹni ibi
For filthy lucre they fete the foulest

Ṣùgbọ́n gbogbo ẹni ọba ayé kò rí
But though terrestrial kings turn blind eyes

Kedere Ọba ọ̀run ńrí wọn
The King above clearly discerns designs

Ìyókù di ọjọ́ ìdájọ́; ọjọ́ ẹlẹ̀rù-jẹ̀jẹ̀
That must unravel come the Judgement Day

Wòó, má fòwúrọ̀ seré ńtìẹ; ọ̀rẹ́ mi
Do not dissipate your youth, my friend

Múra sí IṢẸ́, ọjọ́ ńlọ.
*Apply yourself to LABOUR, time flies.*²⁶

No doubt, this parodic poem is a searing indictment of the prevailing moral economy in contemporary Nigeria, and it speaks eloquently to Nigerians' celebrated talent for fashioning comic material from the abundance of everyday travails.²⁷ But, as is the wont of every effective burlesque, this one also trains its sights on a moral truth. The truth in question is the banalization of pastoring, enfolded within a larger deregulation of (Christian) spirituality in the country, a process in which Pentecostalism has played a key role. For my purpose in this book, what is of interest is not necessarily the ethical indictment of pastoring as encoded in the parody or the fact that the pastor has become a figure of mockery, a phenomenon analyzed in Moradewun Adejunmobi's work on standup comedy and the ethics of popular performance.²⁸ If anything, the targeting of the pastor as a figure of fun merely confirms his social significance. Consequently, my interest is in the emergence of the pastor as a person of consequence, a figure of authority with an undeniable hold on the public imaginary.

A NOTE ON GENDER

Throughout, "he" is my pronoun of choice for a pastor. This is not because there are no female pastors in Nigeria. For instance, Funke

Adejumo, founder and senior pastor of Agape Christian Ministries Inc., Akure, is one of the best-known pastors, male or female, in Nigeria. But, compared to the men, female pastors are few, are less visible, and, evidently, have not had a commensurate impact on the politics, economy, and culture of the country with male pastors. The fact that many of the ministries pair men with women, and some of the women are significant, if not more so than some of their male counterparts, does not invalidate this claim. At any rate, the bulk of pastors who have played a major role in the politics and culture of the Nigerian Fourth Republic (1999–) and whose actions, virtuous or perverse, continue to steal the headlines are male. No doubt, a study of female pastors,[29] whether alone or in relation to their husbands (who, more often than not, tend to be pastors themselves) will deepen and enrich our understanding of the pastorate specifically and of gender dynamics within the church and the broader society more broadly, but that is not the path I have chosen here.

That is not to say that I am foreclosing on the opportunity to consider the gender dimension of my subject. Far from it. In reality, gender is key to my analysis, as evidenced by the idea of the pastor as an erotic subject; my focus on the intersection of gender, patriarchy, seniority, and class; my analysis of the ambiguous agency of pastors' wives; and, finally, my treatment of encounters between four male pastors and the "useless" women who were moved to challenge their authority. In the lattermost aspect, the analysis of gender enables me to show, on the one hand, the disruptive power of individual women in different real-life situations, and, on the other, the socially inscribed limits of the same power.

A NOTE ON DATA; OR, ON THE DIFFICULTY—AND REWARDS— OF INTERVIEWING THE PASTORS

I interviewed several Nigerian pastors for this study, and the process—of trying to set up an interview, of setting up a date, or, as I would discover, of having the nozzle of interrogation dramatically pointed at me for a change—was an eye-opener in terms of my attempt to grasp the sociology of the contemporary Nigerian pastor. With nearly all respondents, my affiliation with an American university was a magic wand that opened doors, though, in a few cases, it was not nearly enough to avert an unmistakable chill in the reception I received. Was this purgatory for the few unflattering essays I had published in the Nigerian media? Difficult to tell. There was the pastor who initially agreed to be interviewed and then canceled as I was pulling into the parking lot of his office on Victoria Island, Lagos, and another who took one sweeping sideways glance at my loafers, blue jeans, and polo shirt and decided that I didn't look sufficiently professorial. He still agreed to be interviewed, but he wore the pain of his disappointment throughout the interview, a reminder that he had not forgiven me for being sartorially underwhelming. Appearance, I was to learn, is everything when you are in the presence of a Nigerian pastor. There were several who exchanged enthusiastic text messages with me, only to go dark as I was on the verge of agreeing to a date for an interview. Lesson number one: I need to look professorial.

And then there is the phalanx of bodies surrounding and surveilling the body of the pastor. Desperate for access to one of the leading Pentecostal pastors in Lagos, the closest I got, through an old media contact, was the number of one of his closest aides. My contact showed me the formula: "You will send the aide credit (airtime), preferably of a generous amount, and then quickly follow up with a call," he said. "That approach never fails," he assured me, and he was right. I quickly purchased 2,000 Naira worth of airtime and sent it to the number the aide had given me. When I called, lo and behold, a voice on the other side answered, something that had not happened after previous multiple tries. I quickly introduced myself, detailing what my research was all about and why I needed to schedule an interview with his boss. I had barely started taking notes when the line suddenly went dead. I dialed back immediately, but after multiple unsuccessful attempts, I gave up. My contact, sitting across the table from me, had figured out what was happening: "He wants you to send more airtime." Lesson number two: There is no easy or free access to the consecrated—and commodified—body of the pastor.

Still, I would go through every disappointment and humiliation I went through again if only for the chance to renew acquaintances with some of those pastors who received me with warmth and, in a couple of cases, gave me extremely confidential information. Most important, I would do it all over again for the sheer frisson of witnessing the arrival of a pastor at an event, an out-of-body experience that I was lucky to have been part of at least once. For, as an index of the social esteem and grandeur of the pastor (and I say this as a one time reporter who has seen state pageantry from up close), nothing compares to it, and there is a real sense in which the totality of everything I am trying to capture about what it means to be a pastor in contemporary Nigeria can be said to be distilled in that single spectacle. Seeing one—and this is the point—the appeal of pastoring to many young people becomes perfectly understandable.

In addition to the sights and sounds of those fortuitous events, my analysis draws on data from interviews with pastors and other key players in the Nigerian spiritual industry, not to forget aides to pastors and members of various churches. Furthermore, I have drawn on secondary data from newspaper reports, church bulletins and announcements, and sundry grey literature. Above all, I have drawn on my own intuitions and judgments on various players and agents in the Nigerian religiopolitical space, "sensory data" accumulated and firmed up across decades of patient apprenticeship in the study of Nigerian political culture dating back to my tentative beginnings as a political journalist in Lagos in the early 1990s. I have tried, as much as possible, to bring this personal, intellectual, and emotional formation to bear on my analysis, drawing out unsuspected connections and pointing out deep currents of interactions and relationships among disparate social forces and agents.

THE STRUCTURE OF THE BOOK

Pastoral Power, Clerical State is the second installment of a projected trilogy on the dynamic interaction of piety and politics in the Nigerian Fourth Republic. Although reading it as a follow-up to *Pentecostal Republic* helps, it is an autonomous work. Its deepest connection with the first book is that it is a consolidation and logical extension of its core argument—just as in *Pentecostal Republic* I posit Pentecostal Christianity as the spiritual lodestar of the Fourth Republic, in this book I argue that the figure of the pastor is the animating spirit of Pentecostalism. But, as I argue, the Pentecostal pastor is not just a religious figure or a subject that can be understood only through the prism of spirituality. Instead, he is a flashlight that illuminates deep fractures in the Nigerian topography, among them the breach opened up by the decline of the intelligentsia, the recession of the state, and the decomposition and realignment of authority, as well as the retreat of ideological systems. Which is why, even though in the book I build on the analysis in *Pentecostal Republic*, securing its core argument on the centrality of the figure of the pastor necessitates that I go further back to the period before the birth of the Nigerian Fourth Republic in 1999.

In chapter 1, "The Social Origins of Clerical Power in Nigeria," I outline and analyze the transformations mentioned above. The main argument of the chapter, and one major contribution of this book, is that the central position occupied by the pastor in today's culture is the culmination of a process dating back to the socioeconomic and political upheaval of the 1980s. In this chapter I show how today's "Man of God" is in fact a beneficiary of the decline of yesterday's "Man of Letters" and how, for its part, the decline of the latter and the social authority that he commanded is incomprehensible without attention to the decline of the university as the fulcrum of knowledge production and intellectual life in Nigeria. In this way, and noting that the Charismatic revolution that has culminated in the enthronement of pastoral authority began within the space of the university, in this chapter I establish a concrete connection between the crisis of intellection in Nigeria, and the efflorescence of religiosity.

In chapter 2, "The Pastor as Political Entrepreneur," I examine the various ways in which pastors are entangled in politics and the political process. I claim, first, that the question of clerical involvement in politics itself triggers the perennial question of the proper limits of religious action, which is central to the secular question in Nigerian politics. Second, I hold that, while it makes sense to speak of a common Pentecostal attitude toward politics, this disguises critical dispositional differences among the cream of the Pentecostal elite, ranging from apparent abstention, on the one hand, to passionate avowal, on the other. Both forms of engagement, I argue, constitute a mode of legitimizing Pentecostal power.

In chapter 3, "Erotic Pentecostalism: The Pastor as Sexual Object," I argue that there is an erotic charge between the pastor and his congregation that enables us to apprehend the pastor as, among other important "roles" he plays, an object of erotic fascination. But the erotic symbolism of the pastor is by no means limited to the economy between him and his congregation. In light of this, in this chapter I seek to place the pastor in a broader economy of pleasure, thus deepening our understanding of gender relations (both within and outside the church), affect, social control, and citizenship.

In chapter 4, "When Women Rebel," I develop a corollary (to the previous chapter's) analysis around the body and authority of the pastor, but this time centering on the unexpected rebellion of four Nigerian women in their interactions with different pastors. I use these counter-hegemonic moments by four "useless" women to illustrate how, even as the (male) body of the pastor continues to be consecrated and his authority revered, resistance to his "hegemony" can erupt quite abruptly, disrupting settled "scripts" and producing fascinating insights into the complexity of women's agency, particularly as it is mediated by class, age, socioeconomic and marital status, education, and the weight of cultural norms.

Now, especially considering the ways in which these insurrections were ultimately throttled, one cannot possibly ignore the irony that they in fact serve to demonstrate the resilience of pastoral power. Nevertheless, the importance of such "unscripted" moments cannot be overemphasized, and, if nothing else, they provide the grounds for juxtaposing the inherently antinomic character of women's agency with the hidden vulnerabilities of a seemingly impregnable masculinity. In addition, they are excellent examples of the kind of subaltern blindsiding rightly valorized in the socioanthropological literature on informal strategies of resistance in African and other postcolonial contexts.[30] That not all the women being analyzed here qualify, properly speaking, to be described as "subaltern," does not diminish, for me, the empirical value of the episodes in which they were involved.

The concluding chapter, "Rule by Prodigy," brings me back to the book's presiding theme of clerical authority, and I have deliberately saved it for last in order not to clutter the flow of the narrative. I use the material presented in the preceding chapters to examine how new forms of rule emerge and substitute for old ones and what the emergence of the pastor as a figure of authority means against the backdrop of people's seemingly insatiable quest for spiritual comfort and meaning. Against the backdrop of problems arising from the exercise of spiritual authority in a secular-democratic order, the analysis in this chapter is guided by two key questions: What happens to state authority as democratically constituted when people trust the pastor more than they trust their governors, if at all? What does the emergence of the pastor as a new category of political actor tell us about transformations in the nature of the state and in the never-ending struggle for power?

As would seem to be the case in any analysis of authority at this historical confluence, I take provocation from the wider literature on the global crisis of authority, zeroing in on the all-important strand of the diminishment of the expert issuing directly from the apparent erosion of established structures of authority.[31] I should emphasize that diminution of expertise is only an aspect of the larger story that this literature aims to capture. Its broader goal, it seems to me, is to make sense of popular disenchantment with elites and elite institutions (the academy and the media, for example) and the implications of that for their meaning-given work. I understand the struggles of the Nigerian intellectual classes as part of this global story of elites under pressure. At any rate, my aim here is to show that the social deposition of the Nigerian intelligentsia, while explicable by specifically Nigerian social forces, gains further intelligibility when read as a "local" manifestation of a wider delegitimizing of expertise due to rapid transformations in culture and technology. In one sense, the seeming rejection of the authority of the Man of Letters predicts the turn toward the Man of God. If the crisis of modern life is the seemingly endless quest for meaning, stability, and certainty, it is one that the Man of God seems perfectly positioned to resolve. His advantage comes from the fact that, contra the tentativeness and self-doubt of the "knowledge" offered by the Man of Letters, the Man of God is possessed of "the Truth," exuding what Richard Sennett describes as "assurance, superior judgment, the ability to impose discipline, the capacity to inspire fear."[32] These are the very qualities, arguably, that the Man of Letters once had and has now forfeited—qualities that the postcolonial state, inarguably, has never really had. The Man of God, especially when he lays claim to a unique divine revelation, offers solidity, belief, and certainty about the future. Small wonder that the Man of God has such appeal. Small wonder that men are on bended knee before him and women, quite literally, are throwing themselves at him.

CHAPTER ONE

The Social Origins of Clerical Power in Nigeria

Whenever the fall of the Nigerian intellectual elite is eventually documented, such an account must privilege the Ibrahim Babangida era (1985–93) as the precise historical juncture when it reached its apogee and, simultaneously, began to unravel. No other class of Nigerians was more fervidly and strategically cultivated by General Babangida; yet none was more demystified and inferiorized in consequence than the Nigerian intellectual elite.

THE EXECUTION OF A SOLDIER-POET

Nothing renders this paradox more vividly than the tragic story of Major General Mamman Jiya Vatsa, who faced a firing squad on March 5, 1986, following his conviction by a military tribunal for his alleged role in a purported conspiracy to overthrow General Babangida. The Vatsa saga is a historic marker. In its tragic afterglow, we see, on the one hand, a class at the peak of its social influence and, on the other hand, omens of its descent into relative desuetude.

When the news broke in early December 1985 of an alleged plot to overthrow the Babangida regime, the Nigerian public reacted with surprise, which turned into utter astonishment in January 1986 after

Major General Vatsa and sixteen others were arraigned before a special military tribunal at the Brigade of Guards Headquarters, Victoria Island, Lagos. Given widely available knowledge of some of the personal details of Major General Vatsa's life, notably his friendship with General Babangida, who had been the best man at Vatsa's wedding, the media and the general public found the idea of Vatsa as the mastermind of an alleged plot against his intimate friend rather jarring.

For various reasons, journalists and the Nigerian public had taken an instant liking to Vatsa. In a profession in which humorlessness tends to be worn like a badge of honor, Vatsa, minister of the Federal Capital Territory (FCT) until the December 1985 debacle, had a certain élan about him. Poets are rarely famous for their conformity, and Vatsa, author of several books of verse,[1] was always liable to push the envelope, for instance devising a cape for his military attire and referring to himself, imprudently in hindsight, as emperor of the Abuja capital territory.[2] Wole Soyinka narrates that in 1983, at the launch of his record *Unlimited Liability Company*, a musical lamentation of the state of the country during the Second Republic (1979–83) and a no-holds-barred indictment of the Shehu Shagari regime, Vatsa had shown up and bought thirty copies of the record, which he then went ahead to distribute to his army colleagues.[3] Clearly, Vatsa was not your run-of-the-mill military officer, a fact he was not loath to parade. According to unconfirmed reports that circulated around the time of his trial, he was not above pointing out syntactical errors committed by tribunal members to whom he literally owed his life. He was a soldier-poet (in an interview, his eldest son, Haruna, confirmed that at the time of death, his father had a library of more than 10,000 books)[4] and was a patron of the Association of Nigerian Authors (ANA),[5] hence someone in whom many Nigerian intellectuals instantly saw a kindred spirit.

Therefore, when, in late February 1986, the Nigerian intelligentsia and a section of the media commenced agitation to spare the lives of Vatsa and twelve other military officers following a guilty verdict by the Tribunal led by Major General Charles Ndiomu, they did so not only because they felt the nation could do without another round of bloodletting but, more important, in the conviction that, in Vatsa, they were defending a member of the literary tribe—an intellectual in uniform, if we can call him that.

This much was clear from what was easily the highlight of the mobilization to plead with General Babangida and the Armed Forces Ruling Council (AFRC) to commute Vatsa's sentence—the visit to Dodan Barracks (at the time, the seat of the military state) by the trio of Chinua Achebe, Wole Soyinka, and John Pepper Clark Bekederemo, three of the most distinguished names in Nigerian letters. While there is no doubt that the three decorated writers (Soyinka would go on to win the Nobel Prize for Literature later that year) saw Vatsa as a kindred spirit, what is interesting in light of the broader argument of the book is their perception of themselves and their social status as writers and intellectuals. Soyinka's narration of J. P. Clark's optimism, rooted in Clark's sense of their eminence, is telling: "If we three walked right up to Dodan Barracks, knocked on the gates and demanded to see the President, who was going to deny us entrance? Our combined stature would open any door in the nation."[6] In his 2001 Nigerian National Order of Merit Award Winner's Lecture, Clark confirmed Soyinka's description of his boundless optimism at the time, asking: "Three distinguished world-acclaimed writers wanted to see him [Babangida] on a national matter of urgency. How could he refuse seeing them?"[7]

As it happens, the three writers were not alone in their awareness of their eminence and status as "the 'elder statesmen' of Nigerian contemporary literature."[8] It was something, apparently, that their host, head of state Ibrahim Babangida, shared, and he assured them that he had promptly suspended a meeting the moment he learned of their arrival, concluding: "Since when has Dodan Barracks been honoured by the presence of the three leading writers of this nation!"[9] The acknowledged dictator had tipped his hat to the nation's three "unacknowledged legislators."

That the three writers failed in their last-minute bid to secure amnesty for Vatsa and his co-plotters is beside the point.[10] What is key for my analysis is the symbolism of their visit, which emerges in retrospect, simultaneously as the high-water mark of the cultural influence of the Nigerian intelligentsia but also as the very moment when a loss of social prestige began to set in. Before Babangida, the military had, to some degree, always depended on the participation of academics, but not with the same focus or deliberateness. That this unraveling happened on Babangida's watch is instructive, given his personal cultivation of the intelligentsia, which is illustrated by his recruitment of top political scientists and other university professors into his administration as ministers, advisers, and heads of government parastatals. Whether Babangida went out of his way to court members of the intelligentsia as part of a cynical ploy to legitimize his administration and, as it turned out, attempt to perpetuate himself in office, is an open question. Typically, that is how elites are co-opted and assimilated into the ruling class. What cannot be doubted, however, is that, by the time he seized power in 1985, although a social transformation was afoot, the social standing of the Nigerian intellectual elite was still such that anyone who courted it could hope to reap some vicarious capital. Thus, when the three writers visited to plead with Babangida, they quite reasonably surmised that their reputation (and that of the elite of which they were a part) was such that not only would it open the gates of Dodan Barracks, it might even tug at the heartstrings of a mercurial military dictator.

That the Nigerian intellectual elite is no longer capable of mustering such symbolic capital and, decisively, that the social prestige and primacy that used to accrue to it has migrated to the Pentecostal pastorate, is precisely the core argument of this book. One way to capture this *transfer*, one of prestige as well as social power, is to imagine a political crisis comparable in gravity to the one in which Achebe, Soyinka, and Clark tried to mediate happening today and then wonder who, in contemporary Nigeria, possesses the kind of authority and aura that can—and at a moment's notice, at that—secure an audience with the president. The reality today is that only a Pentecostal pastor possesses such prestige; as a matter of fact, one does not even have to hypothesize. For instance, and as noted in *Pentecostal Republic* (see chapter 3), in March 2010, as President Umaru Musa Yar'Adua lay dying and as the political struggle for his succession accelerated amid widespread uncertainty, Christian clerics (and their Islamic peers) were the only ones allowed access to him, ostensibly to pray for his recovery. The power of such moments as an illustration of the pastor's social eminence, as well as his role as a political broker poised between civil society and the state, cannot be overemphasized.

But, to have a proper appreciation of why the Man of God is now in fashion and the Man of Letters is out, we need to revisit the era in which the latter was à la mode. Apart from enabling an understanding of the sociohistorical milieu in which the intelligentsia flourished, such an excursion will also allow us to track the essential shifts in the milieu that put the Man of Letters in peril, thus creating the social space for the emergence of the Man of God.

What follows, then, is not an attempt to establish the reality of the decline of the Nigerian intellectual classes, about which even Nigerian intellectuals agree.[11] My aim, modest by comparison, is to argue that, insofar as this decline has had many serious consequences, one of them—the most consequential, in my view—is the concession of social space to Pentecostal pastors and sundry religious agents as centers of a new pole of authority. What is more, I claim, such are the entailments of this surrender (which I attend to in short order) that today, if there is anything that the occupants of the topmost rungs of the intellectual hierarchy desire the most, it is to become known as pastors themselves.[12] This surrender of authority has not taken place in isolation, and I am by no means suggesting that the blame for it—if blame is indeed the right word here—should be shouldered exclusively by the intellectual classes. On the contrary, and accepting that concrete material and structural conditions invariably determine intellectual production and the life of the mind in any society, I wish to show that the process through which the Nigerian intellectual elite has been gradually shorn of its standing and legitimacy has been driven by socioeconomic, cultural, and political factors originating mostly from outside the academy, though interacting, it must be said, with "indigenous" factors inherent in the very conception of the university in Nigeria.

Nor is my reference to a surrender of social space meant to imply that the intellectual elite meekly retreated before the onslaught of an insurgent pastorate. The important thing is to convey the rise and fall of contending social and occupational classes against the backdrop of incessant elite rearrangements and status disruptions. That, for instance, seems to be the larger theoretical point of Bayo Adekanye's analysis of the Nigerian military's ascent from a "low prestige" to a "high prestige" occupation.[13] The point, therefore, is not whether he is right about how, inter alia, military rule "resulted in the distortions of old parities or equivalences"[14] (he is) or whether the military still retains the luster that it evidently had during the military era, when the officer class was more or less *the* quintessential class[15] (it does not). What matters for my analysis is that these elite rearrangements are par for the course, that is, existing parities are being constantly reshuffled as part of a process inextricably tied to issues of social mobility and social privileges. Thus, if, as I contend, the baton of authority has changed hands from the professor to the pastor, it is due only, first, to an entire concourse of events that must be understood within this processual framework, and second, to the power of Pentecostalism, which I have posited as the scaffolding of social life in the Nigerian Fourth Republic.

Finally, although the readiness of the intellectual class to abjure the very basis of its own authority can be upsetting, it is worth emphasizing that there is nothing irreversible about their decline or, for that matter, the contemporary ascendancy of the pastorate. If anything, we may rightly expect that, contingent upon propitious changes in *both* the social organization of knowledge production *and* the broader Nigerian milieu, the intellectual class could very well reclaim its old position in the cultural hierarchy.

The rest of the chapter unfolds in the following order: in the first place, and consistent with my guiding assumption in the book, I show that, at independence in 1960 and well into the late 1970s, Nigerian intellectuals, whether as academics based in the then-emergent university system or as writers with their feet planted in both the academy and the media, enjoyed considerable social prestige. One measure of that status—a crude one, admittedly—was their overall regard in the Nigerian society and the eagerness with which their opinion and expertise were sought on a range of social issues. But that did not last very long, and by the late 1970s through the early 1980s, as Nigerian universities fell on hard times, prompting the attrition of leading academics to European and North American universities, the reputation of Nigerian intellectuals as respected occupants of rarefied ivory towers took a corresponding nosedive. Hence, following this, I examine the causes of the decline in the cultural status of this class, not so much with a view to perform a comprehensive analysis (something I would insist is beyond the scope of the present analysis) as in an attempt to demonstrate that the explanations for the decline of the intelligentsia and the rise of the pastorate are often concurrent. In the final part of the chapter, I attend to the pastor as a new axis of authority, explaining on the one hand the socioeconomic imperatives behind the attraction to pastoring and, on the other, the appeal of pastoring in the context of what, drawing on the relevant socioanthropological and literary literature, particularly the work of Pierre Bourdieu and Jean-Pascal Daloz, I describe as the Nigerian prestige economy.

THERE WAS A CLASS

At independence, most informed Nigerians, if interviewed to indicate their choices of the five topmost prestigious jobs, would probably have suggested a list in the following, albeit impressionistic, rank order: (1) university professor, (2) doctor, (3) high court judge, (4) engineer, and (5) permanent secretary. The lists could vary, of course, depending on how much upwardly mobile and achievement-oriented the individual respondents were. But, whatever the variation, there was no way a listing of the five most prestigious jobs at independence could have included army general or police commissioner.[16]

Viewed in its proper historical context, Adekanye's speculation on the foregoing should not be surprising. Given the widespread expectations at the time regarding the moral and intellectual leadership to be provided by the educated classes, the real surprise would have been if the university professor had ranked lower on the list of the topmost prestigious jobs. Indeed, that superior ranking is consistent with the expectation at the time — not only in Nigeria but across Africa and the "developing" world — that the university as an institution would be responsible for the production of the next generation of "leaders of the nation" as well as skilled manpower for national "development." As well, the ranking reflects the prestige that accrued to university professors as members of the educated classes or intellectuals in general, since at independence in 1960, Nigeria had only one university, the University of Ibadan, established in 1948.[17]

It is not an overstatement to say that there would be no Nigeria without the Western-educated elite, older than the Nigerian state itself, from among whose ranks the nationalist movement drew its leaders and rank and file. Seizing initiative from those Emmanuel Ayandele referred to as the "traditionalist religion-encrusted rulers,"[18] it was this elite that, mobilizing its resentment of British colonial rule, gradually laid the social foundation of what James Coleman describes as an "awakening of racial and political consciousness."[19] Ayandele's portrait of this elite, which cannot be described as flattering, has at least the unintended merit of conveying how the elite saw itself and its role in a future independent Nigeria.

Ever self-centered since the middle of the nineteenth century, the educated elite have all along commented on themselves, presenting themselves as the class around whom history has been revolving in modern Nigeria; as clairvoyant modernists and modernizers who were to create, build, and integrate Nigeria in the developed zone of the world; as the oppressed nationalist crusaders who used their brains, pens, and tongues to expel the British colonial exploiters; and as the wizards of nation-building who were to erect a virile, sphinxlike Nigerian nation on the ashes of British Nigeria.[20]

While Ayandele's portrait, though dismissive, is essentially accurate, it overlooks the most damaging accusation preferred against the educated elite: that it is guilty of cosmopolitan hubris. As Michael Echeruo has noted, educated Africans saw themselves as undertaking "on behalf of Africa, the civilizing duties of Victorian England," and

> in that mission was merged both the dedication of their lives and the irony of their position; for they stood as a testament to the barbarity of Africa as to the intellectual potential of its people. To the extent that they had the privilege of education they seemed very determined to save other Africans from the predicament of illiteracy and godlessness; to the extent, however, that they were black, they realized that they shared a common dilemma with everyone who was not just African, but black.[21]

Unsurprisingly, therefore, and for all their blackness,

> most of them were men and women capable of leading very professional lives in any city of Europe and America of their time. They were men (*sic*), moreover, whose immediate betters could only be found among local white colonial officers or in the middle class families of black America and Liberia.[22]

What explains this mentality, in particular the sharply contrasting lights in which this elite perceived the indigenous and European milieus, demonizing the one and valorizing the other? For Ayandele, alluding specifically to the *Saro*, as the first-generation Western-educated elite were called, it was because they possessed "a different conception of man, his worldview, his religion, his lifestyle, the attributes a leader should have and the course of history society should chart."[23] Nor was this affirmation only a matter of ideological convenience or the elite in question mere echoers of European ideas. Olufemi Taiwo has argued that, in reality, many of them—not least those he calls "prophets without honor"—were genuine protagonists of modernity who, notwithstanding their personal rivalries and contradictions, strove to plant the seeds of "enlightenment" in Africa.[24]

That this did little to diffuse the tension between the educated elite and the majority of the people (not to speak of the European elite, with whom they sought comparison),[25] for whom they became, in the words of Ayandele, "an object of intense aversion, moral and cultural lepers" and "a bunch of pitiable, bumptious and contemptible people,"[26] goes without saying. However, the task before me is neither to draw a comprehensive intellectual portrait of this elite[27] nor to praise or dispraise it, though I would be remiss not to note, especially given the overall objective of this book, that a significant number among them were in fact ardent believers (Taiwo's allusion to "apostles of modernity" is often literally true)[28] who saw no conflict between their calling as intellectuals and their religious identity as Christians, seeing the latter, in fact, as the inalienable foundation of the modernity that they championed. That said, my simple aim is to establish the fact of an educated elite well before Nigeria became independent in 1960 and, more important, to suggest that the contempt for them by the majority of the people for their perceived cultural alienage and moral and philosophical implication in the British colonial project did nothing to temper the respect for their status as intellectuals. That exaltedness, I would argue, not only carried over across different generations of the pre-independence educated elite (many of whom, significantly, did not have any university education) but ultimately redounded to the benefit of the university professoriate in the first-generation universities established in the first decade of independence.

GREAT EXPECTATIONS

If, as argued, the commencement of the Babangida era was the apogee of the cultural influence of the educated elite in Nigeria, the golden age was the 1960s. Jacob Ade-Ajayi's overview of the African university scene during that time was especially true for Nigeria: "Most African universities in the 1960s were treated with great respect. The governments were, on the whole, generous to the universities financially, and were generally unwilling to disturb their autonomy."[29] And, significantly, given what was to ensue between the state and the universities, governments "tended to believe that the universities were above the partisan politics that raged over such issues as the expansion of primary and secondary education. Thus, the universities were not involved in the prevailing power struggle and they enjoyed a temporary immunity."[30]

The unmistakable regard for the universities and, by the same token, the educated elite who operated within them, seems to have owed to two important factors. The first, as already indicated, is that the educated elite in the emerging university system inherited the same respect (with a side of contempt) that the mass of the people had for the pre-independence elite. Second, the universities were viewed with respect often bordering on awe because of the role that universities, rightly or wrongly, were expected to play in the political and economic life of Nigeria and other newly independent nations. In Nigeria and most of emerging Africa, the predominant idea of the university was of "an assembly of skilled manpower essential for the well-being of society,"[31] an institution that would, in the view of T. M. Yesufu, "train and develop the skills and high-level manpower to replace the erstwhile colonial official as well as to staff the new and expanded political, administrative, social and economic institutions."[32]

There is perhaps no better illustration of this overall positive perception—of the university, the university professoriate, and education in general—than official statements on the universities' status. For example, in 1969 Joseph Eyitayo Adetoro, federal commissioner (minister) of health during the Yakubu Gowon administration (1966–1975), weighing in on the question of the control of university policy, insisted that

> the university in Nigeria is the people's institution. General policy and direction should be invested in a body which is composed of well informed, respected and progressive citizens.... The lay composition should not be based on political alignment. It would indeed be a great misfortune if the councils of our universities should degenerate into political battle grounds. The direction of academic policy is, without doubt, the exclusive concern of the Senate.[33]

While the foregoing indicates the high regard in which the university was held, it also anticipates some of the issues and questions over which the educated elite in the universities and the state would soon be crossing swords. Prime among these were questions of university autonomy, funding, and the overall relevance of universities in the search for "national development." The question of "relevance" was of particular significance, given how it tended to be invoked amid broader philosophical conversations on the "identity" of the university. The tension was there right from the beginning, considering Ade-Ajayi's observation that although most ordinary people "tolerated" the universities, it was "in the absence of any real understanding"[34] of what they are about. The rest of his analysis, which speaks to the profound—and persisting—tension between universities and the society in Nigeria, is worth quoting at some length:

> Many people are impressed by the learning of academics. Even more, they are impressed by the enhanced status and earning capacity conferred on its holder by a university degree. For this reason, they patronize the universities. They visit them and show appreciation of the quality of their building and equipment. They show enough curiosity to watch the occasional quaint ceremonies of the universities, the robes, processions and rituals. But [he continues], they hardly look up to the universities to provide answers to the questions that bother them most—improved agricultural methods, questions of historical origin and the purpose and meaning of human life, moral guidance and sense of value, the cure for political instability and intergroup frictions, etc. and when they look up to the universities on these problems, they rarely get answers that they can understand or find relevant to their predicament.[35]

The universities were not unaware of this emergent disconnect between town and gown. As a matter of fact, some of the issues brought up by Ajayi were at the center of many a spirited debate within the African academy for the better part of the 1960s, most of the 1970s, and beyond. The most vigorous debates were provoked by questions over how to end the intellectual dependency of African scholars on ideas and paradigms developed in the erstwhile metropoles, how to "Africanize" or "localize" the teaching curriculum, and how to "adapt" the university to Africa's specific needs.[36]

By the turn of the 1970s, none of this seemed to matter, and the debates themselves, often concerning quaint university rituals, soon paled into insignificance as the strains and stresses already enfolded in the encounter between the town and gown took a steady toll on the latter. Since I am interested only in the decline of the ivory tower as a way of getting to the decline of the intellectual classes in general, I am not obliged to delve *fully* into the complex reasons behind the unraveling of the university system, a process that accelerated in tandem with the country's economic decline in the early 1980s and has otherwise received adequate treatment in the relevant literature.[37] Notwithstanding, I feel constrained to draw attention to Olufemi Taiwo's theory of causality, not only because it touches on the very ontology of the university system in Nigeria but also because it speaks to the character of the intellectual class it would, in fact, seem fated to produce. Taiwo states:

> Because colonialism was not seriously interested in creating a unified vision of reality, nor could it have done so even if it was, given its philosophy of exclusion, the university system it established was not created as an organic part of a mode of life shot through with coherent ideologies and identities. Universities were not established for any high ideals integral to a properly defined way of life. In large part, they were created as training schools for technocrats who would operate the machinery of State and produce goods and services. There was not created an integrated MOKP [mode of knowledge production] for which the university was the apex. Nor was there any effort, unsurprising in light of the pattern of exclusions, to create organic intellectuals, foster scholarly traditions, develop the material structure of knowledge production.[38]

With that in mind, and in lieu of a comprehensive analysis, I want to focus briefly on the impact of military rule on the Nigerian academy. My focus is informed both by a recognition of the deep impact of military rule on the postcolonial Nigerian state and society and by the fact that, of the various reasons often advanced to explain the devalorization of the Nigerian intelligentsia, military rule appears most decisive. To take this approach is not to imply that the crisis of the academy in Nigeria can be reduced to the ups and (mostly) downs of its relationship with the military but to acknowledge that (1) the military was, in fact, the dominant political power for the better part of the period under consideration and that (2) consequently, the military's relationship with the educated elite, especially those based within the academy, exposed flaws and contradictions inherent in the formation of this elite, thus enabling a deeper understanding of its sociology.

FROM GLORY TO IGNOMINY

In order to have a proper appreciation of the interaction of the military with the Nigerian academy, three key ideas should be kept in mind. First, it is worth noting that the by now familiar incivility—discursive and actual—exhibited by the military toward the academy was, in fact, a latter-day development, contradicting the tenor of the initial period of military rule, when it concurred with the rest of society in treating the ivory tower as an intellectual sanctuary and the professoriate as a class apart. When Brigadier General Adeyinka Adebayo, military governor of the then–Western State (1966–71) spoke of his awareness of "the fact that a great university can only emerge in an atmosphere in which the teacher is secure in his tenure and is free to push forward the frontiers of knowledge through unfettered teaching and research,"[39] he essentially captured the posture of the military hierarchy toward the university/teacher at one juncture in postcolonial Nigerian history. Second, the attitude of the military toward the academy cannot be seen in isolation from the military's overall perception of, and attitude toward, civil society. From the perspective of the military, and in a reality that would strengthen as time went on, university teachers were not just harmless researchers but active participants in the mobilization of civil society against military abuse of power. Finally, an undercurrent of class envy seems to have been baked into the military's interaction with the academy from the very beginning. According to Yusuf Bangura, this owes in part to the fact that, "as an institution, the military had low social prestige in Africa during the colonial and early independence period. It was seen as a refuge for less developed ethnic groups and those who could not make it into more intellectually-oriented professions."[40] It comes as no surprise, therefore, that, more than anything else, what the military members of the society most desired was, in the opinion of Adekanye, to elevate "themselves above not just their peers but even other occupational and professional groups hitherto ranked higher in terms of status evaluation."⁴¹ At independence in 1960, no professional group ranked higher than the university professoriate.

In any event, by the early 1970s, such were the transformations in the ideological outlook of the university teachers—initially organized under the aegis of the National Association of University Teachers (NAUT) and, since 1978, the Academic Staff Union of Universities (ASUU)—and the military state's apprehension of the university that both were effectively set on a path of unavoidable confrontation. If the period between 1948, when the University of Ibadan was established, and the end of the 1970s now stands out for being almost conflict-free, it is because, according to Bjorn Beckman and Attahiru Jega, the concerns of university academics during that period "conformed largely to a conventional picture of academics as an elitist, conservative, and vacillating segment of the middle class, preoccupied with conditions of service in a narrow sense. It tended to seek accommodation with the authorities and was easily repressed."⁴² For its part, having tasted political power for the first time in January 1966, by the end of the 1970s, whatever timidity the military may once have had, both about its ability to rule and its assessment of the relative power of contending social forces in Nigeria, was gone. Gone, for instance, was the former resolve, expressed by General Adebayo (above) to leave university teachers to their own devices and allow the system to be self-governing. For instance, in 1975, consolidating a centralist impulse that had seen many powers increasingly moved to the Exclusive list (assigned exclusively to the federal government) from the Concurrent (shared between the federal and state governments), it promulgated Decree No. 23, which removed the power to appoint the university vice chancellor from the university's governing council and vested it in the head of state or visitor to the universities.⁴³ To worsen matters, the bona fides of the university as an institution that could be relied on to produce skilled manpower was being increasingly called into question. Hence, when university teachers under the umbrella of the NAUT embarked on a strike in 1973, the Gowon regime promptly responded with a mailed fist, threatening to evict the teachers from their government-subsidized university quarters and have their leaders arrested.⁴⁴ The contrast with the statements by Adetoro and Adebayo (quoted above) could not be sharper.

It is worth emphasizing that the military state was not alone in its disaffection with the university teachers. By the late 1960s, as the so-called "development decade"—when "African countries immediately found themselves drawn into the vortex of international conferences of varying motivation, rationality, and utility, ostensibly designed not only to analyze but also to prescribe solutions to the problems"[45]— came to a disappointing close, a certain frustration at the way in which things were going inside the ivory tower was already evident. For example, it is difficult to imagine a superior way to read Chukwuemeka Ike's *The Naked Gods*,[46] a campus comedy on the face of it, than as a critical jab at the incipient infestation of the Nigerian university system by the worst sort of academic philistinism.

That some of the emergent misgivings probably had to do with what Ayandele portrays as changes in the cultural and social characteristics of the university community seems evident.[47] What cannot be doubted is that town–gown tensions, some of which can be traced to the constraints of the university idea in an African setting (see Taiwo, above), did gradually constellate with specific pressures from the state to put university teachers in an untenable situation. By the late 1980s, according to Beckman and Jega, "The university system had grown into a mammoth patrimonial edifice characterized by rigid hierarchical structures, arbitrariness in decision-making, and patron-client relations."[48]

The university teachers did not take this lying down, and, if anything, the creeping rot in the system served only to strengthen their resolve. Note Beckman and Jega: "The rapid decline of the material conditions of the universities in the 1980s accelerated ASUU's process of transformation from a timid and accommodationist professional association into a major actor on the national political scene."[49] However, ASUU's transformation had to do with more than the situation in the universities, as important as that was. For Bangura, it, i.e. ASUU's transformation, was, crucially, a function of a change in the philosophical milieu, most especially the fact that "Radical Marxist and dependency ideas were beginning to clash with more conventional modernization approaches which had provided the framework for the state-building and indigenization projects of the 1970s."[50] As a result, and no doubt because the things that ASUU had chosen to devote its energies to "were issues of wide concern, not just to staff and students," "what would otherwise have been simply particularistic demands assumed national significance, broadening the union's popular appeal and ability to attract sympathy when faced with state repression."[51]

Owing to this combination—its radical transformation and the fact that the issues affecting the university system overlapped with urgent national concerns—ASUU naturally found common cause with the Nigeria Labor Congress (NLC),[52] the umbrella association of Nigerian trade unions, and the student movement organized under the National Association of Nigerian Students (NANS). In its pomp, this trinity framed the intellectual agenda for opposition to military rule in the country and provided the organizational spine for civil society during its most emboldened phase. As for ASUU in particular, Bangura writes:

> It became a socially respectable and leading alternative voice, organizing major seminars, public lectures, and conventions on critical economic, social and political issues, issuing communiques after every national convention on burning issues of the day, empowering the national president and branch chairpersons to intervene in public debates, and floating national and branch-level newsletters which were critical of the status quo.[53]

For all its success, particularly in forging an alliance with the NLC and winning some hard-earned concessions for its members after a series of prolonged and bitter strikes (of which the 1992 strike was, by all accounts, the most consequential), ultimately, ASUU was unable to stave off the worst. In a classic case of swimming against the current, the increasing severity of the economic crisis and political dysfunction in the country was such that university teachers suddenly faced the existential risk of not being able to "maintain a respectable position within the changing structure of the national elite."[54] At the same time, "the economic crisis greatly eroded the capacity of academics to defend their social status and forced a sharp differentiation among their ranks, between those who were able to penetrate government bureaucracies, and those who have had to confront radically reduced opportunities at the workplace."[55]

This was the precarious situation of the Nigerian academic by the mid-1980s, and it would be an understatement to say that the Babangida regime exploited it to the fullest. In the next section I will discuss the relationship between the regime and university academics, using political scientists as proxies for the latter. My intention is to show that, as I mentioned earlier, it was during the Babangida era that the crisis of the university system in Nigeria came to a head and that the reason the regime was, on balance, able to have its way with university academics was the underlying conditions that had left the academy short-handed.

"MARADONA" VERSUS THE POLITICAL SCIENTISTS

When, in August 1993, facing sustained civic and political pressure, General Babangida made the decision to "step aside" as president, he brought down the curtain on a tumultuous eight-year regime whose overall legacy continues to divide opinion. Given the controversy surrounding his exit, the idea that, early in his administration, Babangida did in fact enjoy a special bond with a cross section of Nigerians, including the media, sounds almost improbable. This was due partly to the circumstances in which he seized power in August 1985. Babangida's predecessor, General Muhammadu Buhari, had ruled (this was before Sani Abacha) with joyless austerity, taking an axe to many of the freedoms that Nigerians had come to take for granted under the preceding civilian regime of Shehu Shagari (1979–83). Eager to define himself as the antithesis of his scowling predecessor, Babangida immediately went on a charm offensive by releasing political detainees and annulling unpopular and repressive decrees. Furthermore, as Carl LeVan writes, "Babangida used his criticism of the unpopular War on Indiscipline to signal how his policies would differ from Buhari's and to increase his government's credibility with the populace."[56] If these moves did not convince everyone, they at least helped Babangida establish an early reputation as a soldier-populist.

The cultivation of members of the academy was part of that preliminary charm offensive. According to Jibrin Ibrahim, if "a recurring topic of debate in the annual conferences of the Nigerian Political Science Association was the so-called 'failure' of the profession to get a frontline role in the process of political engineering, in the manner in which the leaders of the Nigerian Economic Society were playing a prominent role in economic policy formulation and implementation,"[57] Babangida made sure they could have no further complaints.

Not only were "a fairly large proportion of the leading professors and scholars of political science . . . recruited to design and implement Babangida's Transition Program (BTP),"[58] Babangida literally, and unprecedentedly, assembled what commentators jokingly described as a "Faculty of Social Sciences, Aso Rock" (Aso Rock, Abuja, seat of federal power since December 1991), staffing or heading his Presidential Advisory Council, Political Bureau, National Electoral Commission (NEC), Centre for Democratic Studies (CDS), and Mass Mobilization for Self Reliance, Social Justice, and Economic Recovery (MAMSER) with leading professors of political science. When he was not appointing professors of political science, Babangida was seeking to boost his standing in the social science community through financial contributions to projects dear to the hearts of its members. For example, and no doubt mindful of the standing of the late political scientist Claude Ake in the Nigerian social science community, Babangida donated part of the seed money for the establishment of the Port Harcourt-based Centre for Advanced Social Science (CASS) in 1991.

If Babangida wished to sow the seeds of division in the academy—or, as time went on, in (civil) society in general—he could not have expected more success. While the rank and file of the academy reacted with suspicion bordering on hostility to what, plausibly, was seen as an attempt to split the academy and maintain a modicum of goodwill in civil society, the Babangida professors drowned their benefactor in applause. Even for a society not necessarily wanting in the art of hagiography, the following profile of Babangida by Tunji Olagunju and Sam Oyovbaire is almost unparalleled. They described him as

> a professional, courageous and devoted soldier of the good old days; a military intellectual and strategist; a man with great personable disposition, charm and humour; a very brilliant and witty person; a man of robust heart with tremendous African humanism; a person of manifest devotion to family and friends; a leader with profound knowledge, grasp and appreciation of history, who skillfully combines his visions and dreams with realism and pragmatism in the cause of history; the "Maradona" of Nigerian politics and master tactician; a statesman with abidingly immense convictions and faith in the unity and greatness of Nigeria and in her destiny in world affairs.[59]

Echoing the scholarly consensus, Jibrin Ibrahim posits that, by kowtowing to the military president, Babangida's academic retainers ultimately helped lay the foundation for the subversion of the democratic process in Nigeria.[60] That may be true, but it is beside the point for me. Given the thrust of the chapter, the essential thing is to ask why, ab initio, the academy was susceptible to Babangida's overtures, and the answer, flagged earlier, is that Babangida took maximum advantage of the academy's corporate vulnerability. In danger of pauperization, Bangura writes that university academics responded in ways that either "brought them closer to government"[61] or distracted them from the work of intellection. And, although ASUU battled gamely, it could not "defend the livelihoods of members or . . . regulate individual coping strategies."[62] As a result, "the universities lost their power and glory at the same time they became the major recruiting ground for the numerous institutions floated by the government to manage reforms."[63]

The range of coping strategies embraced by academics as the economic horizon darkened included leaving the country for greener pastures, a trend that shows no sign of abating; becoming consultants to "private companies, foreign research organizations, multilateral agencies, NGOs, and state and federal institutions;"[64] or, when all else fails, sometimes turning on their students by resorting to "the sale of flimsy handouts at exorbitant rates,"[65] as Sanya Osha puts it. As a faculty member at the Obafemi Awolowo University, Ile-Ife, in the 1990s, I had a front-row view of what the average Nigerian academic had to go through in order to keep body and soul together. In an era when, pace two popular ASUU slogans, an academic's "take-home pay could not take him home" and his "wages were a joke because his employer was a comedian," I saw many academics convert their yards into emergency yam and vegetable farms, while at least one colleague in the Faculty of Education set up a successful business as a retailer. The most hard-pressed repurposed their private vehicles—if they were still in service—as *Kabukabu*,[66] and a colleague in the social sciences gained instant fame as a "bush meat" vendor.

The latter subset of "coping strategies" will raise a few eyebrows, as they should. Why, of all possible options, would a PhD opt for a retailing gig, say? The answer offered by Jane Guyer is that, like the majority of Nigerians, Nigerian academics suddenly confronted a profoundly altered world of "rapid, chronic, seemingly directionless and uncontrolled change" in which the best many could possibly aspire to was to "mitigate the effects of confusion."[67] It was a world in which "a synoptic vision of any kind is very hard to come by; people's decisions have to be deeply and intelligently reasonable without, however, benefiting from the luxury of being based on calculation of discrete and stable variables.... Temporal horizons may have to shift suddenly as new configurations of power, price, and plausible social action form and reform."[68] In that situation, if the academics who teamed up with the government or accepted consultancies with NGOs could argue that their new occupations at least involved some form of intellectual work,[69] those who took on side jobs as emergency transporters or vegetable farmers could not. The upshot was what Bangura refers to as a "creeping de-professionalization"[70] and subsequent loss of professional aura that has only worsened with time. While, on the one hand, the entry of academics into the corridors of power and the NGO/human rights space stripped them of the ambience they once enjoyed when they were ensconced in their "ivory towers," their often desperate recourse to occupations normally categorized as "lower class" effectively put them on the path toward proletarianization.

One could conceivably write a whole book on the fate of the professoriate under the military, with some choice data from the Abacha era (1993–98), during which university teachers lost further ground. For example, it was during that era that the appointment of sole administrators as vice chancellors of universities became prevalent, starting with the appointment of Professor Umaru Gomwalk as sole administrator of the University of Nigeria (UNN) in 1994, General Mamman Kontagora as sole administrator of Ahmadu Bello University (ABU) in 1995, and Professor M. I. Isokun as sole administrator of Ambrose Alli University (AAU) in 1997. In terms of the psychic transformation of the office, the most important and enduring effect of this trend is the license it gave to vice chancellors to begin to see and comport themselves as sole administrators.

Rather than present a comprehensive account of the Nigerian university system under military rule, my aim is to show that, much in the same way that one cannot hope to understand the totality of Nigeria's postcolonial history without coming to terms with the military impact, it is impossible to grasp the decline of the intellectual class in Nigeria without attention to the way in which military politics basically gutted the universities of their core values. This is not to say that the blame for the situation can be laid at the doorstep of the soldiers alone. If anything, martial philistinism was always in dynamic interaction with other socioeconomic and cultural factors (both on and external to the university campus), and my argument is that it was these factors operating in tandem—the objective debasement of academics and their self-humiliation—that, ensuing in the depreciation of the intellectual class, created the vacuum into which today's pastor has stepped. I consider these factors next.

AN IDENTITY CRISIS

On September 16, 1991, *Daily Times* columnist Chidi Amuta published what, without exaggeration, is probably one of the most memorable newspaper articles in the history of modern Nigerian journalism. Writing "Off Your Marx (Dead End of Marxism)" was an act of intellectual mea culpa, an expression of a palpable regret by the author at having backed the wrong ideological horse (Marxism-Socialism)[71] in its great Cold War showdown with free-market capitalism, and a passionate appeal to his fellow African intellectuals, who, one presumes, were in denial, to accept the reality of the demise of the old bipolar order as the challenge of "a fundamental reorientation of thought, of the acquisition of a new language of discourse and philosophical premises."[72] It is difficult to imagine anyone better qualified than Amuta to write such an article. Before making the transition to journalism, he had taught at the then–University of Ife (since May 1987 Obafemi Awolowo University), Ile-Ife, for many years, sealing his reputation as a literary theorist with the well-regarded *Theory of African Literature: Implications for Practical Criticism*, which he published in 1989.[73] Most important, not unlike most literary theorists or, for that matter, a majority of university teachers at the time, he was a radical Marxist for whom Marxian precepts were more or less articles of faith: the "proletariat" always innocent and "bourgeois criticism" de rigueur.[74] Amuta's article, coming almost two years after the collapse of the Berlin Wall in November 1989, was therefore significant, insofar as it can be read (and I cannot imagine a different way to read it) as an uncoerced testimony from a believer who had seen the very fundaments of his faith shredded. Amuta's most piercing question in the article, "How does an intellectual with leftist sympathies yesterday fit into today's world where the boundaries of illusion have yielded to the starkness of reality?," was not a matter of rhetorical flourish but an articulation of the dilemma faced by the Nigerian intelligentsia—and indeed the global left intelligentsia—in the aftermath of the fall of the Berlin Wall and the apparent triumph of free-market capitalism.

Three decades after Amuta's much-debated article, it can be difficult to appreciate the meaning of that moment for Nigerian intellectuals. Yet to say it was jarring would be understating it. The rout of Marxism-Socialism as a perceptual frame—an objective, systematic, complete, *hence irrefutable*, way of apprehending reality—was an existential crisis for the Nigerian left and the Nigerian intelligentsia, which were pretty much the same thing, and in Amuta's barefaced surrender one sees the pathos of a class coming to terms with a totally unforeseen, and seemingly irrecuperable, loss of ideological erection.[75] Its ideological merits aside, what Marxism-Socialism did for the Nigerian academy cannot be underestimated. Not only did the ideology give the Nigerian academy a firm handle on the world; at the best of times, it provided a hermeneutical axis around which data about the world could be organized and the philosophical language to analyze it. Such was the ideological pull of Marxism-Socialism at a point in time that to do political science, sociology, literature, or history outside the "political economy" framework was considered sacrilegious. At the apogee of its influence, social thought in Nigeria was Marxist thought, period. In an apocrypha that encapsulates the temper of the times, an eponymous political science professor, finishing work on the draft of a paper for a conference presentation, approaches one of his colleagues and urges him to "*jowo, ba mi fi political economy die si*" ("please, help me incorporate a little political economy"). Such, indeed, was the impress of Marxism-Socialism on Nigerian university academics, and it is hardly surprising that a majority of ASUU leaders since its creation in 1978 (a moment of ideological transformation, as previously noted) have, in fact, been card-carrying Marxists. One of them, Biodun Jeyifo, the union's inaugural president (1980–) had in 1976 teamed up with other comrades to establish a commune in Ode Omu, Osun State, "to prepare for a socialist revolution," according to Ogaga Ifowodo.[76]

To substantiate the claim of the cultural decline of the intellectual class in Nigeria, I have, for the most part, concentrated on the material, political, and economic factors responsible for its devaluation. What I have not done so far is call attention to what the intellectual class can do when it is in its element. Yet it is difficult to appreciate its cultural decline without some basic idea of what the educated elite can do when it is in rude health. What the Nigerian intelligentsia did, consistent with popular expectation at the dawn of political independence, was to serve as a galvanizing force. Whether as public-minded academics like Claude Ake, Yusufu Bala Usman, Edwin Madunagu, Mahmud Tukur, Niyi Osundare, Segun Osoba, Biodun Jeyifo, and Adebayo Williams; "homeless" men of letters like Wole Soyinka, Odia Ofeimun, and Chinweizu; or public intellectuals like Olatunji Dare, Stanley Macebuh, Dele Giwa, Chris Okolie, Gbolabo Ogunsanwo, Doyin Aboaba, Air Iyare, Areoye Oyebola, Tai Solarin, S. Labanji Bolaji, Haroun Adamu, Mvendaga Jibo, Mohammed Haruna, Amma Ogan, Donu Kogbara, Molara Ogundipe-Leslie, Bolanle Awe, and Folake Solanke,[77] the postcolonial Nigerian intelligentsia operated in the best tradition of social engagement, bending public policy to the coruscating force of ideation. It was in his iteration as newspaper columnist, however, that the Nigerian intellectual was most effective, shaping discourse while providing a moral compass on the divisive issues of the day. Ironically, there is no better illustration of the changing fortunes of this class, and its virtual abdication from the public sphere, than the dispiriting poverty of the opinion pages of Nigerian newspapers today. Nor is the connection between the academy and the media a casual one; the correspondence—and collision—between the two is one of the most important drivers of intellectual production in Nigeria. Chidi Amuta's crossover to the media after a stint in the academy (see above) exemplifies a traffic (of personnel and, more crucially, ideas) that was standard, and it is no accident that the Nigerian media was at its most vibrant when the universities were at their best as the centers of what Edward Shils describes as "radical criticism of existing society."[78]

At any rate, given its overwhelmingly leftist leaning, for members of this class, the downfall of Marxism was a disaster, the trigger for a crisis of identity that, I would argue, subsists. For Marxism was, for the Nigerian—nay, the African—intelligentsia, not just another ideology; it was its very lifeblood, the cerebral core of its identity as a class, and the irreproachable lens through which it saw the world. As Andrei Znamenski has shown, faith in the infallibility of the socialist doctrine was shared by "believers" everywhere.[79] One reflection of what Richard Sklar calls "an undoubted partiality for socialism among

Nigerian intellectuals" is that the report of the Political Bureau set up by President Babangida in January 1986 avidly advocated the "nationalization of the entire oil industry and other 'commanding heights' of the economy."[80] My argument is that the contemporary Pentecostal pastor is the ultimate beneficiary of the epistemic chasm created by the ideological bereavement of the Nigerian intelligentsia, paralleling the way in which religious forces (Pentecostalism in the Nigerian case) have profited from the collapse of what Mary Kaldor refers to as "emancipatory ideologies."[81]

One can imagine objections to the claim that Marxism has expended itself as an ideological force among the Nigerian intelligentsia. For instance, alluding to the existence of "Gramscians such as Usman A. Tar" and "the fiery Trotskyite Edwin Madunagu" and the fact that "Nigerian labour leaders evoked ideas and images of class warfare openly," Adam Mayer concludes that Marxism in Nigeria is "far from dead." Furthermore, "Many Nigerian labour leaders still refer to themselves as 'Comrade', and labour personalities such as Dipo Fashina of the Academic Staff Union of Universities and Hassan Sunmonu, formerly of the Nigeria Labour Congress (NLC), or the indestructible Femi Aborisade continue to be Marxists, along with feminist socialists such as Molara Ogundipe-Leslie, Ifeoma Okoye or the expatriate thinker Amina Mama." Finally, Mayer cites as proof of Marxism's continued relevance in Nigeria the fact that "Marxist-inspired movements are still to be found in the country" and writes: "There are a number of diehard Marxist parties, such as the Democratic Socialist Movement and its Socialist Party of Nigeria," and "Two major newspapers, *This Day* and *The Guardian*, are sympathetic to the cause of the left."[82]

Without prejudice to the accuracy of Mayer's observations, it is in his conclusion that he jumps off the rails. To assert on the basis of any of the above random facts that Marxism in Nigeria is in rude health is tantamount to pronouncing the arrival of spring based on the sighting of a solitary swallow. Mayer has written (in his calculation of its prospects) a wishful account that is sympathetic to the left, and there is nothing wrong with that, but it is one thing to wish a thing well and a different thing entirely to wish it into existence. It seems to me that what Mayer trumpets as proof of Marxism's continued vitality in Nigeria are the valiant efforts of disparate agents to keep alive a tradition that continues to struggle for relevance, the so-called renaissance of "Democratic Socialism" in some Western countries notwithstanding. That these agents are earnest and dedicated, as many of them indeed are, is no guarantee of their success, never mind their rightness. Part of the irony here is that Mayer's claim is pointedly at odds with the sober realism of some of the leading participants in the Nigerian Marxist movement,[83] and if the examples he mobilizes as proof of the continued vitality of Marxism in Nigeria tell us anything, it is that he underestimates the power and reach of Nigerian Marxism and the depth of its penetration into the social consciousness in its most successful phase. And as for *This Day* and the *Guardian* being redoubts of Marxian dialectic, I am sure the news would be music to the ears of their proprietors.

To reiterate, then: today, the intellectual elite as a cohort conscious of its group identity, its position in the social hierarchy, its social function, and, most important, its status in the Nigerian society, is greatly devitalized. However, although I have insisted that the intellectual has surrendered his quondam primacy to the pastor and that the intelligentsia's enervation is a prime driver of this surrender, it is not the only one, nor has it operated in isolation. In closing this section, I will touch on a few of the other factors with which the decline of the intellectual elite has been in interaction, the better to place the emergence of the Pentecostal pastor on as wide a pedestal as possible and unveil its property as the creation of several (f)actors acting in concert.

The first of these, also traceable to the ravages of military rule, is the hemorrhaging of specialized expertise from across the professions to various parts of the world, but primarily to the key industrialized societies of the Western Hemisphere. Research showing that, for a variety of reasons, Nigerians count among the most successful immigrant groups in the United States, though partly intended as a celebration of American openness to enterprise, unwittingly underlines the loss to Nigeria of this pattern of emigration.[84] Typically, this loss tends to be calculated in economic terms. My preference is to emphasize an effect that is no less real for being unquantifiable. I speak of the impact of high-skilled emigration on the de-invigoration of civil society, a function, I should emphasize, of the gutting of the middle class in general. I am arguing that the delegitimizing of the educated elite in Nigeria, combined with the aforementioned bleeding of expertise of various stripes, weakens the public space, which then aggravates the generalized metaphysical bafflement that is the foundation of clerical authority. The overall diminution in the quality of (criticism in) the public sphere is, I suggest, inversely commensurate with enhanced pastoral influence. The widespread recourse to and acceptance of prophecy and other forms of revelation-based "knowledge" (about which more in the next chapter) at the expense of expert opinion proves my point.[85]

Complementing this is erosion of trust in the state, especially its capacity to perform the most minimal responsibilities of governance, from law enforcement to provision of essential services. If the state used the Structural Adjustment Program (SAP) partly, and tactically, as a cudgel to corral civil society, the state itself was not unscathed by it, emerging from the many "trimmings" mandated by the SAP considerably diminished, perhaps disoriented, but definitely less confident of its core identity as the institution primarily vested with the organization of "social welfare."[86] I argue that its ensuing retrenchment had two main consequences. In the first place, it created a discursive gap into which a multitude of contending narratives, the most decisive of which is the Pentecostal worldview, have stepped. While there was no inevitability as to this outcome, Pentecostalism's narratological triumph seems to have been aided by, inter alia, the fact that it possesses a coherent theory of history and futurity, including an explanation of the crisis of the Nigerian state and society, not to mention a confidence in its own divinely ordained mission to lead the country out of its morass. Second, state retrenchment unleashed a fury of entrepreneurial (including legally dubious) enterprises in the popular economy, among which is pastoring, a profession that, as it happens (more presently), involves minimal risk-taking and even less "investment" by way of start-up. I use "popular economy" here as formulated by Jane Guyer, LaRay Denzer, and Adigun Agbaje, to describe the range of "livelihood, employment, and capital asset creation that has precipitated out as oil and the state retreated into their own fortress, literally off-limits to the citizens."[87] Accordingly, "The popular economy neither completes a 'national economy' by complementing the formal sector nor constitutes a whole system in and of itself. Rather, it is a series of localized meeting places for economic organizations that have in common their relatively low level of formal regulation."[88] As a model of private enterprise with low barriers to entry that thrives under conditions of minimal regulation, Pentecostal pastoring checks all the boxes.

A final determining factor is the moral and spiritual restlessness that is concomitant to the economic angst outlined above. As the hunger for meaning, power, and salvation has intensified, so has the spiritual economy itself become further deregulated. In this expanded spiritual economy, Pentecostal pastors, standard-bearers of a ubiquitous Pentecostalism, have emerged as prime actors. Yet, as a quick glance at the spiritual landscape will reveal, even they do not command an uncontested view. For all their undoubted visibility and influence, which I illustrate as we go along, they are, in the end, just one of the many avenues of spiritual comfort for people, sharing—and often contesting—authority, and oft-times physical space, with astrologers, palm readers, oracles, and sundry spiritual agents and "consultants."

Accounting for the emergence of the figure of the pastor—which is what I have tried to do in the foregoing—is one thing; explaining the continued attraction of pastoring is another. The latter is the focus of the next section.

THE PULL OF THE PULPIT

Over the past decade the pastor has become the Nigerian society's most successful persona: he possesses both spiritual and physical strength, possesses wealth and power (often in the political milieu), and is held in esteem and respected. The pastor is the human being closest to God and, in a social sense, to the Big Man.[89] Francis Bola Akin-John of the International Church Growth Ministry says of the pastorate:

> It is an avenue to take advantage of people because whether you like it or not, when you become a pastor you have quick access to money, you have quick access to people's life, people trust you with the secrets they won't tell their father . . . and they are bound to take care of you, and you know in African culture we take care of our leaders, we teach it also, we biblicalize it. So, a lot of people that want to be pastors, they see it as opportunity to quick money, quick access, quick power, influence on people. The number three reason I can adduce is the desire for bigness and expansion by many of our mega-pastors and mega-churches; you know, it is as if we are in a competition of who has the largest church, who has the largest members.[90]

Some years ago, on a trip from London to Lagos, I happened on a scene at Heathrow International Airport. As I made my way across the terminal, I sighted a long line of people that, from their dress, I knew right away were my Nigerian compatriots. The line seemed rather long, and more and more people, who clearly knew what was waiting at the front, kept joining at the back, thus extending it. I could not resist the urge to look, whereupon I discovered the reason why a line at the airport that did not lead to the check-in counter had suddenly become the one to join. The person at the front of the line was none other than Pastor Enoch Adejare Adeboye, general overseer of the RCCG and, on this evening (well before his church determined that a private jet would suit his needs better and bought him one), he was about to catch a flight to Lagos, only to be ambushed by people who wanted to take advantage of a rare closeness to his person to ask for his blessings.

Pastor Adeboye (aka Daddy G.O.), suffice to say, is not just an "ordinary" pastor but, in the words of Adedamola Osinulu, one "considered by many in his congregation to be both a prophet whose pronouncements are accurate because they are revealed to him by God and a mediator who is especially qualified to intercede to God on their behalf because of his close relationship with God."[91] He is the one whose church members, if he sneezed, would catch a cold, and his body, imagined to be suffused with the "the power of anointing," is treated with a reverence bordering on beatification.[92] (In March 2002, on the occasion of his sixtieth birthday, a journalist opened an interview with Pastor Adeboye with the question: "Is Pastor Adeboye an ordinary human being?")[93] One could, therefore, understand the importance of the moment for the church members (and, I imagine, members of other Pentecostal denominations) who had suddenly found themselves within touching distance of his hallowed person, minus the retinue of minders that would ordinarily have barred access to him, the management of access being a central principle of pastoral-elite mystique. I stood there for a while, staring as each individual genuflected, received a word of blessing, and quickly yielded to the person behind, and, for a fleeting moment, I wanted nothing more than to become (though I'd readily settle for being treated like) a pastor myself.

Whenever I think about the attraction of pastoring in contemporary Nigeria, my mind always goes back to that Heathrow cameo. What is it like to be Daddy G.O. (or just a regular G.O.), fawned over by millions and treated like royalty wherever you go? What is it like to be above the law, and not just metaphorically, as I will demonstrate with an incident involving Pastor Temitope Balogun Joshua, the late leader and founder of the Lagos-based the Synagogue, Church of All Nations (SCOAN)? Granted, not every pastor is as famous or as revered as Pastor Adeboye or Pastor Joshua, and, as I indicated in the introduction, pastors come in various stripes—as, indeed, do Pentecostal groups. Yet the reverence accorded Pastor Adeboye is not atypical, and this, more than the other reasons I address in short order, is perhaps the greatest draw of pastoring in contemporary Nigeria.[94] To be a pastor is to put oneself in a position to access "the system" at little or no personal or social cost. The special reverence accorded the Pentecostal pastor issues not just from members of his congregation but also, significantly, and, as I show in the next chapter, from members of the political elite eager to leverage the social prestige enjoyed by the leading Pentecostal pastors for political gain.

The more prestigious the pastor, the greater, it would seem, the likelihood that his misdeed(s) will be condoned or overlooked, even when there is probable cause for prosecution. For example, when, in September 2014, a guest house on the premises of his church collapsed, killing at least 115 people, and after a newspaper released tapes of an exchange with journalists in which Pastor T. B. Joshua apparently offered money for an account that exonerated his church,[95] Pastor Joshua was rewarded with condolence visits by then–Lagos State governor Babatunde Fashola and former president Goodluck Jonathan, who was desperate to remain in the "good books" of the leading Pentecostal pastors ahead of the 2015 presidential election.[96] Since then, the criminal negligence case against Pastor Joshua has rumbled on in the courts, where it will most certainly be impaled on the altar of legal technicalities. In the meantime, masquerading as morally conscientious students, members of the church have publicly remonstrated with the Lagos State government, insisting that what happened at the church was a "natural disaster," thus undeserving of a coroner's inquest.[97] "Touch not my anointed,"[98] a popular saying among Nigerian Pentecostals, epitomizes members' conviction that, because pastors have been "called" (I treat this in greater detail in chapter 2), they should be beyond censure, whether in a legal or a moral sense.

To be sure, this privilege of ecclesiastical exception does not extend to all pastors. For instance, it is productive to compare what happened to Pastor Joshua after 115 people lost their lives on his church premises with the fate of Pastor Chukwuemeka Ezeugo (alias Pastor King), general overseer of the Lagos-based Christian Praying Assembly, who was convicted of the murder of Ann Uzoh, at the time of her death a member of Pastor King's church. Without prejudice to the facts of the two cases (King is alleged to have set on fire six members of his congregation, one of whom, Ann Uzoh, eventually died),[99] it is significant that Pastor King was rapidly tried and sentenced to twenty years' imprisonment and death by hanging by a Lagos State High Court (a judgment later upheld by the Supreme Court in February 2016) within four months of his first court appearance. While this proves my point that clerical exception does not, in fact, extend to all clerics, the King case underscores the role of class and social network in the production of this "state of exception," for the key difference between Pastor Joshua and Pastor King, even though, in terms of their pedigrees, they both belong at the lumpen end of the clerical spectrum, is as follows: (1) while Pastor Joshua's congregation comprises the cream of the African political, economic, and sporting elites,[100] Pastor King ministered to members of the underclass on the urban periphery and to others otherwise on the socioeconomic fringe, and (2) while Pastor Joshua's connection to the elite (national and transnational) means that there is a network of influential people who can be relied on to oil the machinery of patronage for him in dicey situations, Pastor King, on the other hand, had no such social capital to draw on.

An indication of Pastor Joshua's connection to the cream of the Nigerian elite could be seen in the stream of condolences and testimonies that poured in from every corner of the country following his unexpected death on June 5, 2021.[101] If one thing is clear from the accounts of his generosity, it is that Joshua devoted himself to building a network of allies and friends among the political and cultural elites while not neglecting philanthropic work among the poor, his kin, and townspeople. From the example of Pastor Joshua (and this applies to anyone similarly placed in the Nigerian social hierarchy) we may reasonably conclude that being socially connected is a way of purchasing a warranty, a sort of advance tariff, against prosecution—in his case, of a future personal scandal, as it turned out. "Knowing people" in this way is a well-known strategy in situations in which institutions are weak, and many depend on "trickle-down" largesse from the elite to get by.

Unsurprisingly, the practice makes those institutions weaker and more prone to personal interference.

Another reason for the attraction of pastoring, one probably not unrelated to the above, is the opportunity it affords for social becoming. What I mean is this: that, for the average young person otherwise unable to access employment (hence unable to discharge normative sociocultural and filial obligations) due to the crunch in the formal labor market, pastoring—which requires, as I have suggested, little by way of seed investment—becomes an attractive option. Leslie Fesenmyer's research among Kenya-born pastors in the United Kingdom and Karen Lauterbach's work among youth pastors in Ghana support this critical linkage between personal ambition and generational opportunity.[102] To appreciate this point, it is important to keep in mind the reality that, for the average young Nigerian, the menu of opportunity tends to be limited to a handful of options: traveling abroad, becoming active in politics (whether as an office-seeker or part of the entourage of an officeholder as an "assistant"), taking up a life of crime (which, in the case of women, often means full-time prostitution), or becoming a pastor.[103] Daniel Jordan Smith's work on young Nigerian men's struggles to "become a man" amid unrelenting economic and social pressures, Charles Piot's on young Togolese citizens' invention amid privation, and Stephen Ellis's wide-ranging analysis of crime and society in Nigeria capture this sociology eloquently.[104] Of all these options, not only does pastoring possess the advantage of being at least mostly legal, with a degree of buffer against economic vagaries, it also, most important, gives the young entrepreneur broad latitude in terms of self-curation. For young people facing the danger of permanent consignment to the social margins, pastoring can be the last opportunity to "become someone." What emerges here, then, is a vital connection between spirituality and the often crushing demand for an "enterprising self," a "Me, Inc.," as posited by Nicolette Makovicky.[105] It is when this desire for a "Me" does not find an outlet in pastoring that we see the desperation to be "worth something" spill over into an assortment of pyramidal ventures: "419," "Yahoo Yahoo," "MMM,"[106] and other get-rich-quick schemes underpinned, if not actively driven, by individuals' need to gamble in order to mitigate the role of chance in their lives. Being themselves forms of the miraculous, it is hardly surprising that some of these schemes (e.g., "MMM") have concrete connections with Pentecostalism.[107] A Russian-originated Ponzi scheme,

MMM (Mavrodi Mundial Moneybox) was active on and off in Nigeria between 2015 and 2017. Several Redeemed Church branches openly advertised the scheme during services, while some pastors participated in the scheme using church names and resources.[108]

Third, and in sum: being a pastor seems the quickest route to the social privileges and social legitimacy ordinarily accruing to other professions—lawyer, doctor, and so on—but without any of their ethical strictures or training requirements. Compared with the material dividends from, say, training to be a lawyer, a profession whose rewards can be uncertain, pastoring promises instant material rewards, a degree of social respect that the ordinary professional can only dream of, and connections to the political and business elites at national and transnational levels. In a credentials-conscious society like Nigeria, being a pastor, then, may well be the ultimate credential.

CONCLUSION

> Lecturers are the bane of the country and most of them have contributed nothing to the nation yet they still print handouts and sell to students, they even harass female students.
> —Olusegun Obasanjo

The reputation of the intellectual class in Nigeria, as denoted by the university professoriate, is in tatters. If a poll of a cross section of Nigerians were to be taken today, it would not be a surprise to see a majority, probably sick as well of recurrent strike actions by the university teachers, agree with the above sentiment expressed by former president Olusegun Obasanjo.[109] Arguably the most important illustration of the ill repute of the academy and of academics is that not only is there no distinction between the physical space of the university (I'm speaking here of its total organization, as expressed in its use) and the world outside it; the mores and rituals that used to set the university apart have been folded into the culture of the "town"—and vice versa.

To cite just one among a plethora of examples: today, there is practically no difference in the process by which the vice chancellor of a Nigerian university, its presumed intellectual leader, is chosen, and the one by which, say, the governor of a state, a political entity, is selected. More to the point, it is practically impossible to become vice chancellor of a Nigerian university without the solid backing of at least one of an array of extra-academic political actors (a commissioner, the governor, or even the president), ethnic allies, or traditional rulers. This explains why it is becoming increasingly rare for universities, even private ones, to choose vice chancellors or other key appointees from outside their ethno-regional locations. *In practice*, and not least because the university is now seen as the "possession" of an ethnic group, a race to be vice chancellor is a race among contestants to curry the favor of powerful actors *outside* the university system. What happened at the University of Calabar (UNICAL) in June 2020 is not atypical: six professors aspiring to the institution's vice chancellorship reportedly declared for the ruling All Progressives Congress (APC), having been told that their candidacies were as good as dead if they were not card-carrying members of the party.[110] Not only must professors aspiring to the highest office of the university necessarily demonstrate their allegiance to the incumbent political party; within the university they often have to make concrete "campaign promises" to faculty (for example, about the number of people who will be elevated to full professorships) and non-academic staff. A de facto political appointee, the average Nigerian university vice chancellor (VC) has the swagger of one, complete with security detail and a fawning entourage.[111]

In the foregoing, I have tried to excavate the sociological soil in which the reputational collapse of the Nigerian intelligentsia germinated and found nourishment, and in doing so, I have argued that there has been a transfer of prestige and authority from the intelligentsia to the Pentecostal pastorate. At the same time, I have suggested that the said centrality of the pastor cannot be divorced from the ascendance of Pentecostalism as a mode of thought and a framework within which, across the Fourth Republic, Nigerians have sought meaning, assurance, salvation, and power. The political is one of the domains in which pastors have exercised and established this newfangled authority. How they do so is the focus of the next chapter.

CHAPTER TWO

The Pastor as Political Entrepreneur

The evolving political language of Africa tends to regard politics as a metaphor for movements in a spirit world rather than vice versa. The real cause of human suffering or prosperity lies in the spirit world, of which human events are a mere reflection: it is in the spirit world that the ultimate cause of events is to be found, and it is here that the ultimate cause of Africa's misfortunes may also be found. Those who have entered the world of spirits, priests and healers, may therefore suggest in all seriousness that what is required is an alliance of forces—governments, priests and healers—to combat evil on the plane where it operates, which is a spiritual one. *The logic of their argument is that African societies will not find political stability until they have found spiritual stability, and it is here that the debate is located at all levels of society.*

—Stephen Ellis and Gerrie ter Haar,
"Religion and Politics in Africa"[1]

A VISIT TO AJAOKUTA

When Pastor Enoch Adeboye paid a courtesy visit to Kogi State Governor Ibrahim Idris in May 2009, he was acting in his capacity as what I have described as a statesman without portfolio.[2] Over the course of the Nigerian Fourth Republic, Daddy G.O. has been the country's most powerful religious figure, and visits like the one he paid to Lugard House, Lokoja, are one of the established rituals through which he demonstrates and projects his authority as Nigeria's foremost "Man of God." During such visits—to Aso Rock, the seat of federal power, governors' offices, governors' private residences, government parastatals, and media houses—the respected pastor and his entourage diligently adhere to the same nonpartisan routine of praying for their hosts and invoking divine blessings on them. In May 2009, Lokoja would have been just another stop on a crowded calendar but for the respected pastor's decision to make a quick stop at the massive Ajaokuta Steel Company in Ajaokuta, 40 kilometers away. According to media reports, following conversations with the staff of the ailing complex, Pastor Adeboye assured them that the company's days as a steel-producing firm that produces no steel would soon be a thing of the past, as he was ready to "put it as a priority in *my* prayers and I am sure God will take control" (italics added). Ajaokuta has not fared better since that May 2009 visit. Contrariwise, its prospects remain gloomy, and as recently as July 2020, the federal government was mulling over plans to commit more money in the umpteenth attempt to "resuscitate" it.[3]

Ajaokuta, it is worth remembering, is not just another steel-producing company but arguably the most enduring testament to the failure of the Nigerian postcolonial state and elite. Daniel Jordan Smith calls it "a national symbol of official graft,"[4] and even he doesn't go far enough. Established in September 1979 under section 2 of the National Steel Council Decree, the Ajaokuta Steel Company Limited (ASCL) was envisioned as the industrial behemoth that would produce various types of steel products to meet the needs of an expanding economy. Not only has Ajaokuta done no such thing, but "the site has become an infamous white elephant, swallowing endless extra costs and suffering long delays well into the 1990s."[5] Today, Ajaokuta remains a notorious graveyard of federal appropriations, the date for its much anticipated opening having been pushed back more times than anyone can remember.[6]

Given how Ajaokuta is seared into the national consciousness in Nigeria and how well-documented its travails, why would someone as knowledgeable as Pastor Adeboye, absent any concrete ameliorative action, insist that a situation that complicated (or simple, depending on how one looks at it) could be rectified through a simple appeal to divine intervention? There are three possible answers to this question, all of which throw into sharp relief Pentecostal approach to politics in Nigeria and the idea of the pastor as a political entrepreneur, which is the focus of this chapter.

The first, as hinted above, is that it fits within Adeboye's brand of politics, the essence of which, a core commitment to "nonpartisanship," is to do everything possible to keep up the appearance of being above the political fray. This typically includes a refusal to take sides in any political contest (which in part explains the welcome extended to *both* Christian and non-Christian members of the political elite at the church's Redemption Camp)[7] and, as in the case of the Ajaokuta Steel Complex, a studious avoidance of questions that members of the political elite might find upsetting. Instructively, only on the rare occasions when the corporate interest of his church or the interest of his church members appears to have been directly affected has Pastor Adeboye acted out of character. For example, the visit to Governor Ayo Fayose of Ekiti State on Christmas Eve 2016, far from providing an endorsement of the controversial governor, as a section of the commentariat hastily concluded, was most probably meant to signal Adeboye's approval of Governor Fayose's hard-line stance against Fulani herdsmen who had reportedly killed many innocent people across the country, including Christians, many of whom were members of the RCCG.[8] Considering, as I emphasize shortly, the way in which Christian-Muslim struggles for supremacy constitute a permanent backdrop to political engagement in the country, it seems plausible to infer that Adeboye, not unreasonably, saw Fayose as a willing ally in the battle against herdsmen who, whatever else we may think of them, are Muslims. A similar calculation would seem to have informed Pastor Adeboye's unprecedented decision[9] in February 2020 to lead a "Prayer Walk against Insecurity in Nigeria" in Lagos during which he held a placard with the message "All Souls Are Precious to God."[10] In the weeks leading up to the rally, the media had been rife with reports of killings of Christians (including, conceivably, members of the RCCG) by insurgents of Boko Haram (the radical Islamist group). Pastor Adeboye's eagerness not to rock the boat and to distance himself from politics—plus the contortions and performances that such a stance must commit him to—is, as I have contended, a form of politics in itself and offers one possible explanation for his action at Ajaokuta.

Second, Pastor Adeboye's reference to the certainty of remedy through prayer must be placed in context, for not only is it not random;

it is a critical lens into Pentecostal understanding of the power of prayer as the weapon given to every believer to mount an assault on all problems—public and private, individual and institutional, secular and spiritual. For Pastor Adeboye—and indeed for every Pentecostal—prayer and divine healing are foundational tenets, and the reference to prayer in the RCCG's mission statement could not be more emphatic:

> A Christian without condemnation of heart has a right to thank God, be in adoration unto the Lord and to ask in prayer always. Prayer should be an evidence of a soul which thirsts for God and those who are unable to pray annoy God. In the absence of prayer, much trouble and danger are encountered. It is God's plan and order that we should pray to receive all the good He has promised in His treasure for us.[11]

If the reference to prayer is far from trivial, equally important is the revered pastor's reference to "my prayers," a tacit acknowledgment of his position as the leading religious figure in the country and the person widely believed by his congregants, if not majority of Nigerian Christians, to have a direct line to God. In public, Adeboye often casually refers to God as "my Daddy" in the manner of one who has unmediated access to God within an intimate Father-son relationship.

Third, and perhaps most important, is that the visit to Ajaokuta throws a light upon what, following Simon Coleman,[12] I describe as the Pentecostal theory of causality, especially how it challenges secular assumptions of causality. Adeboye's assurance that he would "put [the recovery of the Ajaokuta Steel Company] as a priority in my prayers and I am sure God will take control" foregrounds, as discussed in the foregoing, a refusal to wade into partisan politics and an affirmation of the power of prayer. Yet also subsumed in the statement is a conception of how Ajaokuta came to be what it is today not because of the venality of the Nigerian postcolonial elite—which is the secular theory of causality—but a problem that occurred because God allowed it and perseveres because God is not yet interested in terminating it—the Pentecostal theory of causality. Not only does the latter depart from the secular understanding of causality, including, significantly, the role of human agency; by the same token, it rejects the temporality within which human agency unfolds. In this manner, Pentecostal praxeology bolsters Charles Taylor's perspective that secularity, far from being "finalized," is, in fact, a "space" of contention, contestation, and intense debate.[13] Nor is that all. Pentecostal praxeology also accords with a fundamental African cosmological principle regarding the reality of a world of invisible spirits that is the imperceptible driver of secular reality. Hence the assumption (see Stephen Ellis and Gerrie ter Haar in the epigraph to the chapter) that, for things to be settled in political reality, they must be settled ab initio in the spiritual.[14]

Pentecostal politics in Nigeria is grounded in the interaction of these three elements, and while Pastor Adeboye is a key figure in that process, this chapter is not about him per se, though his stature within the Nigerian Pentecostal community means that he must be reckoned with. (As a measure of that stature, not only is Pastor Adeboye indisputably Nigeria's most influential pastor; several of the leading pastors in the Fourth Republic, in fact, cut their teeth under him.)[15] Instead, I focus on the idea of the pastor as a political entrepreneur, meaning someone who reinforces his authority within the religious domain by projecting the same in the political domain—and vice versa. Because of the dispositional and other differences among individual pastors mentioned earlier (see introduction), political entrepreneurship naturally takes different forms. For example, Pastor Adeboye's retiring style (an admirer describes him as "using humility as a weapon of conquest")[16] is the very antithesis of Pastor Tunde Bakare's brash ambitiousness. One is a stabilizer, praying (for reasons explained below) for any government in power; the other, in theory at least, is a disrupter, implacable in his belief that God has destined him to lead the country.[17] And, whatever the current is, Femi Aribisala (who, in fact, insists on not being referred to as a pastor because, as he told me, "Jesus is the only pastor") can be counted on to swim against it. He seems a genuine outlier in the Nigerian theological universe, part curmudgeon and part intellectual oddball.[18] Their differences, indicative of the said attitudinal heterogeneity of the Nigerian pastorate, affirms Majid Yazdi's insight that "the clergy, like any other social group, become involved in politics to promote or protect some interests which they consider vital. How those interests are constituted, and what order of priority they have may, however, vary from one clerical faction to another."[19]

Such differences notwithstanding, I insist that clerical politics is, in sum, a status quo–friendly politics insofar as the Pentecostal theory of causality has the effect, inter alia, of absolving political actors of responsibility for their actions. Clerical status quo–friendly politics often manifests in a gift relationship, as was the case when Pastor Tunde Bakare gave a loan of N160 million (about US$450,000) to his friend Kaduna State Governor Nasir el-Rufai during the latter's campaign for governor. Whether the loan, or their friendship in general, played a role in Bakare's uncharacteristic silence in December 2016 when several Christian villages in Southern Kaduna were sacked and hundreds of villagers killed in attacks believed to have been orchestrated by Fulani herdsmen, is an open question. On a darker note, status quo–friendly politics is often the foundation for collusions between pastors and state officials in which the former—or, more specifically, their churches—are used as channels for money laundering, as would seem to be the case in the alliance between Pastor Emmanuel Omale, founder of the Abuja-based Divine Hand of God Prophetic Ministry, and Ibrahim Magu, acting chairman of the Economic and Financial Crimes Commission (EFCC).[20] The latter extends a pattern of state–church cooperation whereby the church serves as a "parking spot" for illicit monies siphoned from state and other coffers.[21]

To observe that pastors are entangled in politics and the political process in ways that complicate the relationship between the religious and the political is trite. The interesting question, it would seem, is how, in raising the specter of the proper limits of religious action and the boundaries of the political, clerical involvement in politics invites a reflection on the *instruments* used by religious leaders to channel and legitimize their authority. In analyzing three such instruments—calling, prayer, and prophecy, respectively—I wish to demonstrate, first, how they are used to fortify the spines of pastoral claims to exception, and second, how they are operationalized as vehicles of political discipline and social control. Here, calling is understood, pace Max Weber, as "a religious conception, that of a task set by God." In my analysis, being called is the equivalent of a spiritual conscription whereby an agent is drafted by God despite lacking essential qualities or boasting qualities and/or a pedigree that ordinarily ought to have been disqualifying.[22] In this wise, to be "called" is to declare that one's past record has been deleted and that the person who has been called is licensed to start afresh. As a matter of fact, to be called is to become a divine mouthpiece, a medium for the conveyance and implementation of a transhistorical will over which the called has no power or control. Prayer, of course, is any oral or gestural practice in which the believer entreats or petitions God to meet a specific need. More than as a simple petition, however, I approach prayer as the centerpiece of a deregulated spiritual economy in which past, present, and future as well as history, economics, politics, and agency are dissolved via the articulation and acceptance of a divine program in which, no matter the current tribulations, all will be well, perhaps not immediately, but most assuredly eventually. Prophecy is understood as a foretelling of future events, although my analysis also shows that, in the Pentecostal world, the idea is a little bit more complicated.

I must enter three sets of caveats. First: since the interaction of the theological and the political is extremely complex and constantly evolving, the following account is necessarily partial and incomplete. I aim to provide not a comprehensive analysis of religion and politics (for that, the reader is encouraged to turn to *Pentecostal Republic*) but an assessment of how, *with the aid of the three identified theological instruments*, pastoral authority plays out and is asserted within the political domain. Second, I do not discount other instruments of exercising religious authority; I focus on calling, prayer, and prophecy primarily because, often working in combination, they are essential to understanding religious entrepreneurship in a Nigerian context. When I say that they often work in combination, I mean, for example, that prophecy summons, and is indirectly legitimized by, calling and that how a set of prophecies is regarded cannot be disconnected from people's perception of the "spiritual authenticity" of the prophet, that is, whether or not he has been called. Pastors themselves appear to grasp this component of their authority, and I could not help but notice its thematic recurrence in my conversations with various pastors. In the wider framework of Pentecostal politics, calling, prayer, and prophecy cross-fertilize as a basis for "knowledge" grounded in revelation.

Finally, whether I refer to it in passing or not at all, it should be remembered that the Christian struggle for supremacy with its historical competition, Islam, is the perennial subtext to political discourse and engagement in Nigeria and accordingly the all-important backdrop to understanding the movement of Pentecostal politics. As I argued in *Pentecostal Republic*, perhaps the key characteristic of the Nigerian Fourth Republic is the nexus between its inauguration and the ascendance of Pentecostalism as the dominant form of Christianity in the country. It follows that Pentecostalism sets the terms and parameters of political engagement, more or less.

Before moving on to the three instruments, I explain what I mean by political entrepreneurship.

ON POLITICAL ENTREPRENEURSHIP

Any mention of entrepreneurship, especially in this historical moment, will most certainly conjure the specter of capitalism and the centrality of the entrepreneur as the one who ventures, in a process laden with unavoidable risks, to bring labor and capital into a profitable harness. Thus, to speak of entrepreneurship is to speak of innovation, creation, endeavor, and risk-taking, not to forget individual bullishness. Unfolding within the broad rubric of organizational sociology, much of the sociology of entrepreneurship has followed this tack, as evidenced by Patricia Thornton's definition of entrepreneurship as "the creation of new organizations which occurs as a context-dependent, social and economic process."[23] This literature is effectively split between those who favor "supply-side" economics, on the one hand, and those who favor "demand-side," on the other. While "the supply-side focuses on the availability of suitable individuals to occupy entrepreneurial roles," the demand-side privileges "the number and nature of the entrepreneurial roles that need to be filled."[24]

Due in part to frustrations arising from the apparent irreconcilability of these perspectives, some scholars, like Martin Ruef and Lucien Karpik, have suggested that, instead of focusing on who is an entrepreneur, which often leads to an obsession with "personality traits, and achievements," it might be more productive to imagine entrepreneurship as "a series of activities culminating in the process of organizational creation."[25] Recent Africanist literature on the subject has focused on whether the Western emphasis on the entrepreneur as the driver of prosperity is misplaced, with at least one volume of essays, that of Moses Ochonu, explicitly seeking to "temper the entrepreneurial hysteria that has gripped Africa."[26]

I have no dog in this fight, as my purpose is neither to augment the organizational sociology literature nor to judge whether or not the role of entrepreneurship in triggering economic growth, especially in a developing African context, is overly lionized. Instead, and in agreement with Paul Reynolds that "no one discipline or conceptual scheme can provide an adequate understanding of all aspects of entrepreneurship,"[27] I focus on the entrepreneurial behavior of the leading lights of the Nigerian clerical elite in a political context. This refers, pace Reynolds, to individual pursuits of political endeavors and opportunities that redound both to the personal profit of respective pastors and to the corporate gain of the churches that they head.

This is not to deny that Pentecostal pastors are economic entrepreneurs. As a matter of fact, according to James Twitchell, such is the involvement of many of them in the business side of salvation that they are best categorized as "pastorpreneurs," a "market-savvy class of speculators" who, by "clever use of marketing techniques," "promise to shift the entire industry [megachurches] away from top-down denominationalism toward stand-alone communities."[28] For her part, Miranda Klaver has linked pastorpreneurship to the emergence of "a new kind of Christianity that is different from the religious regimes of the past," specifically a religious leadership "no longer legitimized and guaranteed by denominational traditions, confessions and the ordination of clergy but needs to be continuously performed, renewed and authenticated."[29] Undoubtedly, there is something to be said for a view of Pentecostal pastors as corporate titans presiding over complex transnational entities and aiming to be "profitable" in what I have described elsewhere as a competitive Nigerian religious "marketplace."[30] The features of this marketplace include, as I have argued, product saturation (or oversupply of religious goods) and, for the aspiring pastor, low barriers to entry, both of which, it goes without saying, increase the need for an entrepreneurial spirit.

Therefore, even if one were not primarily interested in economic entrepreneurship per se, it would be difficult to dispute that many of the personal traits, skills, and assets required by a pastor to succeed as an economic entrepreneur, or to simply survive as a pastor, are serviceable in a political context. Against this backdrop, I see political entrepreneurship as a series of calculated interventions and mediations by individual pastors who seek opportunities for influence in the political space, with many of such mediations naturally targeted at leading players in the state and the political establishment at large. Just as the economic entrepreneur pursues profit, political entrepreneurship is about leveraging economic *and* perceived spiritual power for individual political access and advantage, which generally favors the consolidation of pastoral authority. As economic entrepreneurs, leading pastors preside over complex financial concerns, from publishing, including broadcasting, to the sale of clothing, anointing oils and handkerchiefs, "blessed" artefacts, and prayer mantles. Their success in the economic realm—their prosperity, so to speak—is foundational to their appeal to their followers, as well as their clout with political authorities.

THE DIVINE SUMMONS

In theory, being "called" is a deeply personal event. It is a moment of deep rupture after which the individual who has been called becomes a different person, and it is an event that catches the individual off guard precisely because, by definition, it is not something you can prepare for. For those who are called, it is a temporal marker of a moral course correction, as many testify to charting a completely different personal path following such "encounters." As it is a biographical milestone, it tends to stay fresh in the memory, which probably explains the ease with which some of the pastors I interviewed were able to call up the precise moment when they believed they received the calling. For Femi Aribisala, it was in the context of a dramatic encounter with armed robbers on his way back from the Murtala Muhammed International Airport, Lagos, where he had gone to collect his wife and six-year-old son, who were returning from a trip to the United States. Having rammed his car into a lamp post as he tried to evade the ambush, and facing certain death as one of the assailants he had tried to overrun approached with menace, he "heard a voice, and it was calm, confident, reassuring, and he said, 'Femi, nothing is going to happen to you here.'" For Aribisala, that was the moment the last of his intellectual reservations against organized religion fell away. As he relates it:

> It's like you're falling down a cliff and you're looking for something to hold on to and someone is at the top and he decides to throw you a thread, he tells you to grab the thread. Now, you know the thread cannot hold the weight and you're an intellectual person, but . . . you have no other plans, no other ideas, so you grab the thread and it holds you. That was what happened to me. So I went inside the car and told my wife what I had heard, "Nothing is going to happen here." Because the other thing that

was peculiar about that situation was that from the first time I heard the voice, "Nothing is going to happen to you here," it was like somebody just brought peace and brought it into the situation. I just was not afraid. It was like I was in a film but I was watching the film.[31]

The theme of finding one's intellectual defense definitively compromised also appears in Pastor Adeboye's account of his calling, or, as he describes it, his "ultimate encounter with God that totally changed my life":

> I was then a senior lecturer in Mathematics at the University of Lagos. It all happened at an evening service at The Redeemed Christian Church of God (RCCG) where I was only a month old. That particular evening, I was so overwhelmed when it became clear that I was close to hell without knowing it. I suddenly realized that it was possible to have all the Ph.D.s in the world and still be on the losing side. I knew all kinds of formulae but did not know the one for eternal life. Sobbing like a baby at that evening service, I made straight to the altar, throwing my hands over my head in total submission to the will of Almighty God by accepting Jesus Christ as my personal Lord and Saviour. From that day, my priorities were re-ordered. Life became different for me, my attitude and approach to world things changed. For instance, extra-marital relationships were totally cut off; I abandoned alcoholism while my wife gained my full attention and love.[32]

The Damascene moment for Pastor Gbade Ogunlana has none of the drama of those described by Pastors Aribisala and Adeboye though, significantly, he too heard a voice. As he narrates it:

> I knew I would become a pastor the day I became born again. 1979. There was one time one preacher came, Evangelist Caleb Oloyede, he has gone to be with the Lord now. He came for a crusade at Christ the King primary school at Oluyoro, Agugu, Ibadan. When he called for Altar call and I was about a go out, inside of me I heard a voice that said you would be a preacher like that man. So since that day, the first day I entered University of Ibadan, I told myself I'm going to graduate here with good colors

but I'm not going to use the certificate because I knew I wouldn't use it. So I've always known from that day.[33]

Sometimes, the call merely consolidates what is believed to be "suggestive circumstances from birth," as we see in the example of Pastor Sam Adeyemi, founder of the Daystar Christian Ministry. While a student at the Federal Polytechnic, Ado-Ekiti, in 1982, his father's civil engineering business upon which he had relied for funding having collapsed unexpectedly, he was

> living on coke and biscuits and I realized things were going to be a little rough for me so I felt I needed God very early, not the fun of drinking, drugs and women. Then, during my Higher Diploma course in 1986, I heard a man of God preach that, "Where your treasure is, there will your heart be also." That day I got to the hostel and I said, "Lord, where have you put my treasure in life, so that I can put my heart there?" And God spoke to my heart; *"You are going to be a preacher, you won't be a contractor."* I was so sure about it, I told my classmates, "Guys, your competition has reduced. I'm not going to be a contractor, I am going to be a preacher." The way God spoke to me is what I call inner witness; that is how my own leading comes.[34]

Prior to the call, Adeyemi's calling seems to have been foretold by a unique set of circumstances surrounding his birth:

> Well, my parents had a child, a boy, before me who died within four days. That was their first child. They were really disturbed and disappointed. But my Dad said that some months later, he was at a tap fetching water, when an elderly man also came for water. (The case of the husband helping out in the home.) He said he stepped aside and asked the man to fetch water. When the man was through, he thanked him and said, *You lost a child but God is going to give you other children and they are going to be great and God is going to use them.* And then my mother told me I was named Samuel and at my dedication, the presiding Reverend, Rev. Chestmore, told them, *You named him Samuel, you must understand what it means. Samuel in the Bible was given back to the Lord to serve God; so you must be willing to let this boy serve God.*[35]

The foregoing illustrations buttress my observation regarding the deeply personal character of being called, but what I find fascinating is its tacit role in the public construction of pastoral authority. In the first place, the public deference given to those who have been called—as an authority not just on spiritual matters but, as I have argued, on secular matters as well—points to the combined weakness and lack of trust in secular institutions and poles of authority. In this regard, being called is the polar opposite of being elected, and it seems reasonable to hazard that, in the long run, consistent resort to, and increased confidence in one, might work to weaken the other. Thus understood, the rise of pastoral authority bodes ill for democratic structures.

A related point to consider is the imagined collision between those who have been called and those with a different kind of calling—what Max Weber calls "a 'calling,' in the most genuine sense of the word"—political leadership. Weber is clear about what happens when both are fused in a single leader, that is, when the political leader is also seen as possessing that intangible but no less real quality called charisma: "Devotion to the charisma of the prophet, or the leader in war, or to the great demagogue in the ecclesia or in parliament, means that the leader is personally recognized as the innerly 'called' leader of men. Men do not obey him by virtue of tradition or statute, but because they believe in him."[36] While Nigerian political history is arguably not lacking in such leaders, their singular rarity is one of the key elements of the Fourth Republic. What obtains for the most part is "the rule of professional politicians without a calling, without the inner charismatic qualities that make a leader"; hence, the political class exists in sufferance to Pentecostal pastors channeling the authority of a spiritual calling.[37] Simultaneously, then, calling—the spiritual one—furthers clerical annexation of power even as it highlights the crisis in the political system, among them the characterological depletion of the political elite and the virtual collapse of political parties as ideologically cohesive formations.

Finally, given the general hunger for credentials and titles in Nigeria, as discussed in the previous chapter, the appeal to calling—and, ipso facto, the status and authority that it confers—can be seen as a way of bypassing the need for formal credentialing; the decisive idea about calling is that, as a credential, it can be neither confirmed nor disconfirmed. That, in spite of this, it is politically potent no less is precisely my point.

POLITICS AS INVOCATION

A Christian without condemnation of heart has a right to thank God, to be in adoration unto the Lord, and to ask in prayer always. Prayer should be evidence of a soul that thirsts for God, and those who are unable to pray annoy God. In the absence of prayer, much trouble and danger are encountered. It is God's plan and order that we should pray to receive all the good he has promised in his treasure for us. The Holy Spirit helps the believer overcome his infirmities in the place of prayer. We must pray only in the name of Jesus. Without faith, our prayer is powerless before God. We are commanded to pray and not to faint and to pray without ceasing. The apostles thus put prayer first in their lives and spent much time in prayer.[38]

Prayer is the beating heart of Pentecostalism, the most important weapon in the believer's spiritual arsenal. Using excerpts from the writings of Pastor D. K. Olukoya of the Lagos-based Mountain of Fire and Miracles Ministries (MFM), I have elsewhere emphasized the centrality of prayer to a litigious Pentecostalism in which the believer is permanently crusading against a host of unseen spirits.[39] So important is prayer as the centerpiece of the Pentecostal devotional repertoire that, if Pastor Adeboye is to be believed (see the interview with CNN quoted above), it is a preferred and more effective *alternative* to political protest. But in the context of the Fourth Republic, prayer, for the Pentecostal, is much more than an item in the individual armory. The Fourth Republic itself, as I have demonstrated,[40] is seen as an answer to Pentecostal/Christians' petition for a "power shift" from the Islamic North to the largely Christian South. Accordingly, the onus is on every believer to preserve it through the power of prayer, which, conceivably, is what Pastor Adeboye and other leading pastors are doing with their well-publicized visits to the residences of high-ranking state officials and government offices.

The focus here is on what I call the politics of invocation, which is about the use of prayer to stabilize the political order and secure clerical authority. This can work in at least two ways. In the first place, and as I have shown with the example of Ajaokuta, state officials can seize upon visits by pastors to "flip the script" on and sabotage civil society by promoting exculpatory official narratives on infrastructural decay and poor governance. At the same time, state governors and other state functionaries have been known to organize public prayer sessions that have essentially pivoted on the idea that (1) public policy problems are, in fact, spiritual problems and (2), being spiritual problems, their *only* solution is to be found in mass prayer.[41] Such spectacles stabilize the political order and disarm the public by creating a distracting buzz around "spiritual problems" while leaving actual public policy problems more or less unattended. Prayer functions in this regard as a technology of acquiescence for the production of governable political subjects.

A complementary way of looking at the politics of invocation is to consider prayer as an element in a discursive frame with which pastors legitimize their authority. This takes place when prayer is subsumed within a grand narrative that frames the totality of Nigerian history as unfolding within a divine master plan. The logic of this framing—the details of which, incidentally, are perceptible only to those who have been called—is that the strings of everyday governance are, in fact, pulled by unseen forces whose rationality or "purpose" can be accessed only through spiritual work, the centerpiece of which is prayer. Seen within this framework, Adeboye's preference for prayer as an alternative to protest makes a lot of sense, for protest as a political activity is redundant if, no matter what the individual citizen does, God's master plan for the nation's greatness is guaranteed. When, for instance, and, as he frequently does in his homilies and speeches, Pastor Tunde Bakare alludes either to the "God-ordained destiny" or to the "prophetic destiny" of Nigeria, he is operating within this mentality,[42] and both Bakare and Adeboye would most probably agree on a future in which the country is won for Christ by prayer, if not politics, presumably after a reconciliation of all the "contrary spirits" that, at the moment, stymie God's divine plan. The key idea is that, as long as this framing can be taken at its face value, one must concede some leverage to those driving it—the clerical class. (I should say that, while the idea of "God-ordained destiny" is reminiscent of "Manifest Destiny," they may or may not necessarily mean the same thing. The former is a straightforward religious conception, while the latter is a secular idea that, depending on context, can be religiously freighted.)

At any rate, the sheer ubiquity of prayer—its visual, auditory, and sensory excess and its apparent inscription into every nook and cranny of social life in Nigeria—makes the case for the success of the politics of invocation. What I am alluding to is the appearance of prayer at multiple social sites, including spaces that are not primarily denominated as either "sacred" or set aside for worship. Prayer within this matrix is not mobilized exclusively within the province of, let alone by, the "religious" or "spiritual"; on the contrary, it is simultaneously a base, a foundational ethos, an aspirational core, and an ever-present scheme of meaning for a majority of the people. It is there in the pre-match huddle by the players of the Nigerian national soccer team, the Super Eagles, trusting God to deliver that all-important victory against usually better-prepared opponents; it is present in the solitary mutter by the occupant of an automobile caught in the perennial vehicular gridlock of Lagos. It is also, as I demonstrated in *Pentecostal Republic*, the political crutch that a new president eager to secure the affections of a watching public falls on and is central to displays of ostentatious humility repeatedly—and desperately—staged by the same president to win the Christian vote.

Overall, and as I have argued elsewhere,[43] within the framework of the struggle for political pre-eminence in Nigeria, prayer is a conduit for channeling Pentecostal power, and the principal medium for this process is the Pentecostal pastor.

FATIDIC POLITICS; OR, WEAPONS OF THE STRONG

When, on November 6, 2016, Prophet T. B. Joshua of the Synagogue, Church of All Nations (SCOAN), decided to share with his congregation the winner of the then–approaching US presidential election as disclosed to him by God, he could not have been clearer: "Ten days ago, I saw the new President of America with a narrow win. The new President will be facing several challenges over many issues, including: passing bills, attempts to possibly pass a vote of no confidence on the new President. The boat of the new President will be rocked. By the way, in order not to keep you in suspense, what I frankly saw is a woman."[44] Such was Joshua's confidence in his prophecy that the church even posted it on the TB Joshua Ministries Facebook page. During the church service, Joshua was quite the tease, holding up a white piece of paper apparently containing the name, mildly threatening not to reveal the name until the end of the service, all the while basking in the growing applause.[45]

Let me pause here to reflect on the clues Joshua's performance in the above episode furnish about his persona. Throughout the video and, as he does in his sermons, Joshua speaks in what, at best, might be regarded as halting English, trampling one syntactical principle after another. His evident discomfort with the English language marks an important difference between him and leading members of the Pentecostal pastorate like Adeboye, Bakare, and Oyedepo—his limited education. From all accounts, Joshua did not even complete one year of high school education, while Adeboye has a PhD in applied mathematics and was once a university professor, Bakare studied law and cut his legal teeth with Gani Fawehinmi Chambers, and David Oyedepo studied architecture at the Kwara State University, Ilorin. Perhaps because of this, Joshua did not seem to have the polish that one finds in these contemporaries. What this means is that he was, relatively speaking, in a world of his own. For instance, one can easily visualize Adeboye, Bakare, and Oyedepo bonding, but the three of them bonding collectively or individually with Joshua, not so much. The trio occupies what we might call, loosely, the "bourgeois" wing of the Nigerian clerical elite, while Joshua belongs to, though he is by no means alone in, the "lumpen" wing. Joshua's status was that of an outsider (so far as I know, he never openly aligned with the Christian Association of Nigeria [CAN] or the Pentecostal Fellowship of Nigeria [PFN]) within the theocratic elite. Confirmation of that status came when, following his unexpected passing on June 5, 2021, no member of the bourgeois wing issued any public message of condolence, and at least one, Chris Okotie of Household of God Church, seemed to gloat over his demise.[46] All this makes Joshua's achievements *despite* the aforementioned educational handicap even more impressive. As discussed in the previous chapter, Joshua boasted a long and enviable list of distinguished friends and devotees, including many incumbent and former heads of state, business executives, celebrities, and sport stars from various parts of the world. In fact, he appears to have had more international "connections" than, say, Pastor Adeboye, even though the latter's church, given its model, has a wider geographic spread. In truth, Pastor T. B. Joshua probably had more "friends in high places" than his better-educated and, inarguably, more sophisticated clerical peers. For example, after the guest house on his church premises collapsed in September 2014, killing scores of people, including an estimated eighty-four South Africans, it was prominent South Africans like former South African Football Association (Safa) chairman, Kirsten

Nematandani and parliamentarian and President of the Economic Freedom Fighters (EFF) Julius Malema who came to his defense. What explains this? First, Joshua's very lack of education could, not implausibly, be a basis for his construal as "authentic" by his enthusiasts and members of his congregation. Second, and relevant to my larger argument in the book, is the way in which being a pastor can override, to the point of canceling, personal limitations that could very well be damaging in a different context. To what extent Joshua's cultivation of the elite was motivated by a feeling of insecurity about his pedigree is an open question. Regardless, his success is an important bit of sociological data for tracking the emergent discorrelation between Western education and personal success in contemporary Nigeria, which proves my point on the emergence of pastoring as a means of short-circuiting existing structures of social mobility.

In any event, and as we now know, Joshua's prophecy about the 2016 US presidential election did not come to pass, as it was a man (Republican candidate Donald J. Trump) who won that election, an unforeseen outcome that sent Joshua scampering for the following face-saving explanation: "We have seen the outcome of the election in America. Having read, you will notice that it is all about the popular vote, the vote of the majority of Americans."[47] Pastor Joshua's bizarre explanation that he had, in fact, meant to pick the winner of the popular vote (in contradistinction to that of the Electoral College) was met with widespread derision across social media, with some commentators accusing him of being a fake pastor and others denouncing him for his "false prophecy." As indicated in the introductory chapter, accusations of "fakery" and "falsity" such as we have seen here have to be understood within the broader Nigerian moral economy, in which the ersatz exists in permanent tension—and contention—with the real. But that is not my focus here.

My focus is on what I am calling "fatidic politics," which is the use of prophecy as a technology of rule by Pentecostal pastors, a phenomenon ironically confirmed by the ferocity and scale of the denunciation that greeted Joshua's unfulfilled prophecy; frustration about a prophecy that did not come to pass became a measure of how much faith people have in prophecies—and those who speak them. Nevertheless, in my judgment, that *a particular prophecy* goes unfulfilled is subsidiary to the fact that *prophecy in general* is seriously regarded, given that, as I explore in short order, being associated with an unfulfilled prophecy hardly correlates to any tangible diminution of pastoral reputation. In the same vein, I am interested neither in the figure of the prophet "as a charismatic leader arising at times of stress to offer a new order, a new vision of society,"[48] nor in the variety of typological distinctions between a "prophet," a "diviner," and a "seer." I do not dispute the importance of the overlaps and departures among such nomenclatures—as we see, for instance, in Weber's comparisons among priest and prophet, magician and prophet, lawgiver and prophet, philosopher and prophet, or even tyrant and prophet. My position, already discussed in the introductory chapter, is that, titular structures in mainline churches exempted, in contemporary Nigeria (these) nomenclatures hardly correlate to any tangible distinctions in job descriptions, and "bishop," "evangelist," "apostle," or "prophet" can be enfolded in the category of "pastor" without any injustice to what the bearers of such titles actually do.

Further, and very much against the grain of the historical literature that analyzes prophecy as a subaltern weapon to challenge hegemonic power,[49] a "weapon of the weak" in the tradition of James Scott, or what Robert Baum captures as "oppositional roles towards institutional authority,"[50] prophecy is understood here as *a weapon of the strong* insofar as it is a tool of political acquiescence mobilized by a powerful clerical elite to reinforce institutional authority and amass power for itself.

Weber describes two fundamental types of prophecy—the "exemplary" and the "emissary." He writes: "Exemplary prophecy points out the path to salvation by exemplary living, usually by a contemplative and apathetic ecstatic life. The emissary type of prophecy addresses its *demands* to the world in the name of a god. Naturally these demands are ethical; and they are often of an active ascetic character."[51] In the same vein, Weber writes of the substance of the prophecy, which he also calls "the savior's commandment," as "to direct a way of life to the pursuit of a sacred value. Thus understood, the prophecy or commandment means, at least relatively, to systematize and rationalize the way of life, either in particular points or totally."[52]

The emphasis in the foregoing on "demands" accords with one of the two ways in which Nigerian Pentecostals think of prophecy. While the common understanding of prophecy as the foretelling of a future event subsists, prophecy is, *in addition*, understood in the sense conveyed by Margaret Poloma and Matthew Lee as "a forth-telling of God's word."[53] Similar to the Mozambican Pentecostals they discuss, Nigerian Pentecostals also regard prophecy as "a gift of the Holy Spirit through which believers experience the usually inaudible 'voice' of God speaking directly to them and/or through the prophetic words of others that lead them and guide their actions."[54] For Nigerian Pentecostals, a prophecy is not merely a prediction of what will happen; it is *also* a prayer regarding what the person speaking the prophecy wishes to see happen. This is the *demand* (command?) aspect and is invariably what Pentecostals have in mind when, in Pentecostal idiom, they "speak a prophecy" into someone's life. It is, often simultaneously, both what the prophet has been commanded to say and his own—there's no better way of putting it—command to God.

Fatidic politics operates in two related ways. In the first, and crucially, at an intimate level, pastors use prophecy—and the implicit trust in their effectivity—to "govern" political leaders. When Stephen Ellis refers to how, in Nigeria—and much of Africa—"older institutions continue to play an important *unofficial* role in politics, including by the use of *their supposed powers to inflict death or to enhance life*,"[55] this is part of what is implied. Among the Nigerian political elite, regular consultation with a variety of spiritual "advisors" or "guides" is par for the course, and not a few have a cluster of such "experts" who are placed on retainer, sometimes at state expense, operating as the last and most trusted line of defense in the "security" apparatus of the concerned officeholder. The explanation for this, as discussed in the introductory chapter, is the belief, common to officeholders as well as the general public, that *real* power is hidden, spiritual power, and such is the strength of their conviction that, as Ellis has documented, many, in fact, go out of their way to swear an oath to deities perceived as the actual (defensive and offensive) "forces" driving secular affairs.[56] Prophecy (also, "vision") here functions as a form of advanced "knowledge" vouchsafed to those in power to help them guard against the nefarious activities of political opponents or to function as approval or disapproval of specific policy moves. Either way, I hold, its *effect* is to "govern" those in power, and the widely publicized reliance of US President Ronald Reagan and his wife Nancy on astrologer Joan Ceciel Quigley for daily "advice" only goes to confirm that the practice is not unique to an African context.

A second way in which fatidic politics operates is seen when prophecy is used to assume control or "take possession" of the narrative of a political dispensation and/or the country. In such a case, the "prophet reveals particular prophecies about a national leader, the outcome of an election,"⁵⁷ the direction of the economy, and so on. For example, and as I discuss in *Pentecostal Republic*,⁵⁸ the Nigerian Fourth Republic was conceived in prophetic controversy after Pastor Tunde Bakare prophesied concerning the newly elected President Olusegun Obasanjo that he is "not your Messiah, he is King Agag and the prophetic axe will come down upon his head before May 29, 1999."⁵⁹ The torrent of counter-prophesies by Obasanjo's supporters among the clerical elite proves that the proclamations of prophesies are political events that may be about *both* foretelling and forth-telling. At any rate, the popularity of prophecies as advance knowledge can be seen in the eagerness with which, in December through January of every year, many Nigerians anticipate and consume yearly prophecies revealed with much fanfare by leading Pentecostal pastors. As I argued in the previous chapter, such popularity is indicative of gaps in Nigeria's economy of knowledge production, gaps that, interacting with global epistemological fragility, instigated a crisis of knowability that, in turn, led to the emergence of pastors as producers of "knowledge" about politics, the economy, and futurity. The claim, via prophecy, of spiritual mastery of this uncertain terrain becomes, I advance, a claim on the power of the state and the subjectivity of citizens.

Notwithstanding, prophecy as a basis of knowledge about the future is extremely contingent, and if the above anecdote about Prophet T. B. Joshua proves anything, it is this inherent precarity. Yet such moments—I call them clerical errors—are no less sociologically instructive. A clerical error can happen in two ways, either when a prophecy is unfulfilled (like Joshua's, supra) or when a prophecy fails to anticipate a momentous event, as happened in 2020, when, to their collective embarrassment, none among the leading Nigerian pastors foresaw the new Coronavirus pandemic. Pastor Adeboye changed his story several times, first saying that he had seen it coming but had refrained from talking about it in order not to create panic, then saying that it would be over within an unspecified number of days, and finally suggesting that perhaps he has been paying more than glancing attention to evolving medical opinion, that "Coronavirus is not going to disappear completely. Just like the flu and Ebola, it would subside. In the mighty name of Jesus, it would subside soon. But that it would leave the world completely, that would take a special miracle."⁶⁰ T. B. Joshua, yet again, was left scrambling for an explanation and facing a barrage of online ridicule after his bold prediction that "Coronavirus will end by March 27, 2020," failed to come to pass.

The frequency with which a large number of prophecies fail to come to pass raises the question of how "prophets" maintain their aura and the trust of their congregations in the aftermath of glaring clerical errors. In their sociopsychological classic Festinger, Riecken, and Schachter show how, counter-intuitively, unfulfilled prophecies may, in fact, engender increased, rather than diminished, fervor on the part of members of a religious community.[61] Evidence from contemporary Nigeria backs up this claim as, thus far, mounting clerical errors notwithstanding, overall, the corporate authority of the Pentecostal pastorate remains unshaken. On the one hand, this makes it interesting to speculate on the extent to which this reflects Nigerian Pentecostals' puzzling reconciliation of the sensible and the nonsensical, particularly the idea "It does not make sense, but it makes spirit." Applied to the analysis of prophecies, it not only increases the latitude that congregants give their pastors but also, more important, the indulgence toward prophecies as precise forecasts of the future. Wariboko sees "It does not make sense, but it makes spirit" as "a yielding to the loss of meaningful rationality or intelligibility provoked by the daily assaults from the Nigerian experience of "governance-as-trauma."[62] On the other hand, there is the idea that a prophecy is not necessarily final but, for Pentecostals, is often provisional and reversible through prayer. We see this idea of prophecy as a form of spiritual alert in Pastor Bakare's retrospective on his unfulfilled prophecy concerning President Obasanjo: "I have not changed any word from that prophecy, because that was the way I received it and that was the way I gave it. It was given so that the nation—the holy nation, the church, *can pray and it would eventually lead to a major prayer move in this country*."[63]

All told, the power of prophecy as a mode of exercising political control, not to mention a continuing source of political intervention, abides.

CONCLUSION

In this chapter I have attempted to demonstrate how the clerical elite manages to exercise control in the political domain through the combined instrumentality of calling, prayer, and prophecy. The overall effect of pastoral manipulation of these instruments—what I call political entrepreneurship—is the enhanced authority of pastors in a cultural context in which many assume that spiritual power is the hidden but constantly active predicate of all forms of power and authority. Of course, the clerical class influences and shapes the political process in multiple ways—by acting as go-betweens between the state and civil society, participating in the determination and resolution of political conflicts,[64] and aiming to reconcile political rivals in times of extreme stress. The often unstated assumption in analyses that emphasize these modes of clerical intervention is that religious leaders are *external* to the political process. In analyzing three related instruments of pastoral legitimization, I have shown how Pentecostal pastors are, in fact, implicated *in* the political process in ways that raise fundamental questions about the location of political authority, especially within the matrix of democratic rule.

As is to be expected from a figure that I have described as an existential micromanager, the influence of the contemporary Pentecostal pastor extends far beyond the political domain. He is also an object of erotic fascination. In the following chapter I discuss how pastoral authority is exercised through the discharge of sexual ardor and the projection of sexual power.

CHAPTER THREE

Erotic Pentecostalism

The Pastor as Sexual Object

"BEAUTY AND THE BEAST"

Judging by the precision and care with which class borders are patrolled and monitored for possible violation in Nigeria, the relationship between Dolapo Awosika and Moses Muyideen Kasali, general overseer of the Ibadan-based Mountain of Mercy, also popularly known as *Baba Alaseyori*, is one that never should have happened. As one blogger, one of the many who took an avid interest in the relationship, was eager to point out, Dolapo is the "educated . . . beautiful, single mother of two children, good social class to mention a few." On the other hand, there is Kasali, "a visually impaired man, married with five children, respected prophet from Ibadan, talented singer, teacher of the Word, illiterate, humble background, etc." This particular blogger then rounds off the descriptions of the two with the question that many a class-conscious watcher had been asking: "So, how did the two get to meet each other?"[1] The angst of class miscegenation also spread to major news dailies. An unsigned commentary in *This Day* (a newspaper so obsessed with social status it has a special weekly pull-out dedicated to the "Glitterati") regretted that "unlike two peas in a pod, Dolapo Awosika and a certain Prophet Muyideen Kasali belong to two different and very distant worlds—in fact, liken them to water and oil which nature and science preclude from mixing, and you would not be mistaken."² It continues in the same disparaging—of Kasali—tone:

> A thoroughbred, London-trained lawyer who has dined and wined with some of the finest male species known to humanity, Dolapo's grin or grimace would effortlessly tug at any man's heartstrings and purse-strings. She is as beautiful as they come (sic). By virtue of education, socialization and marriage, she knows her way through the labyrinth of power and prosperity. And she was once married, and has two kids by Nigerian-born ex-England footballer, the gangling and wealthy John Fashanu. . . . Her path was never supposed to cross with that of her new paramour, a powerful prophet whose church is located in Moniya, a rustic and remote area of Akinyemi LGA, Ibadan.³

As commentators offered various theories in their attempt to unravel Ms. Awosika's inexplicable class betrayal, two themes emerged, both pertinent to the subject of pastoral power, which is the focus of this book. The first and most common "explanation," that Dolapo must have acted "under a spell,"⁴ is consistent with the assumption (see previous chapter) that most everyday decisions are in fact quietly, but steadily, determined by unseen forces and that pastors are uniquely positioned (being in constant touch with the spiritual world) to engineer those forces, in this case apparently to the pastor's selfish end. My naïve attempt during a conversation with one of Ms. Awosika's wounded admirers to point out the obvious class element in the whole saga was quickly dismissed, as she expressed her astonishment at my obvious belittling of the power of "jazz."⁵ A second "explanation," not inconsistent with the first, is that Prophet Kasali had to have enticed Ms. Awosika with his sexual ardor, something that, it is assumed, is integral to the contemporary Man of God's perverse power. In the Nigerian popular imagination, pastoral power and sexual control are so much fused as to become grist for the mill of its fiction.⁶

In all this, Ms. Awosika—especially at the beginning of the ruckus, when she clearly struggled to confirm her new status (marital and otherwise) to her admirers—hardly clarified matters with her explanation: "A friend had issues and she asked me to go there for her. She doesn't live in this country and I was coming back from London to

Nigeria. And that was what I went for. And Baba can say that, he can confirm what I've just said. So, I didn't go to do anything, I don't go to ori-oke."[7]

In the next chapter I discuss class and social status, especially in relation to gender, in more detail. For now I pursue the implication of the latter explanation—which reflects the belief that the Man of God is someone erotically powerful, a figure imbued with an unspecified sexual ardor. In the main, I posit that the erotic sphere is one of the domains within which pastoral authority in contemporary Nigeria is exercised, and that whether we are talking about influence in the political or the sexual sphere, the overall effect of pastoral influence is the same—a concentration of spiritual authority, which helps prepare the ground for mass suggestibility. The discussion unfolds as follows: First, I place Nigerian Pentecostalism within the matrix of the lively contention over sex and sexual matters, both in that country and elsewhere in Africa. Second, against the backdrop of historical tension between religion and sex and drawing on sociological and other writings on the erotic, I elaborate the idea of a Nigerian Pentecostal erotic economy. Finally, in locating the pastor at the center of this economy, I account for the pastor's erotic power, particularly, in a significant number of cases, his access to and seeming control over the bodies *and* sexual organs of his congregants.

STATE OF AROUSAL

A few years ago, when major Nigerians newspapers started tracking the number of people who read and comment on stories posted on their websites, I decided, on a hunch, to track the tracker. I started paying attention to the number of people who look at stories about sex compared to those who view other stories, especially those related to politics. Given the passion with which Nigerians consume news on political matters and engage in debate on them, I automatically assumed that reporting on such matters would attract the greatest attention, judging by the number of views. For my admittedly unscientific survey, I selected stories published in two of the most widely read Nigerian newspapers, the *Nigerian Tribune* and *Punch*. In short order, I discovered an interesting pattern: although stories about politics typically generated the most comments, stories about sex, though with fewer comments, tended to have the most views, routinely exceeding the former, sometimes by a factor of five.

If the recent spate of online sex "clinics," "advisories," and "agony aunts" (akin to advice columnists in American usage, but with a different resonance) about all things sexual is a reliable barometer, the Nigerian public's interest in sex is by no means limited to consumption of stories about it. Not only that, one can easily detect a certain gendered sexual anxiety, especially concerning sexual virility and performance, as a majority of the queries submitted by male-identified patrons to the "Sexperts" who manage these clinics tend to pertain in one way or another to how one can "last longer in bed," how to avoid premature ejaculation, and what measures to take in order to enhance one's manhood or performance in bed. Now, it is not a surprise that people would say one thing about sex while continuing to act differently; people do not readily admit to their actions, never mind their fantasies. This is the problem with any research on sex that, perhaps unavoidably considering the nature of the subject, relies on what people say about it. The real reason that such a robust interest in sexual matters is striking in that it challenges what one would normally expect given (African) Pentecostalism's fixation on sexual restraint as part of its investment in what Melissa Hackman refers to as "transforming sexual acts, gender roles, and sexual subjectivities."[8] It would seem that, ironically, not only has sexual exuberance in Nigeria corresponded to the rise of Pentecostalism as a social force but also Pentecostalism has been implicated in this very process.

In the first place, its seemingly uncompromising position on sex (abstinence before marriage, absolute fidelity after), both within the inviolable matrix of heterosexuality, was primarily what dictated its involvement in the controversy over same-sex marriage on the side of the (Nigerian) state. As I have argued elsewhere,[9] as part of an attempt to keep gays in the closet and keep marriage "heteronormative," Pentecostals and other religious actors were unwittingly lured into the fray of a simmering public debate over intimacy, individual rights, sexual choice, sexual citizenship, and the limits of state power. Outside Nigeria, the most notorious illustration of this paradox of publicizing sex in the process of demonizing a category of sexuality is Ugandan pastor Martin Ssempa, spokesperson for the Ugandan Interfaith Rainbow Coalition Against Homosexuality and an avid campaigner for the country's Anti-Homosexuality Act (2014).[10] Desperate to convince his audience that homosexuality is "socially dysfunctional and non-productive" and "an inherently perverse practice that is threatening the moral order of the country,"[11] Pastor Ssempa had broadcast to his stunned congregation, minors and all, selected footage from online gay pornographic websites.[12] In Nigeria, the anti-same-sex coalition (of the religious elite, the media, and the state), was beneficial to all involved, though the religious elite, having provided the all-important religious grounds, arguably secured the greatest advantage. While there is no suggestion here that African actors were mere ventriloquists for messages originating from elsewhere, and while I find the idea of African agents as naïve pawns of foreign exploiters totally implausible, if not outright insulting; nonetheless, we cannot discount the role of American conservative Christian groups in shaping public opinion against homosexuality in Africa. Since 2008, the US Christian right is believed to have spent up to $280 million in "dark money" in different parts of the world, including more than $50 million in Africa alone.[13]

Second: in a shift from the idea of the pastor as one with the final word on sexual propriety, the embodiment of sexual prudence whose staid domesticity is held up as an inspiration to the faithful, several Pentecostal pastors have been caught up in sex scandals and sexual controversies, leading to a situation in which pastors have become predictable, if unwitting, conveyors of sex to the public domain. For instance, between March and May 2017, the Nigerian public was treated to lurid stories of a sexual liaison allegedly involving Pastor Johnson Suleman of the Omega Fire Ministries and a Canada-Based Nigerian singer, Stephanie Otobo.[14] (Their saga is one of four stories of encounters involving pastors and women analyzed in the next chapter.) Media reportage of such scandals, frequently slipping into the realm of the implausible, seem fueled, on the one hand, by a desire to highlight clerical hypocrisy and, on the other hand, by a realization that such stories, holding a real fascination for the public because of the social prestige of pastors, present a way to make a quick buck. Either way, the mutual entanglement of sex and the pastorate in the popular imagination is solidified.

Third, the emergence of the Pentecostal pastor as a sexual object in his own right (a subject whose sexual and domestic lives are increasingly of public interest) has only assisted in placing Pentecostalism at the center of discussions about sex, sexuality, masculinity, privacy, gender, and eroticism in Nigeria. For example, in recent times domestic controversies involving, in no particular order, Pastor Taiwo Odukoya of the Fountain of Life Church (the timing of his new wife's pregnancy and delivery of the couple's first child together);[15] Pastor Chris Okotie of the Household of God Church International Ministries and his wife, Stephanie Okotie (a messy divorce);[16] and Pastor Chris Oyakhilome of Christ Embassy and his wife, Anita Oyakhilome (another messy divorce), have captured the Nigerian media's attention.[17]

THE PENTECOSTAL EROTIC

The contemporary Pentecostal pastor occupies the center of a Pentecostal erotic economy, one that is rich with implications for scholarly understanding of the character of social citizenship. Charged with representing biblical injunctions on sex against the backdrop of an increasingly sexualized socio-urban landscape that constantly threatens to drown out his message, the pastor is nonetheless drawn into a drama of self-fashioning in which his dress, mode of preaching, aesthetics, personal "tone," automobile—as a matter of fact, his entire vast personal repertory—is sexually charged. He is what, elsewhere, I have called a Charismatic Pornstar.[18]

I should state parenthetically that I am not oblivious of the racially dubious tradition of eroticizing the black male body, one in which that body is typically represented as a sexualized beast.[19] In no way is the argument in this chapter an endorsement of this perverse representation. Nor do I think that, as Rachel Spronk puts it, "there is something peculiar about African cultures regarding sexuality."[20] On the contrary, my analysis focuses on a specific pastor–faithful "communication" in which the person—and not just the body—of the pastor is eroticized. While the emphasis in most writings about religious sects and various kinds of communes is on how leaders appropriate their subject's sexual powers, I emphasize instead how the body of the pastor as the leader of the congregation is imbued with different forms of power (as discussed in the previous chapter), *especially* erotic power. Second, it should be obvious that my observations in what follows about the erotic economy involving the pastor and his congregation apply by and large to all agents operating in the, shall we say, people business, for example teachers, social workers, correctional officers, and medical doctors. My point is that whenever people interact in such close quarters, mostly one-on-one, erotic charges are unavoidable.

For the most part, work on the sexual dimension of citizenship in Africa has tended to emphasize the ways in which contemporary struggles over sexualities and sexual identities have unwittingly opened up conversations over belonging and civic mattering. In this chapter I propose to advance this conversation by examining the sociopolitical implications of the Pentecostal pastor's newfangled erotic agency. The basic question for me, consistent with the overall argument of the book, is how political subjectivity in Nigeria is shaped and determined by erotic communication between the pastor and the congregation, and the kinds of civic praxes thereby enabled by the pastor's sexual ardor. The idea of a Pentecostal erotic economy allows me to press critical questions about gender relations inside and outside of Pentecostal churches, as well as about patriarchy, affect, and social control. Still, a caveat is warranted: when it comes to sex, not only do I confess to a degree of incomprehension; my attitude, emanating from this, is that, ultimately, one is forced to admit to a certain unknowability, bringing to mind what Georges Bataille has referred to as "the darkness that has always beset the vast field of eroticism."[21] Camille Paglia is exactly right:

> Sexuality is a murky realm of contradiction and ambivalence. It cannot always be understood by social models. . . . Mystification will always remain the disorderly companion of love and art. Eroticism is mystique; that is, the aura of emotion and imagination around sex. It cannot be "fixed" by codes of social or moral convenience, whether from the political right or left. For nature's fascism is greater than that of any society. There is a daemonic instability in sexual relations that we may have to accept.[22]

Whether or not Paglia intended his allusion to the "daemonic" property of sexuality as a double entendre, it does open the door to a consideration of the religious dimension of sex, particularly the tension between the two, one of which is, in theory, "otherworldly" and the other "physical." According to Weber, while "originally the relation of sex and religion was very intimate,"[23] a certain tension between religion and sex came to the fore only with the temporary cultic chastity of priests. This rather ancient chastity may well have been determined by the fact that from the point of view of the strictly stereotyped ritual of the regulated community cult, sexuality was readily considered to be specifically dominated by demons. Furthermore, it was no accident that subsequently the prophetic religions, as well as the priest-controlled life orders, have, almost without significant exception, regulated sexual intercourse in favor of *marriage*. The contrast of all rational regulation of life with magical orgiasticism and all sorts of irrational frenzies is expressed in this fact.[24]

Similarly, Bataille, who postulates three types of eroticism—physical, emotional, and religious—nevertheless argues that

all eroticism has a sacramental character, but the physical and the emotional are to be met outside the religious sphere proper, while the quest for continuity of existence systematically pursued beyond the immediate world signifies an essentially religious intention. In its familiar Western form religious eroticism is bound up with seeking after God's love, but the East, intent on a similar quest, is not necessarily committed to the idea of a personal God.[25]

Achille Mbembe, too, sees the erotic as fundamentally inseparable from the religious act. Accordingly, for him,

there is no *religious act* not, at the same time and in some respect, also an erotic act. Like the sexual act, the religious act has never repudiated the tactile element. Neither color no sound, rhythm and melody nor visual phenomena, are alien to the religious act. On the contrary, the religious act has always drawn on their power to involve the senses and realize itself. The religious act thus presupposes interaction with sensuous and motor functions—and, in certain dramatic cases, unleashing of the latter.[26]

Studies on the ecstatic property of Pentecostalism have been generally sensitive to the identified sex-religion tension. For Birgit Meyer, not only is Pentecostalism essentially a religion of the senses; African Pentecostalism, with its "heated calling for bodily and sensational participation," sharply contrasts with "the rather intellectualist profile of 'high church' Protestantism, with organ music inducing stirring, but sober, religious feelings."[27] In his work on the aesthetics of West African Pentecostalism, Nimi Wariboko suggests that "the body and its pleasures are important in understanding the human nature and material form of the Pentecostal worship service."[28] Consequently, he sees Pentecostal worship as "a means of release as much as recreation, devotion as much as display, piety as much as play. Praise and worship is often an intense pleasurable social experience. . . . Together, worship and worshippers' bodies become a site for the production of ecstasy, *jouissance*, and bliss."[29] Annalisa Butticci's stress on Pentecostalism's "emotional charge, its materiality, its objects, bodies and gestures,"[30] and Kwabena Asamoah-Gyadu's allusion to "appropriate gestures—hand raising, prostration, kneeling, weeping, and other symbolic and emotional expressions,"[31] respectively—place their work firmly within this tradition. In a Latin American context, Kevin O'Neill's work on postwar Guatemala demonstrates megachurches' capacity to "use Christian music to excite large crowds, guiding them through emotional peaks and valleys."[32] For him, such music, "dripping with decidedly erotic imagery," has the ability to "place the model listener in constant sexual tension with both the Holy Spirit and Jesus Christ."[33]

My contribution to this literature is twofold. First, and, as already stated, I place the pastor at the center of the Pentecostal erotic economy. This means that, in accepting the sensual as an important component of the Pentecostal formation, I argue that it is best illuminated through a concentration on the figure of the pastor as, among other things, an object of sexual titillation. Second, I suggest that the pastor's erotic pull is not just interesting from the perspective of the sensory experience of Pentecostal worship, as commonly alluded to in the relevant literature (supra), but also is, in fact, politically potent, being one of the ways in which, I claim, the pastor helps to produce "governable" or "suggestible" citizens. (There is an irony here, which is that, even as he produces this effect, the pastor, as evidenced by the slew of sexual controversies and scandals surrounding pastors, seems incapable of governing his own sexuality.)

By insisting that the generation of pleasures is not without constraints but is "produced within the circumscriptions of the social system that envelops the believers and the boundaries patrolled by the clergy," Wariboko sensitizes us to the Pentecostal clergy's often neglected "panoptic power over the people" and how its "disciplinary energy ... is always quick to deploy its moral, aesthetic, suasive, and legal powers to control the meanings, pleasures, and social identities of the people."[34] That the power in question is far from abstract can be seen, for example, in the apparent indulgence granted to Daniel Kwadwo Obinim of the International God's Way Church (IGWC), Accra, Ghana, to massage the penises of male congregants with erectile dysfunction[35] and the authority granted to the Reverend Pastor Njohi's of the Lord's Propeller Redemption Church, Nairobi, Kenya, to command female congregants to come to church without their underwear so that they can be "free in body and spirit."[36] I affirm this power of control, albeit ultimately within a political register. Accordingly, pace O'Neill, who raises the possibility of Christian eroticism re-politicizing the faithful "in ways that prompt concerned citizens to take to the soul rather than the streets,"[37] I focus instead on its capacity to de-politicize insofar as it makes the faithful unquestioning members of the pastor's cognitive entourage. For me, although it is necessary to stress that the faithful derive fulfillment from the erotic charge, it is arguably more important to emphasize how this makes them potentially susceptible to emotional, hence political, manipulation.

While I take the eroticization of the pastor as primarily an imaginative practice in which the pastor is visually consumed by the faithful's gaze, I am also sensitive to how this imaginative practice can evolve into actual dalliances. Across Nigerian Pentecostal churches, near-universal references to "Daddy" (i.e., the pastor, his actual age notwithstanding) and "Mummy" (the pastor's wife) are reminders of the affective feeling that the faithful have toward their pastors. I claim that such tenderness is not just filial in a secular sense, but oftentimes co-exists with a deep eroticization, even if the latter remains, for the most part, dormant.[38] That Daddy is also a patriarch in a Yoruba-African cultural sense is not insignificant and alerts us to an often elided basic epistemological affinity with the Christian idea of masculinity that is central to the success of Pentecostalism. I return to this theme in the next chapter.

Below I describe and analyze the social processes that enable the eroticization of the pastor. Pursuant to the earlier argument on the paradoxical effects of Pentecostal influence, I argue that the pastor as an object of sexual desire is fundamentally inseparable from Pentecostalism's aspiration to produce a "responsible," domesticated man.

OF ECCLESIASTICAL STUDS

As shown above, the sensual aspect of Pentecostalism has aroused the scholarly imagination. Specifically, there have been examinations of Pentecostal worship and prayer as sensory experiences, with Wariboko insisting on the legitimacy of seeing "participation in Pentecostal worship as motivated by pleasure."[39] If that is the case, it becomes doubly legitimate to view the physical church as a place of pleasure where sounds, ululations, music, dance, bodies in motion, bodies flailing and sprawling, and bodies in collision combine to produce ecstatic worship. If the church is a space of pleasure or, in this formulation, a place where the faithful go to find pleasure, the pastor is, I suggest, its throbbing erotic heart. What is the source of this sensuality? What enables the eroticization of the pastor? What kind of light does it throw on Pentecostalism and the broader social space in which it has flourished? In what follows, I advance four related propositions.

First, and as flagged above, the eroticization of the pastor is ultimately inalienable from Pentecostalim's moral project of producing a new kind of male, one disaccustomed from the everyday regimes and profane spaces where he might be easily entrapped. Sexually tamed and emotionally reordered, this "New Man" is the supreme icon of Pentecostal domesticity, and my argument is that this effeminization of the male faithful redounds to the benefit of the pastor, who is allowed to become, if you will, the only man left standing in the church. Enhanced against the backdrop of broken homes and economically emasculated men, the pastor emerges an idealized man, theoretically available to every woman and, as it happens, to some in fact.

Second, having produced this exceptional man, Pentecostalism also provides him with a stage on which to perform. I am referring here to the idea that the altar is a stage on which the pastor more or less holds court. This recalls Martin Lindhardt's argument in a Tanzanian context on deliverance practices and their manifestation of spiritual power as a site for the performance of masculinity.[40] Similarly, Adedamola Osinulu's research on the RCCG underscores the political importance of the altar and the surrounding space in the context of Pentecostal worship. He contends:

> Through their ritualization before the Altar, believers express a desire to negotiate power relations with the society from which

they emerge. This space in front of the Altar can, therefore, be understood as a product of that very society because it is where these believers, who are well aware of their place in the society and who are motivated by the belief that the Altar is a locus of divine power, stake their claim on a better life.[41]

It is in this way, Osinulu holds, that believers "regularly contest the meaning of the Altar and its surrounding space."[42]

While I accept the legitimacy of this reading, *in addition*, I read the altar as the focal point for the expression of a different kind of energy—sexual energy. From this perspective, the altar is a stage of libidinal pyrotechnics, a setting for a certain kind of phallic posturing, rendered intensely sensuous by the constant mixing of light and sound, on the one hand, and the pastor's physical performance, on the other. The idea of the libidinal altar recalls Mbembe's meditation on the theme of the divine libido, especially his insight that the religious act "consists in activating, in a continuous manner, the god's libido."[43] The important qualification is that here I am focused on the pastor's libido, particularly its "activation" due to the enhanced social status of the pastor.

Furthermore, the eroticization of the pastor is enabled by the pastor's individual aesthetics, a vast repertoire combining intangibles such as the manner in which he carries himself, his linguistic affectation (American accent preferred), his automobile, his wardrobe, his education (hence, in part, the scramble for credentialization discussed in chapter 1), and, last but not least, his "appearance."[44] The latter may or may not include physical attractiveness, though the more "attractive" the pastor, we might reasonably surmise, the more eroticized. For instance, I think the good looks and "sex symbol" lifestyle of Senior Pastor Biodun Fatoyinbo might be part of the "attraction" (pun unintended) of COZA (Commonwealth of Zion Assembly), Abuja, Nigeria, for the church's predominantly young (and largely female) congregation. When, in August 2013, two female members of the church came out with allegations that the pastor had seduced them in hotels in London and Lagos, respectively, they were promptly rebuked by other female members of the church, who said the accusers should consider themselves lucky for having been "favored" by such a handsome "Man of God." In short, instead of hurting him, Pastor Fatoyinbo's exposure, as with the modern celebrity, may in fact have boosted his social standing and celebrity status. As for the automobile, it is increasingly no longer the business of the pastor himself but something that he can expect as a gift in the context of a "My-pastor-is-posher-than-yours" race for distinction among churches where the pastor has become more or less an extension of the collective ego of the congregation (see chapter 2). The pastor's wardrobe speaks more to personal taste and may include the type of wristwatch (Rolex, Patek Philippe, Movado, and Gucci are highly favored), suit (Gucci is preferred), shirt (Brooks Brothers), shoes (Gucci, Louis Vuitton, Christian Louboutin, and Alden), and body fragrance (Polo Ralph Lauren, Hugo Boss, Giorgio Armani).[45]

As a consumer of "designer" products, the pastor opens the gateway to avenues of global consumption that are simply beyond the reach, though not the imaginations, of the faithful.[46] In this manner the pastor, at the same time the (conspicuous) consumer as well as the consumed, becomes a crucial lynchpin in the coincidence of eroticization and fantasy. "Consuming" the pastor can take several forms. For certain admirers of Christ Embassy's Chris Oyakhilome, to take just one example, it can involve a wholesale adoption of the pastor's persona, including his manner of speaking, walking, dressing, and perming one's hair (see chapter 2) in the vintage Michael Jackson style favored by the pastor. If that speaks to the newfangled "social eminence" of pastors, likewise, it testifies to the associated imperative to, in the words of Jean-Pascal Daloz, "authenticate their standing."[47] For Daloz, crucially, such "prestigious commodities" as referenced in the foregoing "provide visual information that conveys many different messages by reinforcing identities, *arousing sexual interest*, eliciting difference, etc."[48]

Finally, the pastor's eroticization cannot be separated from his emergence as a social celebrity. This must be approached in the context of what Olivier Driessens calls "the diversification of celebrity," which is the way "several social fields produce celebrity personalities."[49] Accordingly, just as "the celebrity's name, image, hair(style), clothing style, to name but a few, are . . . turned into commodities to be sold and consumed,"[50] pastors can now look forward to their own "branding" or commodification. Similarly, and as we saw previously in the media coverage of Apostle Johnson Suleman's alleged dalliance with Stephanie Otobo (more on which in the next chapter), pastors, like celebrities, can also rely on "leaked" sex videos and nude pictures to boost their social standing and celebrity status.

Though not specifically related to the eroticization of the pastor, other social factors within a rapidly changing broader economy of pleasure must be recognized. These are, first, the sheer proliferation of sex, and, not to forget, new technologies of self-pleasuring, including sex toys. This recalls and is arguably of a piece with my earlier reference to an urban sociality that is saturated in sexual images and urban discourses awash in sex talk. A second factor is what we might call the New Intimacy, which is anchored in the widespread diffusion of electronic technologies that foster connectivity, on the one hand, while deregulating the sexual economy, on the other.

CONCLUSION: EROTIC POWER AND POLITICAL OBEDIENCE

Decades into the era of liberal democracy in Africa, the literature on rule and the organization of power remains by and large in thrall to the vocabulary of coercion. Given the domination of politics by the military for so long—and the accompanying militarization of society in general—this is perfectly understandable. In *Pentecostal Republic* (see chapter 6) I described how traces of this experience of violence continue to materialize in everyday conversation. Nevertheless, the shift in the state–society balance that took place in the wake of the democratization and expansion of the public space necessitates a reappraisal of the techniques deployed for the production of civic consent. If, formerly, such techniques aimed at physically compelling citizens to act in a particular way, the "softer" techniques now favored by the political elite in formally democratic African states are geared toward "nudging" or "orienting" citizens in the direction desired by the elite.

The concern here falls under the theoretical rubric of what, in the wake of Foucault's writings on the idea of governmentality, is now popularly known as "the conduct of conduct." For Nikolas Rose, drawing inspiration from Michel Foucault, this

> refers to all endeavours to shape, guide, direct the conduct of others, whether these be the crew of a ship, the members of a household, the employees of a boss, the children of a family or the inhabitants of a territory. And it also embraces the ways in which one might be urged and educated to bridle one's own passions, to control one's own instincts, to govern oneself.[51]

By definition, this "indirect" form of government mandates radical changes "in the way power is exercised and rationalized," according to Mbembe.[52] In postmilitary Nigeria, the state's alliance with leading Pentecostal pastors allows it to organize this ruse. Strategically inserted between the state and the rump of the citizenry, the pastors emerge as key cogs in the apparatus of democratic governmentality. From this perspective, they help prime the machinery for "the conduct of conduct" in the following ways:

First, and as analyzed in the previous chapter, by developing an interpretive schema that helps people make sense of events, they also, crucially, impose their own (and oftentimes the state's) version of events in a way that eventually redounds to them by bolstering their social power. In this respect, the master narrative is the one that projects political power and those who exercise it as constantly operating under the shadow of invisible and ubiquitous diabolical forces, forces that can only be disciplined—but never completely extinguished—by agents endowed with the appropriate spiritual expertise. A second mode in which pastors assist in the conduct of conduct is through prophetic proclamation, which I have already analyzed in the previous chapter. Erotic power completes the trinity. In its purest manifestation, it is a form of phallic subjugation whereby the pastor's eroticization is leveraged to "sway" the faithful, inducing them to adopt normative ways of seeing and acting and, as such, "program" their agential reflexes.

Suffice it to say, this is by no means the only way in which erotic power can be exercised. For instance, in her essay "The Erotic as Power," Audre Lorde articulates an emancipatory vision of "the erotic as the most self-responsible source of women's power."[53] Therefore, "Recognizing the power of the erotic within our lives can give us the energy to pursue genuine change within our world, rather than merely settling for a shift of characters in the same weary drama."[54] Lorde and I converge on the possibilities of pleasure as a mechanism for political engagement. However, while she valorizes the liberatory potential of the erotic, especially for "women-identified women,"[55] a fact I do not dispute, I differ in emphasizing its possible use for emotional manipulation and the production of political obedience.

That said, it is important to realize that erotic power is mobilized rarely in isolation but typically in conjunction with other factors. Second, the power of pastors to shape the agency of their congregations should not be simply assumed. As a matter of fact, if African postcolonial history furnishes us with any overarching insight, it is that of the sheer creativity of ordinary agents in how they resist political capture, and it is within this crucible of "rule" and "resistance" that political citizenship is forged. Part of Pentecostalism's genius, as I continue to maintain, lies in its capacity to alter the terms of this economy by positing a justification for state action beyond the realm of rational apprehension and endowing a cohort of powerful pastors with the power to "make sense" of it. Eroticization is merely one of the subtle mechanisms deployed by this pastorate. Against this backdrop, this chapter represents an important step toward a more complete understanding of the interplay of sexuality and power within contemporary African religious worlds.

In the next chapter, and with one eye on the kind of "resistance" to political capture that I just mentioned, I analyze four separate encounters between influential Nigerian pastors and women hailing from different social backgrounds and boasting variable funds of cultural capital. I use these examples to show that, on the one hand, resistance to pastoral power can come from the most unexpected places. On the other hand, by showing the limits of such resistance, especially through a portrayal of the complicated character of female agency, I demonstrate the resilience of pastoral power.

CHAPTER FOUR

When Women Rebel

"Useless woman." This is an epithet your ears are bound to pick up once you have spent a fair amount of time around Nigerians. It is mostly used by men, though women themselves are not above using it. The contexts can vary, though you typically hear it in a conversation among a group of men ventilating their annoyance about a particular woman—a wife, a girlfriend, even a female boss. Whether as a question ("That useless woman?") or an exclamation ("That useless woman!"), the same meaning seems to be conveyed—the woman in question has apparently disappointed the utterer of the words through her refusal to conform to a particular normative standard, oftentimes a standard set arbitrarily by men.

ON "USELESS WOMEN"

When a man uses it to describe his spouse, for instance, it usually means that said wife has either refused to *submit* to him or fallen afoul in some unspecified manner of a gender-specific behavioral standard, hence undeserving of the grace and protection of her husband. A "useless woman," at the same time, could be a woman who, in a position of authority, has behaved just as a regular male boss would have, thus falling short of the expectation that, being female, she should indeed have acted *differently*. A "useless" girlfriend is often one who has strayed from the unwritten rules governing relations between an older male "Aristo" (shortened form of "Aristocrat") and his younger female consort and perhaps has declared independence by offering her favors to another man.

A useless woman, in short, is a woman who acts in contravention of the norm undergirding gender and social relations, and it is usually (though not exclusively) in that sense that women, too, use it when describing or remonstrating with another woman. The useless woman is the one who, consciously or otherwise, exposes both the articulated and the inarticulable paradigms and presuppositions regarding female conduct, especially in relation to a male figure or male spaces, whether in a domestic or a public setting. She is the one who breaks ranks, the socially insolent one who, having refused to act in conformity to her expected *role*, is deserving of male-determined, if at times female-enforced, sanction. The Nigerian useless woman, to invoke Sara Ahmed,[1] is a killjoy, the one with no "use" but whose "uselessness" inadvertently points to the male-favoring privileges and contradictions inherent in gender relations.

Naturally, there are "useless men," men who, contrariwise, fail to meet the general understanding of what a man should be and, crucially, how a man should comport himself in relation to women. A man who cannot provide for his family, and in doing so cannot put a woman in her place (in both senses of the term), is considered "useless," not just by his fellow men, but by women, for they, too, have their own expectations regarding how men should *function*.

This chapter focuses on four useless women in their individual encounters with four influential Nigerian pastors. I am drawn to these encounters because, in the final analysis, they provide a forceful illustration of my argument about pastoral power in contemporary Nigeria. At the same time, the role of the various women in the context of their respective encounters shows that resistance to the power of a pastor can often come from the most unexpected places, unleashing social dramas that help amplify the contours of the milieu in which pastoral power has become ascendant. Finally, I argue that the manner in which these encounters were resolved is an object lesson, first, in the power of the pastor and the durability of the structures that underpin and enable it. And second, it is a warning against the common tendency to flatten women's agency by disregarding real and consequential class differences among them. While women often face up to similar political and cultural challenges, as I go on to illustrate, the way in which they combat or push back against such challenges—and therefore their success or failure in doing so—may vary depending on their education, social and marital status, shrewdness with the media, and other personal properties.

In what follows, I describe each of the four encounters in detail, providing as much social context as possible, while establishing connections and making extrapolations that underscore the book's chief argument.

THE "WINCH" WHO BROKE RANKS

There are two things that I could not establish about the incident I am about to narrate, even though I gave it my best shot. The first is the date on which it took place, and the second is the name of the young woman at the center of it. While the first is not material (video of the incident, posted December 29, 2011, is still on YouTube),[2] the anonymity of the young woman is directly relevant to my argument about the cultural capital of women facing social odds. It seems to me that the main reason I could not find the young woman's name anywhere (not even in the suit filed on her behalf, as I explain below) and the reason why nobody in the media thought it worthwhile to find out, is that she is, socially speaking, a nonentity, and she would not have been in the news in the first instance but for the fact that she was resolute enough to stand up to a famous "Man of God."

The subject of the video itself, a deliverance session to cast out demons and "familiar spirits," is really unremarkable as far as Nigerian Pentecostalism is concerned, and when we see Bishop Oyedepo, general overseer of Living Faith Tabernacle, aka Winners' Chapel, looking dapper in his all-white suit, we know that he is about to do something he has done countless times. What we are not prepared for is the roadblock he would soon run into in the form of open rebellion from one of the "possessed" young women and men kneeling in front of the altar, waiting to for their exorcisms.

The following is my transcript of their exchange:

Bishop Oyedepo: You've been there [in a witches' coven, apparently] for how long?
Young woman: I am not a winch [sic], I am a winch for Jesus.
Bishop Oyedepo: You are what?

Young woman: My own winch [sic] is for Jesus.
Bishop Oyedepo [perplexed, voice rising]: You are foul devil. Do you know who you are talking to? Foul devil! [Delivers a slap to loud applause from the congregation.]³
Bishop Oyedepo: Where are you from?
Young woman: I am from Imo state.
Bishop Oyedepo: Where did you get "witch" [sic] from?
Young woman: I am not a winch [sic].
Bishop Oyedepo: Who are you?
Young woman: But I am winch for Jesus.
Bishop Oyedepo: Jesus has no witches, you are a devil!
Young woman: [Mumbles, keeps protesting her innocence.]
Bishop Oyedepo: You are not set for deliverance, and you are free to go to hell!

After this fiery condemnation, the pastor moved on to a second woman, who is also resistant but perhaps not as vigorously as the first woman. Pressed as to the genealogy of her alleged witchcraft, she "confesses": "I am not a witch, but I used to dream that I was with them." Unsurprisingly, it was the encounter with the first young woman that would catch public attention and subsequently dominate the Nigerian news cycle. In fact, such was public anger at the young woman's casual abuse by Pastor Oyedepo that one Robert Igbinedion, a Lagos-based lawyer, filed a suit (in which she is referred to as "Ms. Justice") on her behalf in an Ogun State High Court.⁴

In condemning Bishop Oyedepo—and perhaps rightly so—most of the social and academic commentary on the incident has emphasized the young woman's victimization, originating, it is widely assumed, in the fact of her gender.⁵ In this reading, "Ms. Justice" would not have been on the receiving end of that slap had she been a young man. Gender, of course, is not irrelevant here. After all, a majority of Pentecostal pastors, as I have pointed out (see introduction), are men, while, at the same time, a majority of the individuals who continue to face accusations of engaging in witchcraft and suffering demonic possession are overwhelmingly women—and, in a worrying trend, even little girls.⁶ As a matter of fact—and to buttress the point about gender—many of the abuses and injuries typically inflicted on such individuals in the course of such exorcisms, including sexual abuse, seem, by their nature, gendered.

Yet, important as the emphasis on gender is, we cannot, in this example, see it in isolation from class. As I have suggested, the primary reason Ms. Justice could be so casually maltreated is that she is, in addition to being a woman, of lower social status. The two cannot be separated in this case. More important, to portray her *entirely* as a victim is to miss the crucial point that, for a brief moment, she had mounted a resistance, the ramifications of which, in all probability, she could not have calculated. Perhaps she had freely and happily consented to being paraded in front of the altar and prayed for. We will never know. What comes across clearly is her insistence that she is "not a 'winch'" (*sic*), but that even if she is, she is "a winch for Jesus." As I have argued elsewhere,[7] one thing that the literature on civil society (in Africa and beyond) continues to overlook owing to its obsession with formal civil society organizations (CSOs), is the sheer power of unplanned insurrectionary moments such as the one I am describing here and the continued possibility for such openings despite the risks. Ms. Justice was violated all right. I do not dispute that. Shabbily clad, she was no match for the grandeur and sartorial elegance of Bishop Oyedepo. She was also on her knees, the perfect posture of submission.[8] Yet, in a momentary but powerful show of insubordination, she had refused to adhere to the script, and not even a slap from the frustrated Oyedepo, suddenly in unfamiliar territory, would change her mind. The success of her rebellion could be seen not just in the fact that Oyedepo, threatening, "You are not set for deliverance, and you are free to go to hell!," decided to walk away, but also in the fact that the next woman felt sufficiently emboldened to start her response to him by saying, "I am not a witch."

Of what he has called "hidden transcripts"—"the often fugitive political conduct of subordinate groups"—James C. Scott has remarked:

> The first public declaration of the hidden transcript, then, has a prehistory that explains its capacity to produce political breakthroughs. If, of course, the first act of defiance meets with a decisive defeat it is unlikely to be emulated by others. The courage of those who fail, however, is likely to be noted, admired, and even mythologized in stories of bravery, social banditry, and noble sacrifice. They become themselves part of the hidden transcript.[9]

To be clear, there wasn't much "hidden" in the revolt of Ms. Justice (she was in an open auditorium, and she was mutinying in plain sight), and it would be a stretch to describe the reaction to her dissidence, heated as it was, as a "political breakthrough." Still, there is no doubting the impact of her open defiance. In the first place, it did generate a serious debate among a cross section of Nigerians on the power of Pentecostal pastors like Bishop Oyedepo, and while such debates often come with the risk of turning into a shouting match, as I once argued regarding the controversy over homosexuality in Nigeria, sometimes their real value is symbolic—due to the simple fact that they cause people to feel agitated or concerned enough to want to talk.[10] Second, we can imagine the effect the incident must have had on Bishop Oyedepo as, months later, and with Ms. Justice not there to dispute his account, he would boast to his audience, "I slapped a witch here last year. She came back in February to apologize. She begged me to please forgive her."[11]

Since there is no way of confirming that Ms. Justice did indeed visit Oyedepo to atone for her insubordination, we have to take the pastor's word for it. In any case, and as we shall see in two of the three remaining encounters, entreaties like the one alleged by Bishop Oyedepo are not uncommon but are, in fact, a key aspect of the degradation process through which useless women are "disciplined" and "re-educated" into their social roles as subordinates, either to men or to the "system," the same thing in many cases.[12] The aim of such "degradation ceremonies," consistent with sociological insight on the subject,[13] is to assert the supremacy of the authoritative figure (in this case, the pastor) by humiliating and lowering the status of the "offender," here Ms. Justice. We see further demonstration of this in the examples below. We really don't know if Ms. Justice was brought in for re-education, but the unprovoked allusion to it is enough confirmation that pastoral prestige was besmirched. The "winch" had made her mark.

STEPHANIE OTOBO VERSUS APOSTLE JOHNSON SULEMAN

Early in 2017, Ms. Stephanie Otobo, a Canada-based, Nigerian-born singer-songwriter, became a cause célèbre after she came out to accuse Apostle Johnson Suleman of the Auchi-based Omega Fire Ministries Worldwide of, among other things, going back on a firm promise to her to take her to the altar. As accusations trailed counter-accusations in a protracted and mutually unedifying media spectacle, the only thing that a neutral party could establish was that Ms. Otobo and Pastor Suleman were no strangers to each other and had been acquaintances in some capacity since their first meeting in Canada in 2015. From all indications, Ms. Otobo had become embittered after discovering, much to her chagrin, that the Man of God with whom she was looking forward to a future filled with marital bliss, whom she had gone out of her way to satisfy amorously, and who had once put her in the family way, was in fact married with children. To prove that she was not lying, Ms. Otobo had released Snapchat pictures of herself and Pastor Suleman in compromising positions.

In February 2017, Ms. Otobo escalated her attacks on Pastor Suleman by filing a formal petition through her lawyer, Festus Keyamo, asking the police to investigate the allegations she had made against Pastor Suleman, including the fact that he had induced her to abort a pregnancy and had reneged on a promise to buy her real estate if she agreed to relocate to Nigeria from Canada. In a letter of March 3, 2017, to the inspector general of police, Ms. Otobo asked for N500 million in damages, which the pastor had seven days to make good on.[14] Pastor Suleman retaliated with a defamation counter-suit.

The Otobo-Suleman saga has all the elements of your normal sex scandal, but sex is just one of the reasons that it fascinates me. First, I am fascinated by Ms. Otobo, and though I admit she's a tough sell, I am willing to go out on a limb and defend her as a feminist (an imperfect one, to be sure), and I'd understand perfectly if a lot of people were to disagree with me. The most important thing for me is that she put everything on the line in challenging someone who she clearly knew was in a far stronger position than she was and who could crush her if he so desired. This is not incompatible with the probability that, *at the same time*, Ms. Otobo was seeking fame and money or, at the very least, a much-needed trigger for a music career that had remained largely aspirational.

Second, given the argument of this book, I am interested in sex as a dimension of the pastor's erotic power, as the pastor and sex are, as I have argued, wedded in the Nigerian imagination. In this regard, I find it interesting that Ms. Otobo's attempt to put Pastor Suleman under a moral cloud, inciting pictures and all, failed. It was almost as if the Nigerian public was saying that there was nothing surprising in the sexual disclosures, that they had seen it before, and what else do you expect from a pastor?

Third, having failed to make the pastor pay, whether financially or socially, Ms. Otobo was the one who eventually, and in a significant moment for pastoral power, had to retract her allegations against Pastor Suleman. What is more, she was subjected to a ritual of degradation arguably more humiliating than what Ms. Justice went through, since the ostensible prostration of the latter before Bishop Oyedepo took place behind closed doors. In Otobo's case, in January 2018 she actually showed up in person at Pastor Suleman's church, where she introduced herself as "the lady behind the scandal" and confessed to having fallen "into the wrong hands of some very strong and powerful politicians and some pastors who manipulated me in a very wrong way with the intention to fall [sic] the Man of God."[15] She also claimed, to a chorus of boos from the pews, that she had agreed to lie about Pastor Suleman because of her "desperation" to get her career moving and that she had been paid "a lot of money" in order to do what she did. Finally, fighting back tears, she apologized to "the body of Christ" and "Baba" (Yoruba for "Father"), meaning Pastor Suleman, before dropping to her knees before Pastor Suleman's wife, who went on to pray for her.

An April 2017 interview granted by Mrs. Bukky Otobo, Ms. Otobo's mother, to *Premium Times*, an online newspaper, gives us an indication of the kind of pressure Ms. Otobo may have come under to retract her allegations. In the interview Mrs. Otobo, who disclosed that she had gone to see Pastor Suleman to "beg him" to bring an end to the matter, repeatedly distanced herself from her daughter's reported actions and asked for "pardon" for her. While we may reasonably surmise that Mrs. Otobo's action might have exerted moral pressure on Ms. Otobo, it is the reason that Mrs. Otobo gave for going to beg Pastor Suleman that is interesting from the point of view of the book's argument:

> I told them [her daughter's lawyers] that I want to go and beg the man of God myself to die down the matter. That is what every mother will do. I don't want to see my daughter destroyed. That is why I am saying that all those lawyers should leave my daughter and bring her out of this matter.... Well, we begged the man of God that he should forgive my daughter. *You know when you call somebody a man of God, he can go to any length. So I don't want the man of God to go to any length, to do any evil prayer* because when we heard of it that time, this pastors' association . . . praying

all their sorts of things. I cannot sit down here watching my daughter like that. That is why I said I want to go to the source to beg that man. Nobody tortured me. I went alone. I entered vehicle from Sapele to Auchi.[16]

From Mrs. Otobo's perspective, the merits of the case in which her daughter was involved did not matter as much as the personality she had taken on—a "man of God," one with the capacity to spiritually hurt her daughter and who could "go to any length" if necessary. This goes to confirm the idea of the pastor as the one with the power of life and death, the one who determines who lives and who dies, and the one with the spiritual authority to either save a life (in the *salvation* sense of the word) or destroy it (in the *damnation* sense).

Possibly this particular case received maximum media attention, and dragged on for as long as it did, because of what was at the center of it—sex. At the same time, it is not implausible that Ms. Otobo's foreign connection (the fact that she was "Canada-based"), her facility with social media, and the fact that she had a battery of lawyers working for her, led by the popular Festus Keyamo (who, in July 2019, would be appointed Nigeria's minister of state for labour and employment), kept the story on the front burner of public attention, sparing Ms. Otobo the fate of Ms. Justice—anonymity. Anonymity or not, the pastor, once again, prevailed.

Before moving on to the next example, I want to reflect on the significance of the church altar as the space of the degradation of Ms. Otobo and, as we shall see in the next section, Ms. Kemi Olunloyo. In the first place, I think it has to do with the politics of publicity, as the affected church (as actually happened in both cases) can record the event and post footage on its social media platforms. Second, since the whole point of the entire ceremony is to exonerate the Man of God, it makes sense that the individual who has recklessly put him under a cloud and subjected him to such "unwarranted" duress would perform her atonement in the very presence of the congregation. In this regard, degradation ceremonies work to bolster the moral standing and overall prestige of the pastor, before both his congregation and the Nigerian public as a whole. As a form of absolution, a confession by the degraded individual is technically and morally superior to acquittal by a court of law.

Third, using the altar as the space of degradation is important because—given, as already discussed, the affective connection between pastors and their congregations—it can be inferred that an attack on the Man of God is an attack on his congregation. This inference is not misplaced as, in fact, congregants are known to categorize and resist an attack on their pastor as an attack simultaneously on the specific church and on "the body of Christ." For example, Pastor Suleman's congregants were quick to denounce Ms. Otobo's accusations in the media as "a well-doctored drama to attack the reputation of this Golden Voice and seemingly reduce the volume of his voice even as more evils were planned against the Church. After all the evil efforts, the secret agendas, the heavily funded setup, and the unrelenting pursuits to snare an innocent man, they were futile. The master planner has finally vindicated his church and his servant. This is not only a victory for God's servant; it is a victory for the Body of Christ & The Church in Nigeria."[17] Accordingly, summoning the "offender" to appear before the church is logical, since the congregation, too, counts among the "offended." However, the role of the congregation goes beyond merely listening to the offender's recantation and reveling in her self-flagellation. As these ceremonies also function, especially for the newly degraded, as a form of confession of their faith, part of the role of the congregation is to welcome the offender into the fold. Finally—and perhaps to demonstrate that an attack on the pastor is not just an attack on his church but also, crucially, an attack on his wife and family—it is the pastor's wife (Mrs. Lizzy Johnson Suleman in this case and Mrs. Peace Ibiyeomie in the next) who presides over the ceremony. Nor should we underestimate the symbolic power of two women defending their men against a fellow woman.

KEMI OLUNLOYO VERSUS PASTOR DAVID IBIYEOMIE

Just like Ms. Stephanie Otobo, fifty-five-year-old Ms. Kemi Olunloyo is a complicated actor, and the argument for seeing her as a feminist icon (even an "unruly" one) is not one that many would readily accept.[18] Nevertheless, since I am not interested in saints (in which case this would be a chapter on the dead), I am minded to accept Ms. Olunloyo, warts and all, cognizant of the fact that she is often too inconsistent to take her own side in a quarrel. Not only that; she is prone to the occasional sweeping statement or unfounded claim. For instance: "I don't insult people, I educate u cos I'm the most intelligent Nigerian woman. I refuse to see Nigerians less educated than the Americans I grew up 38 yrs with. Has nothing to do with my 3 First Class degrees."[19] There is no public record of Ms. Olunloyo's having a First-Class degree, let alone three. Or, even more absurdly: "I am actually more intelligent than Einstein."[20] Ms. Olunloyo has claimed in the past that she worked for the American news network CNN for twenty years, a claim that Stephanie Busari, an editor at CNN Africa, has put to rest.[21] As recently as September 2019, she claimed on her Facebook page, and with little by way of substantiation, to be in possession of a doctor of pharmacy (Pharm D) degree from the University of the Sciences in Philadelphia.[22] As of April 17, 2020, she still described herself on her Twitter page as "Kemi Olunloyo (PHD)."

Because of statements and claims like these, many have been quick to dismiss her as a crank or, what is worse, a megalomaniac. My aim here is not to hold a brief for Ms. Olunloyo but to use her encounter with Pastor David Ibiyeomie, founder and general overseer of Salvation Ministries, Port Harcourt, to illustrate the chapter's argument about "useless" women in relation to pastoral power. If anything, it is the personal contradictions of Ms. Olunloyo—and, ipso facto, Ms. Otobo—that make her a fascinating model.

Ms. Olunloyo was arrested by the police in March 2017 after she had circulated rumors linked to one Ebiye Patience, apparently a member of Salvation Ministries, regarding a train of alleged instances of misconduct by Pastor Ibiyeomie, including a reported amorous affair with Nollywood actor Ms. Iyabo Ojo, which Pastor Ibiyeomie vehemently denied. For her troubles, Ms. Olunloyo was arrested and taken to Port Harcourt, where she was charged before Chief Magistrate Alatuwo Elkanah Fubara on four counts of publishing a defamatory and malicious story against Pastor Ibiyeomie. Overall, Ms. Olunloyo would spend several months in custody before her release in January 2018 after Pastor Ibiyeomie decided to drop all charges against her.

Without prejudice to the specifics of the charges brought against Ms. Olunloyo, we have to admit that, in retrospect, some of the facts pertaining to her trial seem rather curious. First is the decision by the authorities to have her trial in Port Harcourt rather than in Ibadan, where she was residing at the time of her alleged offense. Second, given the nature of her alleged offense, the decision to have her remanded to detention in a Port Harcourt prison until her scheduled court hearing in March appears rather high-handed. Third, the fact, disclosed during her March court appearance, that she was being held at the pleasure of the inspector general of police seems totally out of proportion to her alleged offense. I bring up these facts because of what they seem to add up to—and here I am being speculative—that Ms. Olunloyo, having stepped on many powerful toes, and not just those of Pastor Ibiyeomie, was most probably being scapegoated, and the decision to bring her down to Port Harcourt may have been a way to bring her under an informal "pastoral jurisdiction." Born in Bonny and educated at the Rivers State University of Science and Technology, Port Harcourt (RSUST), Pastor Ibiyeomie casts a big shadow in Port Harcourt, and, given what I have already established about pastoral power, it is reasonable to surmise that there Pastor Ibiyeomie would have been able to mobilize enough social capital to bring a useless woman to heel. The fact that, in all of this, Ms. Olunloyo's pedigree as the scion of a distinguished political family counted for very little (granted that her father, who once had reportedly interceded on her behalf with another famous pastor may have had enough of her daughter's antics)[23] and could save her from neither jail nor public humiliation, brings home the point about the scale of pastoral influence.

Having said that, Ms. Olunloyo's confession-degradation was similar to Ms. Otobo's. Delivered in the mode of a testimony, she started with a warning to the congregation:

> Don't let the devil use you. I do want to clarify that I was not paid for this testimony. . . . Pastor Ibiyeomie, somebody used me, the devil must leave. This is a church that I attended yesterday that actually prays for its pastor; I love that, I am a member of this church now and I am going to serve and worship God [applause from the congregation]. . . . I am going to serve God and I am going to serve God in this church. I came here in a police car, and I am not leaving. I am going to fly the colors, stoop to conquer. . . . Pastor Ibiyeomie met with me yesterday in his office privately. He blessed me, he led me to Christ, I gave my life to Christ [more applause]. I told him that the devil used Eve, the snake, after Eve was warned two times by God and by Adam. Somebody used me to genuinely destroy a real man of God.[24]

After reiterating that she had not been paid for her appearance at the altar, she walked down and, sobbing, knelt before Mrs. Peace Ibiyeomie, who proceeded to wrap her in a big hug. In another video, posted on YouTube on August 3, 2019, Ms. Olunloyo would also apologize to Ms. Ojo.[25]

One thing that stands out from Ms. Olunloyo's recantation that is also directly relevant to the theme of the chapter is the reference to Eve's having succumbed to the snake despite being warned by God and Adam. In invoking this as justification for her action, Ms. Olunloyo was, perhaps unbeknownst to her, tacitly empowering a common depiction of women as incapable of forming thoughts of their own, being easily brainwashed, prone to wild mood swings, and therefore undependable—in brief, "useless."

Once again, what had looked at the beginning like a plausible critique of pastoral malfeasance (admittedly by a deeply flawed social agent) ended with the campaigner appeasing the pastor, his church, and his wife. The Man of God had won.

BUSOLA DAKOLO VERSUS "GUCCI PASTOR"

In its overall flavor, and not just because it involves sex (the unwanted type), this case is similar to the Otobo-Suleman saga and is arguably of the deepest moment in sharpening our understanding of relations between contemporary Nigerian pastors and women, and relations between the same pastors and their congregations. Furthermore, and perhaps to an even greater degree than the previous two cases, the encounter between Busola Dakolo and Pastor Biodun Fatoyinbo of the Abuja-based COZA has all the makings of an inter-celebrity face-off. Ms. Dakolo, who announced in June 2019 that she had been raped, twice, by Pastor Fatoyinbo when she was a sixteen-year-old youngster still living with her parents, is a celebrity photographer and popular media personality with a large Instagram following. Her husband, Timi Dakolo, is a popular singer who came into the limelight after emerging as the winner of the inaugural season of Idols West Africa in 2007, which he parlayed into a recording contract with Sony BMG Music Entertainment (now Sony Music). Pastor Fatoyinbo, for his part, is one of Nigeria's most dashing pastors. Born in 1976, he is decades younger than any member of the Adeboye-Bakare-Oyedepo trinity that arguably occupies the apex of the Nigerian Pentecostal elite. He dresses the part as well (hence his alias, "Gucci Pastor"), and, on any given Sunday, can resemble a trend-setting entertainer more than a Man of God. When he preaches, he comes across as more performer than preacher, and in his overall persona he seems the perfect embodiment of the idea of the pastor as modern celebrity.

The star power of the protagonists apart, two other key ingredients went into making Mrs. Dakolo's allegations against Pastor Fatoyinbo a media spectacle like no other. First, and, as many people were quick to point out, this was not the first time that allegations of illicit sex had been leveled against the pastor. Back in 2013, a woman named Ese Walter had disclosed that she had had an affair with Pastor Fatoyinbo after the latter had "gained her trust, favour, and confidence over the one year period she was attending his church before she travelled abroad."[26] To worsen matters for Pastor Fatoyinbo, within twenty-four hours of Mrs. Dakolo's allegation, Nigerian Nollywood star Stella Damasus added fuel to the fire with the allegation that Fatoyinbo had also raped her friend, then fifteen years old.[27] On July 4, it was the turn of another woman, a former member of the church who pleaded anonymity, to level allegations of sexual impropriety against the pastor.[28] Second, Mrs. Dakolo's allegations came at a time when, courtesy of the #MeToo movement that, though it originated in the United States, had caught the global imagination, a new kind of reckoning on sexual harassment and male power seemed to be emerging. In short order, and as a growing number of Nigerians took umbrage on social media at the perceived high-handedness of many pastors and men in positions of authority generally, the hashtags #ChurchToo, #SayNoToRape, and #PastorStepDown provided a unifying banner.

In the days following Ms. Dakolo's allegation, Pastor Fatoyinbo's career as a pastor looked well and truly over. With rallies being organized in Lagos and Abuja (on Sunday, June 30, a group of protesters demanding Fatoyinbo's resignation had staked out a position half a kilometer from the church). On July 1, in fact, it seemed as if the protesters had gotten their wish, as Pastor Fatoyinbo, who continued to deny the allegations, announced on his Instagram account that he was "taking a leave of absence from the pulpit of the church" in order to "submit to the concerns of my spiritual mentors as they consider all the issues that have been raised against me." He then added: "Though I do not understand all that is happening, I trust the Lord to guide and lead me one step at a time. Kindly pray for me and the congregation as we seek the face of the Lord at these turbulent times."[29]

Fatoyinbo's four-week leave of absence would seem to be the most concrete achievement of the protests, for, by August 4, the pastor was back in the pulpit, notably to a thunderous reception from the pews. In retrospect, the tide seems to have turned decisively, if not against the protesters, at least in favor of the pastor, when, on July 15, a CAN delegation led by its FCT chairman, Samson Jonah, visited COZA and declared the association's support for Pastor Fatoyinbo. Just two weeks earlier, when Mrs. Dakolo's allegations were still fresh and the pastor's position was shaky, the same CAN had strongly denounced rape in general, though not the specific allegations, as "ungodly, wicked and reprehensible."[30] Fatoyinbo's strategy all along may have been to pit CAN against the PFN, whose president, Bishop Felix Omobude, had declared the allegations against Fatoyinbo "not only criminal in nature but antithetical to the tenets of Christianity and a violent breach of trust that ought to exist between members of the congregation and a minister of the Gospel."[31] Unsurprisingly, Fatoyinbo declined to appear before a panel of investigation set up by PFN, claiming that "the PFN was already prejudiced and may not conduct an impartial session."[32]

Compared with the other women whose encounters with pastors have been analyzed, Mrs. Dakolo seems to have received far more sympathy from a cross section of the media and CSOs. Conceivably, this had more to do with her—and her husband's—social status, coupled with the global moment in which she approached the media with her allegations against the pastor, than with the specific character or merits of the case. Furthermore, and not unlike Ms. Otobo, Mrs. Dakolo made effective use of her social media presence to bypass the conventional media and take her case directly to the public.

Nevertheless, with the exception of one Obafemi Banigbe, who resigned from the church's board of trustees on July 19, "with immediate effect and for personal reasons,"[33] COZA was united behind its pastor. In addition, just like Mrs. Lizzy Johnson Suleman and Mrs. Peace Ibiyeomie, respectively, Mrs. Modele Fatoyinbo also stood behind her man, insisting that "Not even as an unbeliever will my husband rape someone."[34] As mentioned earlier, the importance of these women's standing firmly beside and defending the honor of their men—as virtuous men, husbands, and heads of their respective congregations—cannot be underestimated, and their unshaken solidarity no doubt went a long way toward vitiating the challenges to their moral authority. At the same time, their declarations of support for their husbands are reminders of the increasing importance of the wife of the contemporary pastor, one who can be powerful in her own right but whose authority is, at the same time, dependent on her being in good standing with her husband. Commonly referred to as "Mummy," "Mummy G.O.," or "Mother-in-the Lord," she is technically a "mother" to the female members of the congregation and the model of what many Pentecostal churches are eager to portray about the woman's subordination to the man under the tent of the Christian family. For instance, Shade Olukoya, wife of Daniel Olukoya of the Mountain of Fire and Miracles Ministries, is described on the church's webpage as possessing a "beloved demeanor" and providing "solid leadership *alongside her husband*."[35] While the pastor's wife is "often limited to dealing with specifically women's issues and guiding congregation women's meetings," in the words of Victor Agadjanian,[36] she can also be a powerful interlocutor (as we've seen in these three examples) whenever there arises a crisis that threatens her husband's—and her own—standing.

DEGRADATION: BETWEEN THE PHYSICAL AND THE VIRTUAL

In lieu of what should have been her routine physical degradation at the altar (Mrs. Dakolo's suit against Pastor Fatoyinbo in a FCT High Court is pending), supporters of Pastor Fatoyinbo, no doubt aiming to unsettle Mrs. Dakolo by pinpointing alleged inconsistencies in her account, have continued to attack her on social media and various online platforms. The following, by one Omotosho Ebenezer Segun (probably an alias) in response to media reports that Mrs. Dakolo had been induced by the police to change her story, is representative: "Busola you have kicked your leg against the pricks [sic], and you must face the consequences, Touch not my annoited [sic], and do my Prophet no harm. Let me tell the truth, You have missed it you better seek for forgiveness, from God and you [sic] Senior Pastor, you are looking for cheap popularity."[37] Apparently, even Pastor Fatoyinbo is not above the occasional self-satisfied online carping. For example, in November 2019, after an Abuja High Court had dismissed Mrs. Dakolo's suit against him, he posted the following enigmatic message on his Instagram page: "He aborts the schemes of conniving crooks, so that none of their plots come to term. He catches the know-it-alls in their conspiracies—all that intricate intrigue swept out with the trash! Suddenly, they're disoriented, plunged into darkness; they can't see to put one foot in front of the other. Job 5: 12–14 (MSG)."[38]

Unlike the kind of physical degradation at the altar that both Ms. Otobo and Ms. Olunloyo were subjected to, online degradation, the kind that has been visited upon Mrs. Dakolo, takes maximum advantage of the anonymity that social media guarantees and can be particularly virulent. While, within the space of the church, the audience/congregation is restricted to intermittent booing, with the declamation at any rate limited to the duration of the ritual, with respect to online degradation, the ritual is not temporally bounded; hence, there is greater scope for the congregation and otherwise dispersed enthusiasts of the pastor to take out their collective rage and visit their retribution upon the person who has dared to challenge the authority of the Man of God and sully his "anointing."

The degradation ritual—if not in fact the crisis as a whole—provides a moment for the strengthening of the affective bond between pastors and their congregations. On the one hand, it allows pastors to declare their faith in their congregations (Fatoyinbo had told his congregation: "I have the most blessed church, if I am not heading it, I'll be glad to be a member.")[39] On the other hand, members of the congregation renew their faith in their pastor and the spiritual mission of his church. For example, and no doubt to take the sting out of Mrs. Dakolo's allegations, several female members of COZA gave testimonies in which "all of them narrated how the singular experience of starting to attend COZA between 2003 and 2013 marked a profound turnaround [in their lives], catapulting them from obscurity to directorship of companies, ownership of businesses and having a great marital life."[40]

Such, instructively, is the quality of this bond between pastors and their disciples (I use the term in the most general sense) that it can motivate the latter to mobilize violence to repel what they perceive as an attack on the honor and integrity of their leader. The experience of Abimbola Adelakun is telling in this regard. A professor of theatre and dance in the African/African Diaspora Department at the University of Texas at Austin, Ms. Adelakun had visited COZA on July 21, 2019, as part of her established research routine of trying "to see if the observations that I made about trends and practices are generalizable across the spectrum."[41] But as this was in the middle of the controversy surrounding its pastor, and as Professor Adelakun had, in her column of July 4, 2019, for *Punch* newspaper arguably taken aim at Mrs. Modele Fatoyinbo,[42] she met a congregation that was literally in a state of mobilization. For her troubles, Professor Adelakun was roughed up, held against her wishes for hours (during which time her phone was seized), before she was eventually taken to a police station, where she managed to secure her release.⁴³

Pace Carl Schmitt's famous friend–enemy distinction,⁴⁴ and allowing for the fact that Schmitt was referring to state actors, COZA's congregants may be seen as partisan actors who, apprehending a fundamental threat to their leader, their church, and ultimately to themselves in their total identity as followers, are willing to deploy violence to repel and deter such a threat. Such, indeed, is the length of the shadow cast by the contemporary Pentecostal pastor.

CONCLUSION

In the foregoing I have used four examples of "useless" women in different interactions with influential Pentecostal pastors to make two related arguments. The first is that, the power and social influence of pastors notwithstanding, resistance to it can and does issue from the most unlikely social agents under the most unpredictable circumstances. The fact that these agents are often women is telling given the fact that, despite some significant exceptions across Nigerian society and within many Pentecostal churches, women continue to receive the short end of the stick. The women in the four examples I have given boasted variable funds of cultural capital, which shaped the evolution (although, vitally, not the outcomes) of their rebellions. Therefore, women's insurrections, while sociologically symbolic, carry no guarantee of success and are often undone by the actions and mobilizations of other women.

Second, not only have the rebellions analyzed in this chapter failed to do any significant damage to the ramparts of masculine pastoral power; I suggest that the pastors may have emerged even stronger and on a surer social footing than before these rebellions, underscoring my argument about the scale and tenacity of pastoral influence. Not all of that can be blamed exclusively on the women, and my aim here is not necessarily to assign a value to what the women did. If anything, I have sought to emphasize the inherent worth of resistance led by women, many of whom carried significant social handicaps. The goal is to show that, regardless of those flaws, women's resistance provides an opportunity to juxtapose the antinomic character of women's agency with the vulnerabilities of a seemingly impregnable pastoral masculinity.

Conclusion

Rule by Prodigy

What follows is (mostly) hypothetical.

Before Daddy G.O. and the current tribe of Pentecostal pastors, there was Emmanuel (later Olufunmilayo) Odumosu, then popularly known as Jesus of Oyingbo. Reading Michael Chambers's profile of Jesus of Oyingbo, written in 1964,[1] one is immediately struck by certain parallels between the milieu in post-independence urbanizing Lagos in which Odumosu emerged and flourished—and, most crucially, on which he capitalized—and postmilitary urban Nigeria. Chambers writes, for instance, "There are virtually no modern welfare services in Lagos. When people need help from outside the tribe or family they turn to the prophets and their religious sects or to the traditional doctors, the juju-men."[2] And when he writes this, he could, albeit with some significant emendations, well have been writing about contemporary Lagos.

The Lagos of today may be a vast megalopolis with all the amenities of which modernity can boast, but the spiritual craving to which Chambers alludes has never been more intense, as previous chapters of this book have shown. As well, the Manichean foundation of this spirituality remains more or less intact:

> The theme of his [Odumosu's] teaching has remained fairly consistent: it is based on the division between the natural world and the world of the spirit. The natural forces are vested in what he calls the "powers and principalities," and the spiritual forces are vested in himself. These two mutually exclusive sets of forces are

today locked in battle, the result of which will be the inevitable triumph of the spiritual kingdom.³

In addition, and not unlike many a Pentecostal pastor today, Jesus of Oyingbo "developed an integrated system of moral values for the guidance of his followers, a system which hinges around discipline as the central virtue."⁴ In other ways, the messianic complex around Odumosu parallels the "Touch Not My Anointed" discursive barrier erected around the figure of the pastor by today's Pentecostals.

Though profound, the parallels can be overdrawn. For instance, the Universal College of Regeneration was just one church—a commune, to be precise—in one city and bears little resemblance to the churches of today's global Pentecostal resurgence. Second, contra the basic working-class character of the Odumosu project—it was also predominantly male and Yoruba—today's Pentecostal movement is a transnational phenomenon that cuts across what Rijk van Dijk describes as "the emergent middle-class, well-educated, urban sections of the population."⁵ Third, while, as I have established, there is an undeniable erotic connection between pastors and their congregations, it appears to exist in permanent tension with, and tends to be reined in by, the injunctions of Christian sexual conservatism. On the contrary, being not particularly conservative or unpretentious in sexual matters, according to Matthews Ojo, Jesus of Oyingbo "possessed sexual privileges over any female member or the wives of his converts," while "women who submitted themselves to Odumosu and even had children for him regarded such as part of their religious obligations to the group."⁶ Finally, Jesus of Oyingbo, even at the peak of his influence, was never a political star, let alone a powerful general overseer of the public and private domains.

The overarching point of comparison for me is the foundation of Odumosu's power over members of his commune. I am referring here to his "calling." Odumosu, it must be said, against the backdrop of nagging personal troubles, had heard "the persistent voice of an angel telling him that he was the Messiah, a voice which he at first ignored but later came to accept."⁷ To Chambers he related

> how, for three months, he slept almost continually, experiencing visions in the form of dreams. One such dream went as follows: dark and heavy clouds of the sky began to roll back, parting to

reveal a bright blue neon light tube descending towards him; he grasped this tube and was trying to fit it into some light sockets, when he woke up. This he had interpreted as meaning that the light had come to him, i.e. that Jesus had entered him and that therefore he was Jesus. In 1952, Emmanuel began preaching to the people of Lagos that he was the Messiah, the Midnight Man, come to redeem the world.[8]

Odumosu's vision was fundamental to his legitimacy as "the Messiah" (much later, he would go a step further and announce to his followers that he was God)[9] and performed for his ministry practically the same function that the trinity of calling, prophecy, and prayer (see chapter 2) performs for today's Pentecostal pastor. Combined, they constitute what may be described as a marvelous portfolio and are essential (though by no means exclusive) components of what I am calling rule by prodigy.

Rule by prodigy harks back to my earlier description of the contemporary pastorate as constituting, in essence, an aristocracy of wonderment, and it is in this sense that I use the word "prodigy" to signify amazing phenomena that are supra-sensory and/or out of the ordinary. In their original usage, writes Lorraine Daston, prodigies were "closely akin to portents, divine signs revealing God's will and things to come."[10] Therefore, rule by prodigy is a claim to authority that is grounded in the claimant's purported access to or possession of special truths (i.e., "things to come") not disclosed to others and his capacity to perform miracles or similar prodigious spectacles as a way of demonstrating or legitimizing that unique access or possession. The contemporary pastor is the agential fulcrum of rule by prodigy, the one ostensibly called to speak prophetically to the country, its leaders, and its people, the one who instantiates that calling through prodigious performances and commands the power to avert the worst through prayer. In this way, rule by prodigy—whose outcome, whether intended or not, is the production of political obedience—is a direct claim on authority that refreshes the nagging question of the ultimate source of rule in a Nigerian-African context. Rule by prodigy expresses clerical dominance over social life.

Within the tradition of personal rule in Africa, the pastor as the axis of rule by prodigy finds a ready ancestor in the post-independence nationalist leader who felt "called upon" to serve the people, who defined policy in terms of an administrative "vision" and generally addressed the populace in the tone of a secular prophet. Tanzania's Julius Nyerere and Ghana's Kwame Nkrumah offer the closest approximations. But there is an essential difference. While Nyerere, to take one example, was a political leader who used the sheer force of charisma to attain secular sainthood, rule by prodigy, founded on spiritual authority and its associated claims, subordinates the political leader to the pastor by the invocation of a marvelous portfolio. As a model of personal rule, according to Robert Jackson and Carl Rosberg, rule by prodigy signposts one of the central features of personal rule as follows: "It is a dynamic world of political will and action that is ordered less by institutions than by personal authorities and power; a world of stratagem and countermeasure, of action and reaction, but without the assured mediation and regulation of effective political institutions."[11]

Maurizio Lazzarato, harking back to Michel Foucault, returns to the theme of "pastoral power" as an enabler of "obedience" outside the law: "Pastoral power is individualizing. The techniques of pastoral individualization are based not on status of birth or wealth but on a 'subtle economy' that combines merits and faults, their trajectory and their circuits. *This economy of souls establishes an overall dependency, a relationship of absolute and unconditional submission and obedience, not to laws or 'reasoned' principles, but to the will of another individual.*"[12] Situating rule by prodigy within the stream of social and political relations in Nigeria, one arrives at a set of tentative hypotheses on its implications for the state, social institutions, state–society relations, and citizenship.

The mutual alienation of state and society is often taken as axiomatic by scholars of African politics. While many have lamented the failure of the state to "dominate" society, others have celebrated the success of society in resisting "capture." Jeffrey Herbst, focusing on the physical side of the problem, emphasizes the cost of projecting "power over distance in Africa because of the combination of a peculiar set of geographic features."[13] Privileging what he calls "the causal provenance of social processes," Olufemi Taiwo postulates the absence of a genuine citizenship owing to the fundamental lack of a "moral-ideological content."[14] Eghosa Osaghae agrees that relations between state and civil society in Africa remain largely "fractured, instrumentalist, and dialectical in the post-colonial period."[15] Tejumola Olaniyan states, rather baldly: "The postcolonial state in Africa is not a friend. It is not considered so by the majority of those it rules over,

given its history and apparent unproductivity so far. Even the minority that has corruptly benefited from it is not saved the high anxiety of the state's instability and inconstancy."[16] These perspectives accurately capture the form and essence of the continued rift between state and society in Africa.

I hold that rule by prodigy is the offspring of this scenario in the sense that it occupies precisely the social vacuum created by the poverty of a state–society compact. On the one hand, it takes maximum advantage of the state's continued crisis of legitimacy, the most blatant manifestation of which is its failure to monopolize legitimate violence; on the other hand, it capitalizes on the disintegration of the moral and ideological systems that once galvanized social forces.[17] Either way, it appears to diminish the prospect that state and society will be mutually reconciled.

It does this, first, through its narrative about the state and other sociopolitical institutions, which are portrayed either as totally dispensable or, in the best scenario, as supplemental to an established divine plan. According to this narrative, state officials are mere pawns on a metaphysical chessboard, prone to decisions and initiatives that even they may struggle to explain or justify rationally. Political leaders warm to this view of their vocation because it furnishes advance exculpation for their action, making rule by prodigy the antithesis of political accountability. Thus, rule by prodigy consecrates the existing divorce between action and consequence in Nigerian public life. Second, rule by prodigy deepens the wedge between state and society by portraying social action without divine license as doomed to failure, thus undermining the basis of any kind of collective organizing. Its theory of social change, to the extent that it is decipherable, tends to boil down to an absolute reliance on the agency of prayer. In its individual emphasis, prayer facilitates the social atomization that, weakening the civic bond, makes society all the more governable. But there is a politically performative dimension to prayer as well, as is seen most clearly in those "spectacles of piety" whereby a fleeting "affective proximity" or "momentary neural binding" between rulers and their subjects sustains the ideological work of manufacturing consent.[18] Effectively, then, rule by prodigy keeps state and society mutually enchanted—and alienated.

Rule by prodigy hurts social and other institutions in another way. Because it claims both the private and the public domains as its legitimate jurisdiction, honoring few distinctions between them (as a matter of fact, seeing both as equally susceptible to demonic manipulation), rule by prodigy, by relentlessly interspersing the supernatural with the natural, postulates a banal spirituality that delegitimizes human agency. For example, in the universe of Pastor D. K. Olukoya of the Mountain of Fire and Miracles Ministries, one struggles to find any kind of secular intermission amid a host of invisible spirits besieging the believer every day and *everywhere*. The social consolidation of this Weltanschauung manifests, for instance, in the changing definition of a "miracle," which may range from finding a job, giving birth to a child, or being absent from the scene of an armed robbery to successfully completing a journey between two towns. By championing a form of total spirituality whereby every aspect of daily life requires a miracle or some form of supernatural intervention, rule by prodigy renders the investment of time, energy, and resources in the reform of public institutions redundant.

The main object of rule by prodigy—spiritual as well as political—is the conversion of citizens into disciples, with discipleship not necessarily the endpoint but rather, to borrow an idea made popular by Achille Mbembe, zombification. Zombification suggests a kind of radical de-invigoration in which, having been relieved of its will to resistance, the agent is transformed into a permanent ally of the state. Rule by prodigy, I would argue, creates civic zombies precisely because, as Mbembe writes, "it appeals *not* to reason as a category of public life, but to sensations (the eye, the ear, the mouth, the phallus, taste, smell, a range of pleasures and pains of varying intensities)."[19]

Pentecostalism, furnishing the ideological software for rule by prodigy, appears modern in every sense. In Nigeria and elsewhere, its appeal among the urban, educated, and middle and upper classes is evident, and its leaders are plugged into the "right" political, educational, and financial circuits. What is more, it is widely asserted, Pentecostalism lionizes the individual by creating the space for the renegotiation of identity. I claim, conversely, that because it does not appeal to reason, and at times positively repudiates it, Pentecostalism is the antithesis of individualism, hence anti-modern. Within Pentecostalism, the individual is "free" only to the extent that he or she is empowered to combat various spirits, the existence and active malevolence of which are taken for granted.

Rule by prodigy, I have shown, is mediated through prophecy, sexuality, and gender. In his work on what he describes as "prophetic invention," Ramon Sarró suggests that "prophets bring new religious discourses and convince followers that they have to abandon old religious cultures and convert to these innovative ones."[20] While that may be true, I have approached "prophets" and "prophetic work" differently, taking these appellations at face value even as I have taken seriously how the very act of laying a special claim to "knowledge" of the future through the possession of supernatural power paves the way to political power. The foregoing is why, for me, prophecy, contra the direction and emphasis in the literature, is a "weapon of the strong" rather than the weak. Significantly, too, in the context of rule by prodigy, prophecies do not have to come to pass since, for a variety of reasons, nonfulfillment (I call it "clerical error") compromises the social standing of the Man of God only minimally, if at all. Within this framework, sexuality and gender operate interdependently. Sexuality refers to the erotic masculine power of the pastor over his congregation, whether as evidenced by his access to the bodies of female congregants or as seen in pastoral freedom to, quite literally, shape the masculinity of male congregants.

Regarding the democratic consequences of rule by prodigy, the future does not look promising, although it is worth remembering that the Nigerian iteration of the commerce of Pentecostalism and politics analyzed here is just one among many possible constellations of spirituality and democracy. At any rate, if, by my own lights, all indications point to a perversion of democracy in Nigeria, it is because of the theory of democracy that I uphold. At the heart of that theory is the conviction that argumentation is the cornerstone of a democratic order, whether argumentation between citizens or between citizens and the state. This much is settled in the otherwise rancorous literature on deliberative democracy or deliberative politics,[21] the idea of which is that, since moral conflict and political difference are inevitable in a plural society, it is incumbent on citizens, mutually committed to the principle of equality under the law, to subject their agreements to debate and discussion. But what does this principle of argumentation have to do with rule by prodigy? Resting as it is on revelation and prophetic "foresight," rule by prodigy is incompatible with—and, as matter of fact, corrodes— democracy *as* argumentation insofar as the latter entails reason-giving in a spirit of give and take. There is damage to civil society as well, since systematic and prolonged disinvestment in institutions and spaces where citizens learn the techniques of public debate will most likely eventuate in their atrophy. To worsen matters, and amid repeated clerical assurances about future security, citizens forfeit the capacity to argue and gradually come to see rational debate as pointless.

Yet, and, as I have tried to illustrate with the examples of women who, in their own ways and with varying degrees of success, stood up to powerful pastors, rule by prodigy is not impregnable. Hence, while, for the moment, all the evidence seems to point to a dark future for Nigerian democracy under the spiritual auspices of rule by prodigy, an alternative clustering is indeed possible.

NOTES

Introduction

1. All my information is from a friend of the family who was present at the scene.

2. For more on the problems of infrastructure in urban Nigeria and how they illuminate politics and policy, see the work of Ulrika Trovalla and Eric Trovalla, especially "Infrastructure as a Divination Tool: Whispers from the Grids in a Nigerian City," *City* 19, nos. 2–3 (2015): 332–43, and "Infrastructure Turned Suprastructure: Unpredictable Materialities and Visions of a Nigerian Nation," *Journal of Material Culture* 20, no. 1 (2015): 43–57. See also Ulrika Andersson Trovalla, *Medicine for Uncertain Futures: A Nigerian City in the Wake of a Crisis* (Uppsala, Sweden: Uppsala Universitet, 2011). For a different, if no less productive, approach to infrastructure in Nigeria, see Brian Larkin, *Signal and Noise: Media, Infrastructure, and Urban Culture in Nigeria* (Durham, NC: Duke University Press, 2008).

3. See Ihuoma Chiedozie, "Confusion as 'Prayer Warriors' Compete with Medical Doctors for Patients," *Punch* (Lagos), June 22, 2019.

4. My original title for this book, or at least the first part of it, was "My Pastor Says." During my research I was quite fascinated to hear this phrase recur among Pentecostals in different congregations and across a variety of contexts, universally employed to justify or defend particular acts by individual congregants. I don't imply, of course, that people always act in accordance with whatever their pastor says; what is useful here is the constancy of the appeal to the figure of the pastor as the ultimate validator of a wide variety of actions and opinions.

5. See, for instance, Nimi Wariboko, *Nigerian Pentecostalism* (Rochester, NY: University of Rochester Press, 2014); Olufemi Vaughan, *Religion and the Making of Nigeria* (Durham, NC: Duke University Press, 2016); Asonzeh

E.-K. Ukah, *A New Paradigm of Pentecostal Power: A Study of the Redeemed Christian Church of God in Nigeria* (Trenton, NJ: Africa World Press, 2008); Ruth Marshall, *Political Spiritualities: The Pentecostal Revolution in Nigeria* (Chicago: University of Chicago Press, 2009); Annalisa Butticci, *African Pentecostals in Catholic Europe: The Politics of Presence in the Twenty-first Century* (Cambridge, MA: Harvard University Press, 2016); Simeon O. Ilesanmi, *Religious Pluralism and the Nigerian State* (Athens: Ohio University Center for International Studies, 1997); J. Kwabena Asamoah-Gyadu, *Contemporary Pentecostal Christianity: Interpretations from an African Context* (Eugene, OR: Wipf and Stock, 2013); Ogbu Kalu, *African Pentecostalism: An Introduction* (New York: Oxford University Press, 2008); Matthews A. Ojo, *The End-Time Army: Charismatic Movements in Modern Nigeria* (Trenton, NJ: Africa World Press, 2006); Afeosemime U. Adogame, ed., *Who Is Afraid of the Holy Ghost? Pentecostalism and Globalization in Africa and Beyond* (Trenton, NJ: Africa World Press, 2011); Ebenezer Obadare, *Pentecostal Republic: Religion and the Struggle for State Power in Nigeria*, African Arguments (London: Zed, 2018); Gina Lende, "The Rise of Pentecostal Power: Exploring the Politics of Pentecostal Growth in Nigeria and Guatemala," PhD dissertation, Norwegian School of Theology, Oslo, 2015; Richard Burgess, *Nigerian Pentecostalism and Development: Spirit, Power, and Transformation*, Routledge Research in Religion and Development (London: Routledge, 2020); Adoyi Onoja, "The Pentecostal Churches: The Politics of Spiritual Deregulation since the 1980s," in *Religion in Politics: Secularism and National Integration in Modern Nigeria*, edited by Julius O. Adekunle, 263–73 (Trenton, NJ: Africa World Press, 2009).

6. Karen Lauterbach, "Becoming a Pastor: Youth and Social Aspirations in Ghana," *Young: Nordic Journal of Youth Research* 18, no. 3 (2010): 259–78; Richard A. van Dijk, "Young Puritan Preachers in Post-independence Malawi," *Africa* 62, no. 2 (1992): 159–81; Martin Lindhardt, "Men of God: Neo-Pentecostalism and Masculinities in Urban Tanzania," *Religion* 45, no. 2 (2015): 252–72; John F. McCauley, "Africa's New Big Man Rule? Pentecostalism and Patronage in Ghana," *African Affairs* 112, no. 446 (2013): 1–21; Matthew Engelke and Birgit Meyer, "Mediating Tradition: Pentecostal Pastors, African Priests, and Chiefs in Ghanaian Popular Films," in *Christianity and Social Change in Africa: Essays in Honor of J.D.Y. Peel*, edited by J.D.Y. Peel and Toyin Falola, 275–306 (Durham, NC: Carolina Academic Press, 2005); Obvious Katsaura, "Theo-Urbanism: Pastoral Power and Pentecostals in Johannesburg," *Culture and Religion: An Interdisciplinary Journal* 18, no. 3 (2017): 232–62; Rafael Cazarin and Marian Burchardt, "Learning How to Feel: Emotional Repertoires of Nigerian and Congolese Pentecostal Pastors in the Diaspora," in *Affective Trajectories: Religion and Emotion in African City-Scapes*, edited by Hansjörg Dilger, Astrid Bochow,

Marian Burchardt, and Matthew Wilhelm-Solomon, 160–84 (Durham, NC: Duke University Press, 2020); Leslie Fesenmyer, "Pentecostal Pastorhood as Calling and Career: Migration, Religion, and Masculinity between Kenya and the United Kingdom," *Journal of the Royal Anthropological Institute* 24 (2018): 749–66; Abimbola Adunni Adelakun, "Pastocracy: Performing Pentecostal Politics in Nigeria," in *Africa's Big Men: Predatory State-Society Relations in Africa*, edited by Kenneth Kalu, Olajumoke Yacob-Haliso, and Toyin Falola, 161–76, (New York: Routledge, 2018); Gregory Deacon, George Gona, Hassan Mwakimako, and Justin Willis, "Preaching Politics: Islam and Christianity on the Kenya Coast," *Journal of Contemporary African Studies* 35, no. 2 (2017): 148–67; Amy S. Patterson and Tracy Kuperus, "Mobilizing the Faithful: Organizational Autonomy, Visionary Pastors, and Citizenship in South Africa and Zambia," *African Affairs* 115, no. 459 (2016): 318–41.

7. See Heyck's "From Men of Letters to Intellectuals: The Transformation of Intellectual Life in Nineteenth-Century England," *Journal of British Studies* 20, no. 1 (1980): 158–83. For a full development of the same thesis, see, by the same author, *The Transformation of Intellectual Life in Victorian England* (London: Croom Helm, 1982).

8. See Ben Knights, *The Idea of the Clerisy in the Nineteenth Century* (New York: Cambridge University Press, 1978), 41.

9. I am aware that both the definition and the social role of the intellectual are fiercely contested (see, for example, Edward W. Said, *Representations of the Intellectual* [New York: Vintage Books, 1996]) and cognizant of the rich African literature on peasant and local intellectuals (see, for example, Steven Feierman, *Peasant Intellectuals: Anthropology and History in Tanzania* [Madison: University of Wisconsin Press, 1990] and the essays in the special issue of *Africa* 87, no. 1 [2017] dedicated to "Africa Local Intellectuals"). This category of intellectuals is not included in my analysis. On the relationship between the media and intellectuals and whether journalists can be classified as intellectuals, see Nicholas Garnham, *Emancipation, the Media, and Modernity: Arguments about the Media and Social Theory* (New York: Oxford University Press, 2000). For an analysis of the same question in a Nigerian context, see Wale Adebanwi, "Introduction: Media Intellectual and the Social Conscience," in *Public Intellectuals, the Public Sphere & the Public Spirit*, edited by Wale Adebanwi, 1–27 (Ibadan: Ibadan University Press, 2014).

10. William Ellery Channing, "On the Elevation of the Laboring Classes," in *The Harvard Classics: Essays English and American*, edited by Charles W. Eliot, 321–80 (Norwalk, CT: Easton Press, 1994), quote on 335.

11. Lewis A. Coser, *Men of Ideas: A Sociologist's View* (New York: Free Press, 1977), xvii. Italics in original.

12. See Syed Hussein Alatas, *Intellectuals in Developing Societies* (London: Franc Cass, 1977), 10.

13. See, for example, Robert H. Jackson and Carl G. Rosberg, *Personal Rule in Black Africa: Prince, Autocrat, Prophet, Tyrant* (Berkeley: University of California Press, 1982); Joan Vincent, *African Elite: The Big Men of a Small Town* (New York: Columbia University Press, 1971); John L. Comaroff and Jean Comaroff, eds., *The Politics of Custom: Chiefship, Capital, and the State in Contemporary Africa* (Chicago: University of Chicago Press, 2018); Tejumola Olaniyan, ed., *State and Culture in Postcolonial Africa: Enchantings* (Bloomington: Indiana University Press, 2017); Jeffrey Herbst, *States and Power in Africa: Comparative Lessons in Authority and Control* (Princeton, NJ: Princeton University Press, 2000); Olufemi Taiwo, *Africa Must Be Modern: A Manifesto* (Bloomington: Indiana University Press, 2014); Achille Mbembe, *On the Postcolony* (Berkeley: University of California Press, 2001); Sebastian Elischer, "Burkina Faso: State and Religious Authority in Turbulent Times," in *Faith in the Balance: Regulating Religious Affairs in Africa*, edited by Haim Malka, 111–36 (Lanham, MD: Rowman and Littlefield, 2020); Martin Doornbos, "Church & State in Eastern Africa: Some Unresolved Questions," *Religion & Politics in East Africa: The Period since Independence*, edited by Holger Bernt Hansen and Michael Twaddle, 260–70 (London: James Currey, 1995); A.H.M. Kirk-Greene, "His Eternity, His Eccentricity, or His Exemplarity? A Further Contribution to the Study of H. E. the African Head of State," *African Affairs* 90, no. 359 (1991): 163–87.

14. See Obadare, *Pentecostal Republic*.

15. Isaac Terwase Sampson, "Religion and the Nigerian State: Situating the de Facto and de Jure Frontiers of State-Religion Relations and Its Implications for National Security," *Oxford Journal of Law and Religion* 3, no. 2 (2014): 311–39.

16. Jean Comaroff and John L. Comaroff, eds., *Law and Disorder in the Postcolony* (Chicago: University of Chicago Press, 2006), x.

17. Patrick Chabal and Jean-Pascal Daloz, *Africa Works: Disorder as Political Instrument* (Oxford: James Currey, 1999).

18. See Joseph Raz, "Introduction," in *Authority*, edited by Joseph Raz, 1–19 (New York: New York University Press, 1990), 2.

19. See Obadare, *Pentecostal Republic*.

20. J.D.Y. Peel, "The Pastor and the *Babalawo*: The Interaction of Religions in Nineteenth-Century Yorubaland," *Africa* 60, no. 3 (1990): 338–69.

21. See Adéléke Adéèkọ́, *Arts of Being Yorùbá: Divination, Allegory, Tragedy, Proverb, Panegyric* (Bloomington: Indiana University Press, 2017).

22. Elnathan John, *Be(com)ing Nigerian: A Guide* (London: Cassava Republic Press, 2019), 13.

23. For more on this, see Wale Adebanwi and Ebenezer Obadare, "Paper Games: Consularity and Ersatz Lives in Urban Lagos," in *Everyday State and Democracy in Africa: Ethnographic Encounters*, edited by Wale Adebanwi (Athens, OH: Ohio University Press, 2022). Cf. Jesse Weaver Shipley, "Comedians, Pastors, and the Miraculous Agency of Charisma in Ghana," *Cultural Anthropology* 24, no. 3 (2009): 523–52.

24. See Wale Adebanwi, "The Clergy, Culture, and Political Conflicts in Nigeria," *African Studies Review* 53, no. 3 (2010): 121–42.

25. Ebenezer Obadare, "State of Travesty: Jokes and the Logic of Socio-Cultural Improvisation in Africa," *Critical African Studies* 2, no. 4 (2010): 92–112.

26. I am grateful to Tade Ipadeola and James Yeku for assistance with translation.

27. Ebenezer Obadare, "The Uses of Ridicule: Humour, 'Infrapolitics' and Civil Society in Nigeria," *African Affairs* 108, no. 431 (2009): 241–61.

28. Moradewun Adejunmobi, "Standup Comedy and the Ethics of Popular Performance in Nigeria," in *Popular Culture in Africa: The Episteme of the Everyday*, edited by Stephanie Newell and Onookome Okome, 175–94 (New York: Routledge, 2014). Adejunmobi's work provides a lead into how Nigerian popular culture imagines Pentecostalism in general and pastors in particular. For example, in addition to being regular targets of mockery by standup comedians, pastors and their shenanigans are recurrent fixtures in many Nigerian Nollywood films. Akinwumi Adesokan sees a deeper sociological process at work, arguing that "the explosion of Nollywood films is very much linked to the logic of informalization at work in the growth" of Pentecostal churches. See his "'Jesus Christ, Executive Producer': Pentecostal Parapolitics in Nollywood Films," in *State and Culture in Postcolonial Africa: Enchantings*, edited by Tejumola Olaniyan, 191–206 (Bloomington: Indiana University Press, 2017). The union of Pentecostalism and Nigerian cinema is cemented by the recent emergence of pastoring as a career among an increasing number of retired Nollywood stars and other celebrities. Among retired movie stars who have gone on to establish themselves as Pentecostal pastors are Eucharia Anunobi-Akwu, Ernest Azuzu, Kanayo O. Kanayo, Zack Orji, Larry Koldsweat, and Liz Benson. See Ebenezer Obadare, "On the Theologico-Theatrical: Explaining the Convergence of Pentecostalism and Popular Culture in Nigeria," *Africa at LSE* (blog), August 1, 2018, https://blogs.lse.ac.uk/africaatlse/2018/08/01/on-the-theologico-theatrical-explaining-the-convergence-of-pentecostalism-and-popular-culture-in-nigeria/. For a complementary analysis, particularly of the idea of Pentecostalism and Pentecostal rituals as performance, see, for example, Abimbola Adunni Adelakun, "Godmentality: Pentecostalism as

Performance in Nigeria," PhD dissertation, University of Texas at Austin, 2017, and Jonathan Haynes, *Nollywood: The Creation of Nigerian Film Genres* (Chicago: University of Chicago Press, 2016).

29. See, for instance, Nandera Ernest Mhando, Loreen Maseno, Kupakwashe Mtata, and Mathew Senga, "Modes of Legitimation by Female Pentecostal-Charismatic Preachers in East Africa: A Comparative Study in Kenya and Tanzania," *Journal of Contemporary African Studies* 36, no. 3 (2018): 319–33.

30. See, for instance, Ebenezer Obadare, *Humor, Silence, and Civil Society in Nigeria* (Rochester, NY: University of Rochester Press, 2016); Ebenezer Obadare and Wendy Willems, eds., *Civic Agency in Africa: Arts of Resistance in the 21st Century* (Rochester, NY: James Currey, 2014); James C. Scott, *Domination and the Arts of Resistance: Hidden Transcripts* (New Haven, CT: Yale University Press, 1992).

31. From a growing literature, see, for instance, Barbara Kellerman, "Leadership—It's a *System*, Not a Person!" *Daedalus, the Journal of the American Academy of Arts & Sciences* 145, no. 3 (2016): 83–94; Martin Gurri, *The Revolt of the Public and the Crisis of Authority in the New Millennium* (San Francisco: Stripe Press, 2018); Thomas M. Nichols, *The Death of Expertise: The Campaign against Established Knowledge and Why It Matters* (New York: Oxford University Press, 2017). One way in which my thought differs from what is seen in this literature (including Gurri and Nichols) is that the origins of the phenomenon I am grappling with antedate the digital era, though there is no doubt that it has been accentuated by it.

32. Richard Sennett, *Authority* (New York: Knopf, 1980), 17–18.

ONE. The Social Origins of Clerical Power in Nigeria

1. For example, *Reflections on Warminster* (1975), *Will Live Forever* (1977), *Nupe Dance Poems* (1978), *The Poetry of Abuja: Nigeria's Capital* (1983), and *Reach for the Skies* (1985).

2. See Wole Soyinka, *You Must Set Forth at Dawn: Memoirs* (Ibadan: Bookcraft, 2006), 262.

3. Ibid, 260.

4. See Arukaino Umukoro, "I Don't Believe My Father Plotted a Coup, He Told Me He Didn't—Mamman Vatsa's Son," *Punch* (Lagos), January 8, 2017.

5. The ANA Writers' Village in Abuja, named after him, is built on land allocated by Vatsa when he was FCT minister.

6. Soyinka, *You Must Set Forth at Dawn*, 265.

7. J. P. Clark, "When Soyinka, Achebe and I Pleaded with IBB to Spare Vatsa's Life," *NEWS* (Lagos), September 3, 2016, available at https://www.thenewsnigeria.com.ng.

8. Soyinka, *You Must Set Forth at Dawn*, 265.

9. Ibid., 266.

10. This does not make it any less interesting to speculate as to the reasons that Babangida went ahead with the execution. First and foremost, coup-planning being the deadly business it is, it would have been highly unusual for general amnesty to have been extended to the coup-plotters. Whatever one thinks of the Babangida regime, it stands to reason that a mass pardon would have made him appear weak, an impression he could not afford, given that he himself had seized power only four months earlier, in August 1985, deposing the duo of Muhammadu Buhari and Tunde Idiagbon. As he was a student of history, the reality could not have been lost on him that many military rulers (in Africa and elsewhere) had been either edged out of power by, or lost their lives in putsches spearheaded by, close associates. Given this backdrop, Babangida may actually have been telling the truth later in his secret message to Soyinka saying that he, Babangida, had tried his best but had been overruled by the other members of the Armed Forces Ruling Council (AFRC) (see Soyinka, *You Must Set Forth at Dawn*, 270–72). Second, and, perverse as it may sound, it is not far-fetched to think that Vatsa's fate may in fact have been sealed by his friendship with Babangida. While a case for amnesty for a "random" person might have been plausible, amnesty for Vatsa, even if defensible on other grounds, could very well have been easily interpreted as giving an undeserved pass to a friend, thus portraying Babangida as an emotionally unstable leader who could not be entrusted with dispassionate decisions. Such, it appears, is the strange conflation of affinity with fatality. For a deeper exploration, see Wale Adebanwi, "What Are Friends For? The Fatality of Affinity in the Postcolony," unpublished manuscript, 2013. Finally, and relevant to the subject of this chapter, is the possibility that Vatsa was doomed once he was arrested because of how he consistently portrayed himself: as an outsider intellectual. Did he go too far, perhaps, in his versification of what Soyinka calls "social themes and private thoughts" (Soyinka, *You Must Set Forth at Dawn*, 260), his insistence on being seen as a litterateur in uniform? Had he stepped on the toes of powerful people in the armed forces who had found his ostentatious posturing as an intellectual too irksome? Put differently: Did Vatsa die for being an intellectual?

11. The real disagreement is about the causes of this decline and the role of intellectuals themselves in its precipitation. The following provide representative points of view: Samuel O. Atteh, "The Crisis of Higher Education

in Africa," *Issue: A Journal of Opinion* 24, no. 1 (1996): 36–42; Adebayo Williams, "Intellectuals and the Crisis of Democratization in Nigeria: Towards a Theory of Postcolonial Anomie," *Theory and Society* 27, no 2 (1998): 287–307; Wole Soyinka, *The Open Sore of a Continent: A Personal Narrative of the Nigerian Crisis* (Oxford: Oxford University Press, 1996); Yann Lebeau and Mobolaji Ogunsanya, eds., *The Dilemma of Post-Colonial Universities* (Ibadan: IFRA, 2000); Attahiru Jega, "Nigerian Universities and Academic Staff under Military Rule," *Review of African Political Economy* 22, no. 64 (1995): 251–56; Ebenezer Obadare, "Brain versus Brawn in Nigerian Universities," *CODESRIA Bulletin* 1 (1997): 6–9; Arthur Agwuncha Nwankwo, *African Dictators: The Logic of Tyranny and Lessons from History* (Enugu, Nigeria: Fourth Dimension Publishing, 1990); Adekunle Amuwo, "Between Intellectual Responsibility and Political Commodification of Knowledge: Nigeria's Academic Political Scientists under the Babangida Military Junta, 1985–1993," *African Studies Review* 45, no. 2 (2002): 93–121.

12. Reverend Professor (sometimes Professor Reverend) Eghosa Osaghae, political scientist and former vice chancellor of Igbinedion University, is a case in point, though by no means an isolated one. To be sure, the traffic of "status imitation" is not unidirectional, as pastors, too, for reasons of social prestige analyzed later, long for PhDs, "professorships," and associated pendants of academic distinction. As a matter of fact, in the context of the nascent prestige economy in Nigeria, acquiring a PhD is de rigueur, with honorary PhDs and awards from online diploma mills being the most frequented paths for the most eager. For a growing segment of the elite, the PhD is typically augmented with an expensive "leadership training" class (usually between two and four weeks in duration) at a prestigious American or other Western university, which guarantees that the individual in question can be introduced or referred to as, for example, "Harvard-trained." Those who wish to stand apart from the crowd and show that their PhDs are "legitimate" often go out of their way to post their award certificates on their social media sites. For instance, in October 2019 media personality Japhet Omojuwa posted the certificate of his PhD in Digital Media and Communications (from Escae-Benin University), no doubt to signal his new status, but at the same time to convey that it was "real." See https://twitter.com/Omojuwa/status/1185582592512483328. Others, aiming to separate themselves from their "peers" with legitimate PhDs, go out of their way to accumulate multiple PhDs. An example is Pastor Funsho Odesola, assistant general overseer of the RCCG, who apparently boasts a personal war chest of six PhDs and four master's degrees. See Olayinka Latona, "OLIVER TWIST! Redeemed Pastor Who Has Six PhDs Wants More," *Vanguard* (Lagos), July 7, 2019. The extreme opposite of acquiring multiple

academic titles is what I call honorific austerity. In honorific austerity, which is in essence another mode of acquiring eminence, the agent, perhaps conscious of the existing scramble for titles in the society, makes clear a desire not to be associated with any but instead to be referred to as simply "Mr." Some recent examples are Ogbeni (Yoruba for Mr.) Rauf Aregbesola, Osun State governor, 2010–18, and "Arakunrin" (also Mr. but, colloquially, closer to "That Man") Rotimi Akeredolu, Ondo State governor, 2017–present. What immediately comes to mind here is Jean-Pascal Daloz's discussion of the idea of "conspicuous modesty" or "studied understatement." See Jean-Pascal Daloz, "Political Elites and Conspicuous Modesty: Norway, Sweden, Finland in Comparative Perspective," *Comparative Social Research* 23 (2006): 171–210, and Jean-Pascal Daloz, "Elite (Un)conspicuousness: Theoretical Reflections on Ostentation vs. Understatement," *Historical Social Research* 37, no. 1 (2012): 209–22. Cf. Elizabeth Currid-Halkett, *The Sum of Small Things: A Theory of the Aspirational Class* (Princeton, NJ: Princeton University Press, 2017). The foregoing raises the key question of how to account for the hunger for status in Nigeria. I'd hazard a guess that, inter alia, it is a reflection of all-too-real blockages and misdirections in conventional routes to elite recruitment, access, and mobility. See the discussion in Gavin Williams, *State and Society in Nigeria*, 2nd ed. (Lagos: Malthouse Press, 2019), 223–24. At the same time, status anxiety in Nigeria can be explained as a product of "deindividualization" created by a prolonged economic crisis. Here the struggle for status is an attempt to push back against the massification induced by the forces of economic erasure. The idea of status anxiety is from Richard Hofstadter, who used it in reference to demographic or ethnic groupings. See his *The Age of Reform: From Bryan to F.D.R.* (New York: Vintage Books, 1955).

13. J. Bayo Adekanye, "Military Occupation and Social Stratification," Inaugural Lecture, University of Ibadan, Ibadan, 1993, 8.

14. Ibid., 1.

15. Perhaps the only thing matching the military's importance in the society at the time was its higher echelon's self-importance, evidenced by the many projects of self-monumentalization it found time for, including commissioned hagiographies. See Gbemisola Adeoti, "Narrating the Green Gods: The (Auto)Biographies of Nigerian Military Rulers," in *Intellectuals and African Development: Pretension and Resistance in African Politics*, edited by Bjorn Beckman and Gbemisola Adeoti, 49–64 (London: Zed, 2006). For an analysis of African soldiers as a new political class, see Ali A. Mazrui, "The Lumpen Proletariat and the Lumpen Militariat: African Soldiers as a New Political Class," *Political Studies* 21, no. 1 (1973): 1–12.

16. Adekanye, "Military Occupation and Social Stratification," 8.

17. Independence brought a rash of new universities, including the University of Nigeria, Nsukka, in 1960, the University of Ife in 1961 (though classes would commence only in 1962), the University of Lagos and Ahmadu Bello University, Zaria, in 1962, followed by the University of Benin in 1970.

18. See E. A. Ayandele, *The Educated Elite in the Nigerian Society* (Ibadan: Ibadan University Press, 1979), 2.

19. James S. Coleman, *Nigeria: Background to Nationalism* (Benin City: Broburg & Wilstrom, 1986), 145.

20. Ayandele, *The Educated Elite in the Nigerian Society*, 3.

21. Michael J. C. Echeruo, *Victorian Lagos: Aspects of Nineteenth Century Lagos Life* (New York: Macmillan, 1977), 113.

22. Ibid.

23. Ayandele, *The Educated Elite in the Nigerian Society*, 9.

24. See Olufemi Taiwo, *How Colonialism Preempted Modernity in Africa* (Bloomington: Indiana University Press, 2010). Cf. Wale Adebanwi, "Elites and the Enlightenment: Reflections on the Question of Progress in Contemporary Nigeria," Metropolitan Club 60th Anniversary Lecture, Lagos, Nigeria, October 15, 2019. See also Nozomi Sawada, "The Educated Elite and Associational Life in Early Lagos Newspapers: In Search of Unity for the Progress of Society," PhD thesis, University of Birmingham, England, July 2011.

25. For an analysis of European attitudes toward the educated elite, See Coleman, *Nigeria*, 145–66.

26. Ayandele, *The Educated Elite in the Nigerian Society*, 11.

27. See, in this regard, Philip Serge Zachernuk, *Colonial Subjects: An African Intelligentsia and Atlantic Ideas* (Charlottesville: University Press of Virginia, 2000).

28. Taiwo, *How Colonialism Preempted Modernity in Africa*, 100.

29. J. F. Ade-Ajayi, "Towards an African Academic Community," in *Creating the African University: Emerging Issues in the 1970s*, edited by T. M. Yesufu, 49–64 (Ibadan: Oxford University Press, 1972).

30. Ibid., 14.

31. Ibid., 12.

32. T. M. Yesufu, "Introduction," in *Creating the African University: Emerging Issues in the 1970s*, edited by T. M. Yesufu (Ibadan: Oxford University Press, 1972), 4.

33. Quoted in Adekunle Amuwo, "The Discourse of the Political Elites on Higher Education in Nigeria," in *The Dilemma of Post-Colonial Universities*, edited by Yann Lebeau and Mobolaji Ogunsanya (Ibadan: IFRA-Nigeria, 2000), 3.

34. Ade-Ajayi, "Towards an African Academic Community," 12.

35. Ibid.

36. To get the flavor of these debates, see, for instance, O. Onoge, "Revolutionary Imperatives in African Sociology," in *African Social Studies: A Reader*, edited by Peter Gutkind and Peter Waterman, 32–43 (New York: Monthly Review Press, 1977); Bernard Magubane, "Crisis in African Sociology," *East African Journal* 5, no. 12 (1968): 21–40; and Carl K. Eicher, "African Universities: Overcoming Intellectual Dependency," in *Creating the African University: Emerging Issues in the 1970s*, edited by T. M. Yesufu, 27–34 (Ibadan: Oxford University Press, 1972).

37. For an excellent overview, see Said Adejumobi, "Knowledge for Sale? The Politics of University Education Reform in Africa, with a Nigerian Example," in *Manoeuvring in an Environment of Uncertainty: Structural Change and Social Action in Sub-Saharan Africa*, edited by Boel Berner and Per Trulsson, 179–206 (Aldershot, England: Ashgate, 2000).

38. Olufemi Taiwo, "Colonialism and Its Aftermath: The Crisis of Knowledge Production," *Callaloo* 16, no. 4 (1993): 891–908, quote on 907. Mahmood Mamdani has made a variant of this argument. See his "The African University," *London Review of Books* 40, no. 4 (2018): 29–32.

39. Quoted in Amuwo, "The Discourse of the Political Elites," 3.

40. Yusuf Bangura, "Intellectuals, Economic Reform and Social Change: Constraints and Opportunities in the Formation of a Nigerian Technocracy," *Development and Change* 25, no. 2 (1994): 261–305. The same point is underscored by Robin Luckham in *The Nigerian Military: A Sociological Analysis of Authority and Revolt* (Cambridge: Cambridge University Press, 1971), and by Paul E. Lovejoy and Jan S. Hogendorn in *Slow Death for Slavery: The Course of Abolition in Northern Nigeria, 1897–1936* (New York: Cambridge University Press, 1993).

41. Adekanye, "Military Occupation and Social Stratification," 2.

42. See Bjorn Beckman and Attahiru Jega, "Scholars and Democratic Politics in Nigeria," *Review of African Political Economy* 22, no. 64 (1995): 167–81, quote on 173.

43. See J. Isawa Elaigwu, "Nigerian Federalism under Civilian and Military Regimes," *Publius: The Journal of Federalism* 18, no. 1 (1988): 173–88; Dennis Austin, "Universities and the Academic Gold Standard in Nigeria," *Minerva* 18, no. 2 (1980): 201–42; A. A. Adeogun, "The Law and the Institutionalization of Labour Protest in Nigeria," *Indian Journal of Industrial Relations* 16, no. 1 (1980): 1–23. We may add to this centralist logic the establishment of the National Universities Commission (NUC) in 1962 and the Joint Admissions and Matriculations Board (JAMB) in 1978. Effectively, both transferred power from the universities to the federal government, thus further eroding the former's autonomy.

44. See Sanya Osha, *African Postcolonial Modernity: Informal Subjectivities and the Democratic Consensus* (New York: Palgrave Macmillan, 2014), 73.

45. Yesufu, "Introduction," 3.

46. London: Harvill, 1970.

47. He laments, for example, that "Nigerian traits have begun to dominate staff quarters, including the pounding of yam in flats and the cultural habit of noise-making." Ayandele, *The Educated Elite in the Nigerian Society*, 176.

48. Beckman and Jega, "Scholars and Democratic Politics in Nigeria," 174.

49. Ibid., 173.

50. Bangura, "Intellectuals, Economic Reform and Social Change," 270.

51. Ibid., 174.

52. Notably, one of its declared objectives at its founding in 1978 was to align itself with "such other objects as are lawful and not consistent with the spirit and practice of trade unionism." See Sanya Osha, "Violence and Decay within the Nigerian University System: Notes from Ladoke Akintola University of Technology, Ogbomoso," in *The Dilemma of Post-Colonial Universities*, edited by Yann Lebeau and Mobolaji Ogunsanya (Ibadan: IFRA, 2000), 96.

53. Bangura, "Intellectuals, Economic Reform and Social Change," 271.

54. Ibid., 264.

55. Ibid.

56. A. Carl LeVan, *Dictators and Democracy in African Development: The Political Economy of Good Governance in Nigeria* (New York: Cambridge University Press, 2015), 81.

57. See Jibrin Ibrahim, "Political Scientists and the Subversion of Democracy in Nigeria," in *The State and Democracy in Africa*, edited by Georges Nzongola-Ntalaja and Margaret C. Lee, 114–24 (Trenton, NJ: Africa World Press, 1998), quote on 117.

58. Ibid.

59. Tunji Olagunju and Sam Oyovbaire, eds., *Portrait of a New Nigeria: Selected Speeches of IBB*, vol. 1 (London: Precision Press, 1989), ix.

60. Ibrahim, "Political Scientists and the Subversion of Democracy in Nigeria."

61. Bangura, "Intellectuals, Economic Reform and Social Change," 262.

62. Ibid.

63. Ibid.

64. Ibid., 274.

65. Osha, "Violence and Decay within the Nigerian University System," 98.

66. Nigerian slang for an unofficial taxi. In retrospect, this must have been one of the most excruciating things that the average Nigerian academic had to do for survival, for, in Nigeria in particular, the automobile is not just a mode of conveyance but a significant index of social stratification. It is, in the words of Achille Mbembe and Janet Roitman, "an object of appropriation as a sign, belonging to a logic that is partly inspired by class affiliations." See Mbembe and Roitman, "Figures of the Subject in Times of Crisis," *Public Culture* 7 (1995): 323–52, quote on 330. An idea of what, status-wise, the automobile (typically a Volvo 240 or 244 DL) meant to the Nigerian university professor can be gleaned from the following elegy to a bygone era by Adegoke Olubummo:

> In 1965, I had a reliable car which I drove with confidence to any part of Nigeria. In 1985, I do not have a car: oh, all right, I have a car which needs at least four tyres, which is very much in need of a battery and which has hardly any brakes so that the only way I can stop it is by uttering appropriate incantations. So if I need to go, for instance, to Lagos on a personal, professional or even official business, I often have to go by public transport. Actually, I now enjoy these journeys, but sometimes on such journeys, when I see an expensive, brand-new, chauffeur-driven car zoom past me, with a young man sitting in the owner's corner, I cannot help asking myself, "Is this what it all adds up to?"

See Adegoke Olubummo, "What Does It All Add Up To?" Valedictory Lecture Delivered at the Send-Off Function Organized by the Faculty of Science, University of Ibadan, on July 17, 1985 (Akure: Afrografika), 19. Whether as a rueful passenger like Professor Olubummo or as an emergency entrepreneur who had to press his private car into service, for the academic, the loss of prestige from having to operate in a different psychosocial space, and with citizens on the lower rungs of the social ladder, could not be more real.

67. Jane I. Guyer, "Preface," in *Money Struggles & City Life: Devaluation in Ibadan and Other Urban Centers in Southern Nigeria, 1986–1996*, edited by Jane I. Guyer, LaRay Denzer, and Adigun Agbaje, ix–xv (Ibadan: BookBuilders, 2003), quote on xi.

68. Ibid.

69. The incorporation of academics into the orbit of NGOs and human rights organizations was not without cost, as involvement with them, apart from distracting academics from their legitimate research, often served to "reduce attention to connections between local problems and the wider political analyses of experts." See William Reno, "The Politics of Public Intellectuals under Abacha and After," in *Vision and Policy in Nigerian Economics: The Legacy of Pius Okigbo*, edited by Jane I. Guyer and LaRay Denzer, 129–47 (Ibadan: Ibadan University Press, 2005), 135. For more on NGOs

and the transformation of the civic and intellectual landscape in Africa, cf. Ebenezer Obadare, "Revalorizing the Political: Towards a New Intellectual Agenda for African Civil Society Discourse," *Journal of Civil Society* 7, no. 4 (2011): 427–42.

70. Bangura, "Intellectuals, Economic Reform and Social Change," 264.

71. I write "Marxism-Socialism" because (1) Marxism is just one variant of socialism and (2) both tend to go together in Nigeria, where most socialists are Marxists. Suffice it to add, you don't have to be a Marxist in order to be a socialist.

72. Chidi Amuta, "Off Your Marx (Dead End of Marxism)," *Daily Times* (Lagos), September 16, 1991.

73. In his 2017 foreword to the book, Biodun Jeyifo, who should know, describes it as "irreplaceable in being the very first systematic attempt to give us a cognitive map of where African literary theory came from in colonial Africa" (Chidi Amuta and Biodun Jeyifo, *Theory of African Literature: Implications for Practical Criticism* [London: Zed Books, 2017], xiv).

74. For example, see the account in Tajudeen Abdulraheem and Adebayo Olukoshi, "The Left in Nigerian Politics and the Struggle for Socialism: 1945–1985," *Review of African Political Economy* 37 (1986): 64–80.

75. A full history of the Nigerian left is outside the remit of this chapter. But see, for instance, A. A. Amakiri, *The Left in Nigerian Politics* (Lagos: Amkra Books, 1997). For a more recent—and, arguably, more comprehensive—account, see Adam Mayer, *Naija Marxisms: Revolutionary Thought in Nigeria* (London: Pluto Press, 2016).

76. The commune would be dissolved within a year. See Ogaga Ifowodo, "The Communist as Teacher—the Example of Biodun Jeyifo," *Premium Times*, February 18, 2016.

77. The list is selective. It is also largely male, flagging gender issues in Nigeria's intellectual formation that are outside the purview of this book.

78. Edward Shils, *Selected Papers of Edward Shils: The Calling of Sociology and Other Essays on the Pursuit of Learning* (Chicago: University of Chicago Press, 1980), 338.

79. See Andrei Znamenski, *Socialism as a Secular Creed: A Modern Global History* (Lanham, MD: Rowman and Littlefield, 2021).

80. Richard L. Sklar, "Beyond Capitalism and Socialism in Africa," *Journal of Modern African Studies* 26, no. 1 (1988): 1–21, quote on 8.

81. See Mary Kaldor, *Global Civil Society: An Answer to War* (London: Polity, 2004), 146.

82. Mayer, *Naija Marxisms*, 1–2.

83. See, for instance, Biodun Jeyifo's illuminating interview with *The News* and *PM News*: "Biodun Jeyifo: Reflections of a Radical Literary Critic, Theorist, Unionist and Columnist," *PM News Nigeria*, February 6, 2016,

available at https://www.pmnewsnigeria.com/2016/02/06/biodun-jeyifo-reflections-of-a-radical-literary-critic-theorist-unionist-and-columnist/.

84. See, for example, Amy Chua and Jed Rubenfeld, *The Triple Package: How Three Unlikely Traits Explain the Rise and Fall of Cultural Groups in America* (New York: Penguin Books, 2014).

85. I should point out that, as indicated in the previous chapter, this problem is not unique to Nigeria and probably has more to do with a global transformation in the economy between "experts" and their audience, enabled by digitization.

86. The essence of the SAP, advertised by the World Bank and the International Monetary Fund (IMF) as the panacea for African countries' economic woes, was a drastic pullback of state involvement and investment in social services, a move that, in principle, would free up space for private investment and make the state "smarter," if not smaller. For more on SAP, see Adebayo Olukoshi, ed., *The Politics of Structural Adjustment in Nigeria* (London: James Currey, 1993).

87. Jane I. Guyer, LaRay Denzer, and Adigun Agbaje, "Introduction: The Nigerian Popular Economy—Strategies Toward a Study," in *Money Struggles & City Life: Devaluation in Ibadan and Other Urban Centers in Southern Nigeria 1986–1996*, edited by Jane I. Guyer, LaRay Denzer, and Adigun Agbaje, xvii–xlv, quote on xxi.

88. Ibid., xxii.

89. Katrien Pype, "Of Fools and False Pastors: Tricksters in Kinshasa's Television Fiction," *Visual Anthropology* 23, no. 2 (2010): 115–35, citation on 130.

90. Dr. Francis Bola Akin-John, International Church Growth Ministry, personal interview, Lagos, June 16, 2016.

91. See Adedamola Osinulu, "The Road to Redemption: Performing Pentecostal Citizenship in Lagos," in *The Arts of Citizenship in African Cities: Infrastructures and Spaces of Belonging*, edited by Mamadou Diouf and Rosalind Fredericks), 115–35, quote on 124–25 (New York: Palgrave Macmillan, 2014).

92. Osinulu references Asonzeh Ukah's (2008) report that "in the old auditorium, after Adeboye departed the stage, people would rush to the area where he had previously stood." Ibid., 125. The media is replete with reports of church members hoping to experience a healing miracle stampeding to touch Pastor Adeboye's body, sit on a chair in which he had sat, or occupy a pulpit he had just vacated. See, for example, Bisi Daniels, "Pastor Adeboye at 76—How He Made Osinbajo Believe in Supernatural," *Premium Times*, March 4, 2018. For his followers, whatever the man they affectionately refer to as "Daddy" has either touched or prayed upon is as good as his physical

presence, as we saw with the anointing oil in the vignette with which I opened the introduction to this book. The same thing applies to his image. For example, in one of the many hagiographic accounts of his life, A. O. Oshorun describes the case of a man who was apparently delivered from "Satanic bondage" after touching a picture of Pastor Adeboye "on a calendar in his house." In another example, a woman whose child had taken ill and died was able to raise the child from death with "a handkerchief anointed by Pastor Adeboye under general ministration." See Oshorun, *Pastor E. A. Adeboye: A Man of Life of Submission and Service to God: The General Overseer of the Redeemed Christian Church of God* (Ibadan: Ethical Financial & Investments Consultants, 2014), 33 and 29. Often Pastor Adeboye's voice produces the same effect, as seen in the example of a woman apparently cured of cancer after hearing Adeboye's voice on the radio. See Biodun Odunuga-Samuel, "He Touched Me: How I Got Victory over Cancer through Adeboye's Voice on Radio," *Sunday Tribune* (Ibadan), June 21, 2019. The idea of the uniqueness of the body of the pastor as a conveyor of divine charge seems common among Nigerian Pentecostals. Meyer has pointed out that "though in principle all born-again believers are able and entitled to *embody* the Holy Spirit, charismatic pastors are prime exponents of divine power. Indeed, this is what their charisma depends upon and what draws people into their churches." Italics in original. See Birgit Meyer, "Religious Sensations: Why Media, Aesthetics, and Power Matter in the Study of Contemporary Religion," in *Religion: Beyond a Concept*, edited by Hent de Vries, 704–23 (New York: Fordham University Press, 2008), 709. The reverence for the body (and the person) of the pastor also manifests in the wholesale adoption by church members or junior pastors with a founding pastor's style, including his manner of dressing and hairstyle. This seems to be the case, for instance, with Pastors Chris Okotie and Chris Oyakhilome, whose permed coiffures and impeccable suits have launched a train of imitators. Pastor Biodun Fatoyinbo's taste in designer shirts, suits, and shoes has not gone unnoticed among a group of young members of his church. A different kind of investment in the body of the pastor is seen in the "My pastor is more elegant than yours" competition among Pentecostal churches to either dress up their pastors in choice clothes or treat them to the most prestigious automobiles, the most common (as of July 2020) being either a Rolls Royce or a G-Class SUV Mercedes-Benz, popularly known as a "G Wagon." A private jet remains the premium mode of conveyance, and for many churches remains at the level of aspiration. See Mfonobong Nsehe, "Wealthy Nigerians, Pastors Spend $225 Million on Private Jets," Forbes, May 17, 2011, https://www.forbes.com/. Further, as Ibrahim's work on Christ Embassy shows, the body of Murtala the pastor can be an entity on which members of a congregation can "sow a seed." According to Ibrahim, "Sowing seed on the pastors means giving money as a gift to the pastor personally instead of donating to the church as an institution." This is because "seed sowing is tacitly projected as an investment that people can make so as to incur a significant profit." See Ibrahim, "Sensational Piety: Practices of Mediation in Christ Embassy and NASFAT," PhD thesis submitted to Utrecht University, Utrecht, Netherlands, 2017. Quotes from 115 and 116, respectively. All told, Pentecostalism "is about bodies," says Nimi Wariboko. "Just visit any of its churches or turn on the television and you will see bodies falling, laughing, talking, shouting, singing, praying, tearing, quivering, gesticulating, dancing, circulating, touching, hugging, weighing against one another, self-positing, and . . . ." See Wariboko, *Nigerian Pentecostalism* (Rochester, NY: University of Rochester Press, 2014), 52.

93. Sam Eyoboka, "Adeboye at 60: 'The Secrets of My Success,'" *Vanguard*, March 2, 2002, 22.

94. To have an idea of what I am talking about here, it is necessary to witness the arrival of a pastor at a social event, something, I have to say, that is a spectacle in itself. Once I was lucky to witness Pastor Adeboye arrive at an event on the campus of the Obafemi Awolowo University, Ile-Ife. It was a sight to behold, befitting of a head of state, what with the smartly dressed security entourage speaking into walkie-talkies and generally making a racket. This was sometime in the late 1990s, and since then, the very act of arriving at an event has become, for many pastors, an opportunity to "make a statement" by projecting their newfangled social power, that is, their having "arrived," status-wise. See, for instance this video of Pastor Alph Lukau of the Johannesburg-based Alleluia Ministries arriving at an event: https://www.youtube.com/watch?v=gUoHk1gOwzw. Part of what we see on display here—and in similar spectacles of "arrivals"—is the idea of the pastor as a celebrity and Man of God rolled into one.

95. See Nicholas Ibekwe, "Synagogue Building Collapse: Why I Exposed T. B. Joshua for Bribing Journalists," *Premium Times*, September 23, 2014.

96. I have taken this from my account in *Pentecostal Republic*, 131.

97. See "Synagogue: NANS Protest in Lagos, Demands Halt in Coroner Inquest," *Vanguard*, February 25, 2015.

98. A reference to 1 Chronicles 16:22: "Touch not my anointed, and do my prophets no harm."

99. See Eric Dumo, "A 'King' Sentenced to Death on His Birthday," *Punch* (Lagos), February 27, 2016.

100. Joshua received many international dignitaries in his church, including former Malawian president Joyce Banda; former Ghanaian president John Atta Mills; Julius Malema, leader of South Africa's Economic Freedom Fighters (EFF), former Zimbabwean Prime Minister Morgan

Tsvangirai; and former president of the Central African Republic (CAR) Andre Kolingba.

101. See, for instance, the testimonies by media-political personalities Femi Fani-Kayode and Dele Momodu, respectively: Musikilu Mojeed, "Why Some Nigerian Pastors Hated T. B. Joshua—Fani-Kayode," *Premium Times*, June 8, 2021, available at https://www.premiumtimesng.com/, and "Dele Momodu Visits Evelyn, TB Joshua's Wife," *MAD News*, June 13, 2021, available at https://mirrorafricandiaspora.com/dele-momodu-visits-evelyn-tb-joshuas-wife.

102. Leslie Fesenmyer, "Pentecostal Pastorhood as Calling and Career: Migration, Religion, and Masculinity between Kenya and the United Kingdom," *Journal of the Royal Anthropological Institute* 24 (2018): 749–66.

103. I often wonder whether statistics on the rate of unemployment, useful as they are, can fully capture the sense of hopelessness one finds among many young people in Nigeria today. You can hardly open a Nigerian newspaper and not find a story like the one that recently caught my attention involving Chigozie, a twenty-five-year-old school dropout from Imo State who committed suicide, leaving a note with the following terse message: "Die, die, die. Let nobody weep for me, because I am tired of this wicked world." The report describes Chigozie as having become "frustrated after leaving secondary school many years ago, without securing a job." See Charles Ogugbuaja and Dom Ekpunobi, "25-Year-Old School Leaver Commits Suicide in Imo," *Guardian* (Lagos), July 23, 2017, 3.

104. See Daniel Jordan Smith, *To Be a Man Is Not a One-Day Job: Masculinity, Money, and Intimacy in Nigeria* (Chicago: University of Chicago Press, 2017); Stephen Ellis, *This Present Darkness: A History of Nigerian Organized Crime* (New York: Oxford University Press, 2016); and Charles Piot, *Nostalgia for the Future: West Africa after the Cold War* (Chicago: University of Chicago Press, 2010). For an analysis of similar pressures on the opposite end of the generational spectrum, see Stephan F. Miescher, *Making Men in Ghana* (Bloomington: Indiana University Press, 2005).

105. Nicolette Makovicky, "Me, Inc.? Untangling Neoliberalism, Personhood, and Postsocialism," in *Neoliberalism, Personhood, and Postsocialism: Enterprising Selves in Changing Economies*, edited by Nicolette Makovicky, 1–16 (Surrey, England: Ashgate, 2014).

106. Referencing the relevant section of the Nigerian criminal code, "419" is the catch-all phrase for crimes whose basic modus operandi is to deceive the targets into parting with their money. "Yahoo Yahoo" (named for Yahoo!, the American web services provider) refers to young criminal elements who use their electronic savvy to bilk unsuspecting targets, often citizens—and, in a growing trend, institutions and governments—in Western countries. "MMM," as seen below, is a Ponzi scheme that originated in

Russia. The common thread among these schemes is the element of using a ruse to defraud one's targets.

107. I am not necessarily suggesting that these are the only options for young people in Nigeria. It is worth remembering, for instance, that the high-tech industry in Nigeria—which, against all odds, has had remarkable success—is driven by the young.

108. See, for example, Anthony Ogbonna, "RCCG Warns Pastors, Members against Participating in MMM, Other Ponzi Schemes, *Vanguard* (Lagos), January 24, 2017.

109. See Rudolf Ogoo Okonkwo, "This Obasanjo Sef & Other Unreplied Letters," *Sahara Reporters* (New York), December 18, 2013.

110. See Judex Okoro, "UNICAL Professors Declare for APC over Vice Chancellorship Contest," *Sun* (Lagos), June 24, 2020.

111. The parallels do not end there. VCs also tend to boast of their "accomplishments" the way political officeholders do, using "words such as 'commissioned,' 'built,' 'contract awarded,' and 'under his/her able leadership.'" See Moses E. Ochonu, "Vice-Chancellors and Trends of Embarrassing 'Accomplishments,'" *EduCeleb*, April 5, 2021, https://educeleb.com/vice-chancellors-and-trends-of-embarrassing-accomplishments/.

TWO.   The Pastor as Political Entrepreneur

1. The epigraph is from Stephen Ellis and Gerrie ter Haar, "Religion and Politics in Africa," *Afrika Zamani* 5 (1997) and 6 (1998), 221–46. Italics added. Although I quote this with approval, I wish to emphasize that I do not necessarily think that the sentiment it expresses applies only to African societies. On the contrary, and given that where similar causes operate, similar effects seem to follow, the same relationships are bound to operate where more or less similar spiritist logics and beliefs operate. For example, MMM (cited in the previous chapter) was a problem in Russia and Albania (where it effectively bankrupted the entire country and brought down the Democratic Party government) before it found its way to Nigeria. For more on the Albanian case, see, for instance, Chris Jarvis, "The Rise and Fall of the Pyramid Schemes in Albania," *IMF Staff Papers* 47, no. 1 (2000): 1–29.

2. In *Pentecostal Republic* (2018), 143.

3. See Victoria Onehi, "FG to Spend $1.45bn on Ajaokuta Steel, Iron Ore Coy," *Daily Trust* (Abuja), July 7, 2020.

4. Daniel Jordan Smith, *A Culture of Corruption: Everyday Deception and Popular Discontent in Nigeria* (Princeton, NJ: Princeton University Press, 2008), 50.

5. Andrew H. Apter, *The Pan-African Nation: Oil and the Spectacle of Culture in Nigeria* (Chicago: University of Chicago Press, 2005), 217.

6. For a glimpse into the financial cesspool that Ajaokuta has become, see Theophilus Abbah, "Vultures of Steel: Ajaokuta Where Corruption Is the System," *Daily Trust* (Abuja), July 9, 2019. In contrast to this, and in fact to mainstream critical opinion of Ajaokuta, Dirk Kohnert—unsurprisingly, given his assumption that "most cases of grand corruption in Africa, for example, have been instigated by global corporations"—invokes Ajaokuta as an example of how African agency is "obstructed" and blames its travails on "several failed attempts at privatization." See his "Trump's Tariff Impact on Africa and the Ambiguous Role of African Agency," *Review of African Political Economy* 45, no. 157 (2018): 451–66, quotes from 460–61. Not only is his theory of corruption in Africa ahistorical; the notion of Ajaokuta as simply a matter of failed privatization rather than the most concrete evidence of the financial incontinence of a political elite is, frankly, absurd.

7. Pilgrimage to the Redemption Camp is obligatory for members of the Nigerian political elite and state officials, including practicing Muslims.

8. See Kamarudeen Ogundele and Bayo Akinloye, "Adeboye Commends Fayose's Boldness, Prays for Him," *Punch* (Lagos), December 25, 2016.

9. Unprecedented given his well-known aversion to taking a political stance and also considering that he is on record as favoring prayers over protests, the latter being not just pointless but also potentially dangerous. Responding to CNN correspondent Christian Purefoy's question as to whether it is not "better to protest outside government house" instead of thronging the church in the millions to pray, Adeboye responded: "Prayers can move mountains. Protesting outside government house—how much has it achieved? You go there— you carry placards, if you're fortunate you will return home alive, if you are not fortunate some overzealous police officer might accidentally discharge some bullets. And you protest day after day after day and after some time you get tired." See full transcript of interview at https://www.bellanaija.com/2011/02/pastor-enoch-adeboye-of-the-redeemed-christian-church-of-god-on-cnns-african-voices-this-weekend-read-the-interview-transcripts/.

10. See Anthony Nlebem, "Pastor Adeboye Leads Prayer Walk against Killings and Insecurity in Nigeria," *Business Day*, February 2, 2020.

11. See Tony Ojoibukun, *The Redeemed Christian Church of God in Prophecy: The History of the Explosion and a Call to Divine Service* (Laurel, MD: Honeycombs Publishers, 2010, 65. The conviction that prayer is the solution to every problem—and a perfect example of the influence of Pentecostalism on the Nigerian society—is seen in the widespread acceptance and practice of "spiritual warfare." For instance, in September 2019 the Nigerian Army headquarters organized a widely publicized Spiritual Warfare Seminar on the theme Countering Insurgency and Violent Extremism in Nigeria

through Spiritual Warfare. See Femi Owolabi, "EXTRA: Army Organizes Spiritual Warfare against Boko Haram," *Cable* (Abuja), September 30, 2019, https://www.thecable.ng/.

12. Simon Coleman, "'Right Now!': Historiopraxy and the Embodiment of Charismatic Temporalities," *Ethnos* 76, no. 4 (2011): 426–47.

13. Charles Taylor, *A Secular Age* (Cambridge, MA: Belknap Press, 2007).

14. To reiterate my earlier caveat, this is not an exclusively African phenomenon. For instance, this is what Muslims generally believe. Besides, across instances too numerous to recount, people have been victims of religious demagogues in various parts of the world for sharing this belief.

15. Although Adeboye's status as the doyen of the Nigerian theocratic class remains more or less intact, it is worth noting that today, for various reasons, his overall reputation is arguably no longer what it was about a decade ago, when his utterances (whether on sex or the economy) were treated as almost incontrovertible. Since then, he has had some reputation-denting run-ins with other leading pastors and younger members of his own congregation on a variety of social issues. For example, in July 2020, on the occasion of his wife Foluke (Mummy G.O.) Adeboye's seventy-second birthday, Adeboye praised her for her many sacrifices for their marriage, adding, "The husband is the head of the wife. No matter how educated or successful you are, your husband is your head and you must regard him as such at all times." Then he was roundly condemned by a section of Nigerian feminists and younger members of his congregation for making his wife's birthday about himself and championing a retrograde view of marriage. See Eniola Akinkuotu, "Feminists Tackle Adeboye over Wife's Birthday Message," *Punch* (Lagos), July 15, 2020. The point here is not whether Adeboye is right or wrong but that the challenge itself, arising from a coterie of factors not directly relevant to my analysis, would have been unimaginable a decade ago. Sociologically, part of what comes to my mind here is Goode's analysis of "long-term changes in prestige processes" and how "prestige and the processes of attaining and losing prestige change over time." See William J. Goode, *The Celebration of Heroes: Prestige as a Social Control System* (Berkeley: University of California Press, 1978), viii. Adeboye, it seems, has finally run into a perfect storm caused by the emergence of a new generation vigorously extolling new ideas around feminine power at the expense of an ossified patriarchy and taking advantage of new technological tools for articulating them. It is also not impossible that, just due to the sheer fact of having been in the public eye for so long, during which time he has expressed his fair share of controversial ideas, more and more people feel emboldened to take a shot at him. Whatever it is, there is no gainsaying that his once seemingly impregnable armor now carries more than a few chinks.

16. See Gbolabo Ogunsanwo, "The Man They Love to Call 'Daddy,'" *Guardian* (Lagos), March 17, 2002, 11.

17. Pastor Bakare is almost unique among the Nigerian Pentecostal elite in his singular fixation on the presidency, an office for which, if anything, he believes God Himself put him on this earth. As a matter of fact, if we are to believe Bakare, he is in line, courtesy of a personal assurance from God, to succeed the incumbent President Buhari as the country's sixteenth head of state in 2023. During a sermon at his Lagos Latter Rain Assembly Church in 2018, he declared to a cheering congregation: "Take it to the mountain top, if you have never heard it before, I am saying it to you this morning, in the scheme of things as far as politics of Nigeria is concerned, President Muhammadu Buhari is number 15, and yours sincerely I am number 16. I never said that to you before. I never said that to you before. I make it plain this morning, I let you know it this morning, nothing can change it. In the name of Jesus, he is number 15, I am number 16. *To this end was I born, and for this purpose came I into the world, I prepared you for this for more than thirty years.* That's why if he [Buhari] wants to run in 2019, I do not oppose, he is still number 15. It's when he steps out that I step in. His assignment is that of Moses, to take Nigeria to River Jordan, but he can't cross it. It would take a Joshua to go to the other side and begin to distribute resources to the people of this nation." Italics added. The video is available at https://www.pmnewsnigeria.com/2019/09/23/watch-bakares-video-declaring-himself-nigerias-next-president/. If, broadly, the aim of Pentecostal politics is to portray Christianity in a favorable light and give it a competitive edge in its geopolitical rivalry with Islam, the end of Bakare's politics is, not to put too fine a point on it, Bakare, and part of what the italicized portion of the foregoing speech captures is how easily he can segue from himself to God and back. This is not to say that Adeboye's politics is not also, in some fundamental sense, about Adeboye but to insist that, if indeed Adeboye has a *personal* design on the Nigerian presidency, he has been quite successful in masking it. Bakare's confidence in his uniqueness as an individual, and his certainty that he is the one destined by God to shepherd Nigeria to greatness, is evident in statements such as the following: "By the grace of God, I have the means to leave the shores of this nation to relocate to climes of much greater comfort and never come back here but *the promptings of destiny would not permit me*. Like a pregnant woman, I cannot sleep like others sleep. Like one in the season of birth, I cannot ignore the pangs that rouse my spirit in the night seasons regarding my beloved nation Nigeria. Like one taken by labour pains, I cannot disregard the quickening of the New Nigeria, *a seed divinely implanted in my womb of destiny from infancy*, whose delicate life I have grown, with the sense of responsibility to

nurture through its full gestation, on behalf of the One who planted it and to Whom I owe account." Italics added. See Tunde Bakare, "The Nigeria of My Dreams: Text of Speech by Pastor Tunde Bakare at the Thanksgiving Service for His 60th Birthday on Sunday the 16th of November, 2014," http://tundebakare.com/. No one can accuse Bakare of not preparing himself for the role that he sees himself destined to play, and to the best of my knowledge, he is the only Nigerian pastor who goes out of his way to deliver regular "State of the Nation" broadcasts. Part of what I find fascinating about these broadcasts is the mode of their delivery, particularly Pastor Bakare's occasional shift of pronoun from "I" to "We," consolidating the impression of an éminence grise addressing and sharing some bitter truths with his communitas. Some of the broadcasts can be found at http://tundebakare.com/videos/, available July 22, 2020. We do not have the tools to divine whether or not Pastor Bakare has the celestial imprimatur that he so boldly advertises, but I can't help but speculate on the extent to which his will to power may have been shaped by something as banal as the effect of being firmly anchored in some of the most powerful social and business networks in the country. My point is this: for someone of Bakare's pedigree (a trained lawyer with deep pockets, deep enough to have extended a credit of US$450,000 to Kaduna State Governor Nasir El-Rufai when the latter was running for office), extended familiarity with the Nigerian political leadership at all levels might well have opened his eyes to its intellectual, not to mention ethical, poverty, leading to the not unreasonable conclusion that if so-and-so could be, for example, president, why not he? If my speculation is valid, a conclusion that Bakare is using a divine mandate to justify an urge that would be perfectly reasonable for any individual in his situation is not unwarranted. Ultimately, and significantly, Bakare's identity as a Pentecostal pastor not only conduces to his ambition but in fact indulges the ardor and singular self-mythologization with which he has pursued it. As a widely heralded founder-owner of his church, he is, in the final analysis, accountable only to himself.

18. He is also, for my money, the most intellectually stimulating, if intermittently frustrating, at least among the pastors with whom I managed to secure an audience. For example, he is the only one with the chutzpah and contrarian imagination needed to write a book with the title *The Foolishness of God* or *Why Christians Won't Go to Heaven*, and it is easy to see why other pastors, never mind a good number of Pentecostals, would conclude that he is not even a Christian like them. In a way, Aribisala is the anti-Adeboye, especially in his willingness to embrace controversy. Incidentally, he is also the only one liable to ever break ranks and criticize Adeboye openly. See, for example, his *Premium Times* "Article of Faith" column of

May 11, 2014, "Daddy G.O.," https://www.premiumtimesng.com/. I think he is able to pull this off partly because, unlike some of the others (Bakare, Ituah Ighodalo, and Madojemu easily come to mind), he is not a former protégé of Adeboye and is not therefore bound by the unwritten "father-son" honor code that prevents them from speaking openly against him. Nor is he morally indebted to him as is, say, David Oyedepo. It was Adeboye who both ordained Oyedepo and his wife, Faith Abiola Oyedepo, as pastors and officially commissioned their Living Faith Church in 1983, and, if Oyedepo himself is to be believed, it was Adeboye who helped Oyedepo avoid death in a plane crash by showing up uninvited to pray for him ahead of an international trip. See the article by Ifreke Inyang, "How Adeboye Saved Me from Death in Plane Crash," *Daily Post* (Nigeria), October 21, 2017, https://dailypost.ng/. Beyond this, it's also clear that Aribisala is intellectually uncomfortable with not a few of the normal practices taken for granted across Nigerian Pentecostalism. For instance, while Adeboye and a significant number of Pentecostal pastors see tithing as a matter of salvation for the believer, with Adeboye once saying in a widely reported April 2018 sermon, "Make it clear to them. Anyone who doesn't pay tithe is not going to heaven," Aribisala insists, to the contrary, "Every pastor who collects tithes is nothing but a thief and a robber." See his "Pastors Are the Real Robbers of God," *Vanguard*, November 19, 2017, https://www.vanguardngr.com/2017/11/pastors-real-robbers-god/. As an endlessly renewing fount of theological controversy, Aribisala can be exasperating, muddling, as many of the pastor are wont to do, the boundaries delineating wish, prayer, and prophecy. For instance, in his April 3, 2020, column titled "There Is No Coronavirus in Nigeria," he wrote: "This is not a prophecy: it is a decree. The word of God says: 'You will also declare a thing, and it will be established for you.' . . . Therefore, I issue this decree: 'There is no coronavirus in Nigeria.'. . . Join me in proclaiming this righteous decree: 'There is no Coronavirus in Nigeria.' The Lord God Almighty will establish it in Nigeria and confound the rest of the world. He will use it to confound the reports you have been hearing here and there." See *Vanguard*, April 3, 2020, https://www.vanguardngr.com/2020/04/there-is-no-coronavirus-in-nigeria/. At this point, the coronavirus was already a global phenomenon, with more than six hundred cases and at least twenty deaths in Nigeria according to the Johns Hopkins University dashboard.

19. See Majid Yazdi, "Patterns of Clerical Political Behavior in Postwar Iran, 1941–53," *Middle Eastern Studies* 26, no. 3 (1990): 281–307.

20. See Taiwo Adebulu, "Magu Probe: We Mistakenly Transferred N573m to Prophet Omale, says FCMB," *Cable*, August 10, 2020, https://www.thecable.ng/.

21. One example is the case involving the leaders of two Catholic churches (St. Monica Catholic Church and St. Augustine Catholic Church, both in Ibusa, Delta State), who reportedly received the sum of N45 million (believed to be stolen depositors' funds) as a "tithe" from Francis Atuche, former managing director of Bank PHB. See "EFCC to Arrest Catholic Priests over Atuche's N45 Million Tithe," *Premium Times*, October 3, 2012. The first of such cases to grab the headlines way back in 2002 involved one Lawrence Agada, a cashier at the Sheraton Hotel, Lagos, who stole the sum of N39 million from his employers and handed the bulk of it to a parish of Christ Embassy as a "tithe." Not only did the church refuse to return the money to Mr. Agada's employers; the head of the church, Pastor Chris Oyakhilome, actually "wrote him a special letter of commendation read to his entire parish." See Femi Aribisala, "Money Laundering in the Churches," *Vanguard*, October 7, 2012, https://www.vanguardngr.com/2012/10/money-laundering-in-the-churches/. The use of churches as financial shelters for stolen money raises all sorts of questions, one of which is the appeal that churches hold: their status as tax-exempt nonprofit institutions. Furthermore, it is not too difficult to imagine how the idea, championed by most Pentecostal leaders, that members should "sow a seed" as a form of "investment" from which they can expect bountiful "dividends" (spiritual and otherwise) can be a driver of this practice. For example, when pastor Chibuzor Nnaegbo was arrested in February 2015 for allegedly defrauding four businessmen, he confessed as follows: "My problem started while I was pastoring a church in Onitsha. I read a book written by Bishop Oyedepo on how to sow a seed. After reading the book, *I sold all the church properties and sowed the proceeds in another church*. When I relocated to Lagos, I started collecting money from people, deceiving them that I am in Israel. I told them that I had issues trying to set up a church and needed money to grow the ministry. *I used all the money I collected from them to sow seed in Redemption Camp*. I collected N1.9 million from one of the victims, N1.255 million from another, N2.5 million from the third and N900,000 and a Toyota Camry from the fourth victim. *I sowed the Camry as seed in Winners Chapel in Otta*." Italics added. See Esther Onyegbula, "Fake Pastor in Police Net over Alleged N10m fraud," *Vanguard*, February 11, 2015. For an analysis of this practice, see Asonzeh F.-K. Ukah, "'Those Who Trade with God Never Lose': The Economics of Pentecostal Activism in Nigeria," in *Christianity and Social Change in Africa: Essays in Honor of J.D.Y. Peel*, edited by Toyin Falola, 253–74 (Durham, NC: Carolina Academic Press, 2005). Tax breaks and seed-sowing aside, "transfers" of resources from notionally "public" to "private" institutions raises the interesting possibility that people may see the church as an institution embedded within what

Ekeh has called a primordial public, hence deserving of the kind of "moral" treatment that the same people would not accord to institutions within the civic public. (For a classic analysis of this moral antinomy, see Peter P. Ekeh, "Colonialism and the Two Publics in Africa: A Theoretical Statement," *Comparative Studies in Society and History* 17, no. 1 [1975]: 91–112. See also Kato Gogo Kingston, "Concealment of Illegally Obtained Assets in Nigeria: Revisiting the Role of the Churches in Money Laundering," *African Journal of International and Comparative Law* 28, no. 1 [2020]: 106–21.) That said, Ekeh's theory seems unable to explain increasingly rampant corruption *within* the church, part of a primordial public in regard to which, in theory, people should behave morally. See, for example, "Corruption: Oyedepo Blows Hot over Millions Stolen by Church Officials," *Vanguard*, January 12, 2020. For a critique of Ekeh's framework, see Browne Onuoha, "Publishing Postcolonial Africa: Nigeria and Ekeh's Two Publics a Generation After," *Social Dynamics* 40, no. 2 (2014): 322–37.

22. A biblical model is Moses, who was drafted by God even though, as Moses himself pleaded, "I am not eloquent, neither heretofore, nor since thou hast spoken unto thy servant: but I am slow of speech, and of a slow tongue." Exodus 4:10.

23. See Patricia H. Thornton, "The Sociology of Entrepreneurship," *Annual Review of Sociology* 25, no. 1 (1999): 19–46.

24. Ibid.

25. Martin Ruef and Lucien Karpik, *The Entrepreneurial Group: Social Identities, Relations, and Collective Action* (Princeton, NJ: Princeton University Press, 2010), 7.

26. See Moses E. Ochonu, "Introduction: Toward African Entrepreneurship and Business History," in *Entrepreneurship in Africa: A Historical Approach*, edited by Moses E. Ochonu, 1–28 (Bloomington: Indiana University Press, 2018), 1.

27. Paul D. Reynolds, "Sociology and Entrepreneurship: Concepts and Contributions," *Entrepreneurship Theory and Practice* 16, no. 2 (1992): 47–70, quote on 67.

28. See James B. Twitchell, *Shopping for God: How Christianity Went from in Your Heart to in Your Face* (New York: Simon & Schuster, 2007), 3.

29. See Miranda Klaver, "Pentecostal Pastorpreneurs and the Global Circulation of Authoritative Aesthetic Styles," *Culture and Religion* 16, no. 2 (2015): 146–59, quote on 157.

30. Ebenezer Obadare, "On the Theologico-Theatrical: Popular Culture and the Economic Imperative in Nigerian Pentecostalism," *Africa: Journal of the International African Institute* 92, no. 1 (2022): 93–111.

31. Femi Aribisala, interview with the author, June 2016.

32. See Bisi Ojediran, Isaac Achor, and Ohi Alegbe, eds., *How I Was Called: Testimonies of Ministers of God* (Lagos: Booksplus Nigeria, 2003), 18.

33. Pastor Gbade Ogunlana (aka *Paito Wa*), Bible City Church, Ibadan, interview with the author, July 2, 2016. Due to his conviction that "the essence of the gospel is to reach people, and your effectiveness is measured in the understanding," and "since [his] purpose is to be understood, the wisest thing is to communicate in the language they can perfectly understand," Pastor Ogunlana preaches in Yoruba and has written several books in that language. As a matter of fact, he sees communication in Yoruba as not just "sensible" but also part of his calling.

34. Ojediran, Achor, and Alegbe, *How I Was Called*, 25. Italics in original.

35. Ibid., 25–26. Italics in original. This is by no means unique to Pastor Adeyemi—or even pastors, for that matter—as it is common for successful or highly placed people in the Nigerian society to describe their births in similarly "miraculous" terms.

36. Hans H. Gerth and C. Wright Mills, eds., *From Max Weber: Essays in Sociology* (London: Routledge, 1991), 79.

37. As I have shown in my work (see *Pentecostal Republic*) and earlier in this book (see the introduction), this space is not exclusively occupied by pastors, who willy-nilly must contend with other players offering a wide range of spiritual goods in an increasingly competitive religious marketplace.

38. From "The Mission of the RCCG," in *The Redeemed Christian Church of God in Prophecy: The Story of the Explosion and a Call to Service*, edited by Anthony Ojoibukun (Laurel, MD: Honeycombs Publishers), 65–66.

39. *Pentecostal Republic*, chapter 6.

40. Ibid., chapters 1 and 2.

41. For a discussion of these mass prayer sessions, see Ebenezer Obadare, "Spectacles of Piety: Prayer and the Politics of Mass Arousal in Democratic Nigeria," in *Crowds: Ethnographic Encounters*, edited by Megan Steffen, 51–61 (New York: Bloomsbury Academic, 2020). Such spectacles are by no means limited to Nigeria but are to be found in various "developed" and "developing" contexts as parts of efforts by state officials to spiritualize power. For instance, in April 2011 Texas governor Rick Perry proclaimed a statewide prayer for rain in the following words: "Now, therefore, I, Rick Perry, Governor of Texas, under the authority vested in me by the Constitution of the United States, do hereby proclaim the three-day period from Friday, April 22, 2011, to Sunday, April 24, 2011, as Days of Prayer for Rain in the State of Texas. I urge Texans of all faiths and traditions

to offer prayers on that day for the healing of our land, the rebuilding of our communities and the restoration of our normal and robust way of life." See Ben Smith, "Praying for Rain," *Politico*, April 4, 2011, https://www.politico.com/. For an analysis of political spectacles in general, see Simonetta Falasca-Zamponi, *Fascist Spectacle: The Aesthetics of Power in Mussolini's Italy* (Berkeley: University of California Press, 2000).

42. In the case of Pastor Bakare and as already noted, this "prophetic destiny" is inextricable from his own conviction regarding his assumed personal destiny to rule Nigeria. For Bakare, Nigeria's destiny and his are joined at the hip.

43. Ebenezer Obadare, "The Muslim Response to the Pentecostal Surge in Nigeria: Prayer and the Rise of Charismatic Islam," *Journal of Religious and Political Practice* 2, no. 1 (2016): 75–91.

44. See "Nigerian Preacher TB Joshua Deletes Prophecy of Clinton Win," *BBC News*, November 9, 2016, https://www.bbc.com/news/world-africa-37924086.

45. The full video is available at https://www.youtube.com/watch?v=7DkSP-7e4bU.

46. Three days after Joshua's death, Okotie posted a cryptic message on his Instagram account that included the following: "The wizard at Endor who assumed the title Emmanuel has been consumed by divine indignation. And now his disciples bewail his ignominious exit. . . . Let those who swear by the Lord and by Malcham and the descendants of Haman, now tremble in fear. The day of the vengeance of our God has fully come to Nigeria. And they shall not escape. Operation Hupopodion (footstool) has commenced." See Jayne Augoye, "TB Joshua: Wizard Called Emmanuel Has Been Consumed—Chris Okotie," *Premium Times* (Nigeria), June 8, 2021, available at https://www.premiumtimesng.com/. The subtext here should be noted, and it is the idea that, unlike the power of the more "enlightened" members of the pastoral elite, Joshua's was grounded in "unclean" and dubious forces (Okotie meant for "the wizard" to be taken literally), which, if true, would mean that he was not a "true" Christian. For Joshua, matters were not helped by the fact that, unlike the other leading members of the Pentecostal elite, he was at no time a protégé of the undoubted doyen, Enoch Adeboye, hence never felt a need to kowtow.

47. See Conor Gaffey, "Nigeria's T. B. Joshua Explains Unfulfilled U.S. Election Prophecy," *Newsweek*, November 14, 2016.

48. David M. Anderson and Douglas H. Johnson, eds., *Revealing Prophets: Prophecy in Eastern African History* (Athens: Ohio University Press, 1995).

49. For an overview, see Robert H. Jackson and Carl G. Rosberg, *Personal Rule in Black Africa: Prince, Autocrat, Prophet, Tyrant* (Berkeley: University of California Press, 1982).

50. Robert M. Baum, *West Africa's Women of God: Alinesitoué and the Diola Prophetic Tradition* (Bloomington: Indiana University Press, 2016), 4.

51. Gerth and Mills, *From Max Weber*, 285.

52. Ibid., 327.

53. See Margaret M. Poloma and Matthew T. Lee, "Prophecy, Empowerment, and Godly Love: The Spirit Factor in the Growth of Pentecostalism," in *Spirit and Power: The Growth and Global Impact of Pentecostalism*, edited by Doland E. Miller, Kimon H. Sargeant, and Richard Flory (Oxford: Oxford University Press, 2013), 282.

54. Ibid., 280.

55. Stephen Ellis, "The Okija Shrine: Death and Life in Nigerian Politics," *Journal of African History* 49, no. 3 (2008): 445–66, quote on 447–48. Italics added.

56. Oath-taking can take three additional forms, all affirmative of the widespread belief in its supernatural potency and suggestive of a deeply embedded mistrust of institutions and protagonists in the struggle for power. One form is the oath of loyalty a chief executive of a state or occupant of a powerful office demands that members of his cabinet take at a specified shrine, as Governor Chinwoke Mbadinuju apparently did as governor of Anambra State (1999–2003). See ibid., 459. A second form is oath of loyalty a political "godfather" demands that a client take at his shrine of, as was the case when Governor Mbadinuju demanded that of his successor-in-waiting, Chris Ngige. See ibid., 458–59. In a third form, a political chieftain mandates such an oath (of *continued* loyalty) in his presence, as Ayodele Fayose required of his followers to prevent them from defecting to a rival in the same political party. See Rotimi Ojomoyela, "Drama as Fayose-Led Ekiti PDP Camp Takes Secret Oath," *Vanguard*, July 21, 2020, https://www.vanguardngr.com/2020/07/video-drama-as-fayose-led-ekiti-pdp-camp-takes-secret-oath/. My point here is less about oath-taking in general, which is a common phenomenon across political contexts (for example, Republican candidates in the United States are often made to swear oaths to the National Rifle Association [NRA] and the Federalist Society), and more about the belief in the efficacy of the supernatural.

57. Election-related prophecies can be said to constitute a special category of prophecy and may or may not instigate political conflict, depending on the prevailing circumstances. See, for instance, Emmanuel Sackey, "Election Prophecies and Political Stability in Ghana," in *Christian Citizens and*

the *Moral Regeneration of the African State*, edited by Barbara Bompani and Caroline Valois, 49–62 (New York: Routledge, 2019).

58. See chapter 2.

59. Obadare, *Pentecostal Republic*, 58.

60. See "Pandemic Won't Disappear Completely, Says Adeboye," *This Day*, May 25, 2020, https://www.thisdaylive.com/.

61. See Leon Festinger, Henry W. Riecken, and Stanley Schachter, *When Prophecy Fails: A Social and Psychological Study of a Modern Group That Predicted the Destruction of the World* (New York: Harper, 1990). For a critique, see J. Gordon Melton, "Spiritualization and Reaffirmation: What Really Happens When Prophecy Fails," *American Studies* 26, no. 2 (1985): 17–29.

62. See Nimi Wariboko, "Governance as Trauma in Nigeria: Turning Evangelicalism into Pentecostal Incredible," unpublished manuscript, 2019.

63. Italics added. See Victorson Agbenson, *Moment of Truth: The Compelling Story of Pastor Tunde Bakare* (Ibadan: Safari Books, 2014), 5–6.

64. For more on this, see Wale Adebanwi, "The Clergy, Culture, and Political Conflicts in Nigeria," *African Studies Review* 53, no. 3 (2010): 121–42.

THREE. Erotic Pentecostalism

1. See https://yorubavoiceofreason.wordpress.com/.

2. See "Holy Trap! Dirty Portrait of Dolapo Awosika and Prophet Kasali," *This Day* (Lagos), November 18, 2018, available at https://www.thisdaylive.com/. The photos of Ms. Awosika and Prophet Kasali, respectively, used to illustrate the story and the rider, "For God or Mammon? The Sordid Tale of Dolapo's Romance with Oyo Cleric," perfectly encapsulate the blatant "beauty-and-the-beast" (the writer's words) tone of the commentary. Nor can we overlook the implication, even though it's not so stated, that a dark-skinned Mr. Kasali is a poor match for the light-skinned Ms. Awosika. For an analysis of "colorism" in the wider context of the politics and discourses of beauty and beauty standards in Nigeria, see Oluwakemi M. Balogun, "Cultural and Cosmopolitan: Idealized Femininity and Embodied Nationalism in Nigerian Beauty Pageants," *Gender & Society* 25, no. 3 (2012): 357–81.

3. "Holy Trap!"

4. Ibid.

5. Not to be confused with the musical genre, "jazz" (sometimes "charms" or "juju") is the popular appellation for a set of mystical powers

believed to be transmissible through—though not always the same thing as—specific material objects. The real puzzle, or perhaps the sting in the tail here, is that, in general, it is (Nigerian) women who are supposed to use their charm, failing which, their "charms," to entrap men, and it is rarely, if ever, the other way around. This idea of women as agents who have to rely on their cunning and wiles in order to get ahead in a male-dominated society provides the cultural backdrop to the sexually freighted idea of "bottom power," which basically suggests that women have to traffic their bodies and deploy their sexuality in order to access social goods they should be legitimately entitled to.

6. See, for instance, Obinna Udenwe's highly entertaining *Holy Sex: A Church Erotica* (Chicago: Brittle Paper, 2016).

7. See "Dolapo Awosika, John Fashanu and Prophet Kasali Controversy: The True Story," *Elites Nigeria*, November 14, 2018, https://www.theelitesng.com/dolapo-awosika-john-fashanu-and-prophet-kasali-controversy-the-true-story/. The reference to ori-oke, literally "prayer mountain," is far from trivial, revealing a discourse about a certain nefarious spirituality (as opposed to the "good" spirituality of mainline Christianity) that many Christians, especially of a certain social status, are always eager to distance themselves from. The broader tension that I cannot accord an elaborate treatment in the book is the suspicion by mainline Christians of Aladura, or "White Garment" churches like Cherubim and Seraphim and the Celestial Church of Christ of not being really "Christian" because of their proximity to and accommodation of "traditional" beliefs and practices. See, for instance, Benjamin C. Ray, "Aladura Christianity: A Yoruba Religion," *Journal of Religion in Africa* 23, no. 3 (1993): 266–91. Cf. J.D.Y. Peel, "Syncretism and Religious Change," *Comparative Studies in Society and History* 10, no. 2 (1968): 121–41. One other reason that Ms. Awosika may have struggled for a coherent explanation initially is that, as noted by the blogger, at the time that rumors of their affair started circulating, Prophet Kasali was married with five children. Ms. Awosika may have feared being labeled a "homewrecker" (the Nigerian equivalent of the classic femme fatale), an epithet used (by both men and women) to describe women whose entanglements with married men create domestic problems for the latter, sometimes leading to the dissolution of their marriages. Here, we see the power of a discourse, championed by members of both sexes, regarding the centrality of women to the nuclear heterosexual family, whether as faithful, submissive, and married insiders—stabilizers—or as wayward, unamenable, footloose outsiders—disrupters.

8. See Melissa Hackman, *Desire Work: Ex-Gay and Pentecostal Masculinity in South Africa* (Durham, NC: Duke University Press, 2018), xii.

9. See Ebenezer Obadare, "Sex, Citizenship and the State in Nigeria: Islam, Christianity and Emergent Struggles over Intimacy," *Review of African Political Economy* 42, no. 143 (2015): 62–76.

10. Available at https://www.refworld.org/pdfid/530c4bc64.

11. See Adriaan van Klinken and Martin Zebracki, "Porn in Church: Moral Geographies of Homosexuality in Uganda," *Porn Studies* 3, no. 1 (2015): 89–92, quote on 89.

12. See "Martin Ssempa, Anti-Gay Ugandan Pastor, Shows Church Gay Porn Videos," *HuffPost*, May 25, 2011, https://www.huffingtonpost.com/2010/02/18/martin-ssempa-anti-gay-ug_n_467157.html.

13. See Lydia Namubiru and Khatondi Soita Wepukhulu, "Exclusive: US Christian Right Pours More Than $50m into Africa," *Open Democracy*, October 29, 2020, https://www.opendemocracy.net/en/5050/africa-us-christian-right-50m/.

14. See, for instance, "Stephanie Otobo Battles Apostle Suleman, Discloses Account, Payments Details," *Vanguard* (Lagos), April 9, 2017.

15. Pastor Odukoya's South African wife, Nomthi Rosemary Simangele Odukoya, gave birth to their first child together seven months after their wedding, leading to speculations that her pregnancy predated their wedding, which, if true, means the child was conceived out of wedlock.

16. See Opeoluwani Ogunjimi, "Chris Okotie's Crashed Marriage: Ex-Wife Opens Up," *Vanguard*, July 6, 2012.

17. See "Anita Finalizes Divorce from Pastor Chris Oyakhilome," *Vanguard*, February 19, 2016.

18. Obadare, "Sex, Citizenship and the State in Nigeria."

19. For a discussion, see, for instance, D. N. Hopkins, "The Construction of the Black Male Body: Eroticism and Religion," in *Loving the Body: Black Religious Studies and the Erotic*, edited by D. N. Hopkins and A. B. Pinn, 178–98 (New York: Palgrave Macmillan, 2004).

20. See Rachel Spronk, *Ambiguous Pleasures: Sexuality and Middle Class Self-Perceptions in Nairobi* (New York: Berghahn, 2015), 269.

21. Georges Bataille, *Erotism: Death and Sexuality* (San Francisco: City Light Books, 1986), 16.

22. Camille Paglia, *Sexual Personae: Art and Decadence from Nefertiti to Emily Dickinson* (New York: Vintage Books, 1991), 13.

23. Hans H. Gerth and C. Wright Mills, eds., *From Max Weber: Essays in Sociology* (London: Routledge, 1991), 343.

24. Ibid., 344. Italics in original.

25. See Bataille, *Erotism*, 15–16.

26. See Achille Mbembe, *On the Postcolony* (Berkeley: University of California Press, 2001), 212–13. Italics added. On the same subject, he also

says: "Even asceticism, an exercise supposed to allow desire to be mastered, and the flesh and its concupiscence mortified, does not escape the carnal. The experience of asceticism in fact shows that bodily pleasure and spiritual union are in no way incompatible. On the contrary, they support each other. The malady of lust, the movement of the members, ejaculation during prayer . . . —in short, sensual impulses—all indicate very clearly that religious ecstasy simulates physical pleasure." Ibid., 232.

27. See Birgit Meyer, *Mediation and the Genesis of Presence: Towards a Material Approach to Religion* (Utrecht: Universiteit Utrecht, 2012), 27.

28. See Nimi Wariboko, "West African Pentecostalism: A Survey of Everyday Theology," in *Global Renewal Christianity: Spirit-Empowered Movements Past, Present, and Future*, vol. 3, edited by Vinson Synan, Amos Yong, and Kwabena Asamoah-Gyadu, 1–18 (Lake Mary, FL: Charisma House Book Group, 2014), 5.

29. Ibid., 6. Italics in original.

30. Annalisa Butticci, *Na God: Aesthetics of African Charismatic Power* (Padua: Dipartimento de Filosofa, Sociologia, Pedagogia e Psicologia Applicata, Universita Degli Studi Di, 2013), 7.

31. See J. Kwabena Asamoah-Gyadu, *Contemporary Pentecostal Christianity: Interpretations from an African Context* (Eugene, OR: Wipf and Stock, 2013), 21.

32. Kevin Lewis O'Neill, "I Want More of You: The Politics of Christian Eroticism in Postwar Guatemala," *Comparative Studies in Society and History* 52, no. 1 (2010): 131–56, quote on 135.

33. Ibid.

34. Nimi Wariboko, "West African Pentecostalism," 4.

35. See Ashitha Nagesh, "Bishop Claims to Make Men's Penises Larger by Massaging Them with His Hands," *Metro* (London), December 6, 2016, http://metro.co.uk/2016/12/06/bishop-claims-to-make-mens-penises-larger-by-massaging-them-with-his-hands-6304158/.

36. See Radhika Sanghani, "Bra and Knickers? Sorry, Not in My Church," *Telegraph* (London), March 4, 2014, http://www.telegraph.co.uk/women/womens-life/10675818/Bra-and-knickers-sorry-not-in-my-church.html.

37. O'Neill, "I Want More of You," 134.

38. The key phrase here, of course, is "for the most part," for it is difficult to make a case, to take one example, for Daddy G.O.'s being a sex symbol. While he can be charismatic in his own austere, tranquilizing way, he doesn't quite have the frisson of, say, Pastor Biodun Fatoyinbo of the Abuja-based Commonwealth of Zion Assembly (COZA)—about whom more in the next chapter. What Adeboye undeniably possesses, sex-wise, is a

discursive influence, particularly on issues bordering on constructions of male sexuality, as it is shaped by marriage, social expectations, gender relations, and the imperatives of domesticity. For instance, in February 2020, in two statements that caused a public uproar, he advised his male congregants not to "marry a lady who cannot cook. She needs to know how to do chores and cook because you cannot afford to be eating out all the time," and then followed this up less than twenty-four hours later with another statement in which he urged the female members not to "marry a man who has no job." See Taiwo Okanlawon, "Don't Marry Man Who Has No Job—Pastor Adeboye," *PM News Nigeria*, February 19, 2020, https://www.pmnewsnigeria.com/2020/02/19/dont-marry-man-who-has-no-job-adeboye/.

39. Wariboko, "West African Pentecostalism," 5.

40. See Martin Lindhardt, "Men of God: Neo-Pentecostalism and Masculinities in Urban Tanzania," *Religion* 45, no. 2 (2015): 252–72.

41. See Adedamola Osinulu, "The Road to Redemption: Performing Pentecostal Citizenship in Lagos," in *The Arts of Citizenship in African Cities: Infrastructures and Spaces of Belonging*, edited by Mamadou Diouf and Rosalind Fredericks, 115–35 (New York: Palgrave Macmillan, 2014), quote on 126–27.

42. Ibid., 127.

43. Mbembe, *On the Postcolony*, 213.

44. See, for example, Nicholas Ibekwe, "COZA Abuja Senior Pastor in Sex Scandal," *Premium Times* (Abuja), August 25, 2013, https://www.premiumtimesng.com/. I say more about this episode in the next chapter. Nor is this unusual in other churches or, generally, in settings where the intimacy between the leader and his followers is such that both are, literally, mutually identified. Pastor Andy Savage of Memphis-based evangelical Highpoint Church received a standing ovation from his congregation after he had admitted to a 'sexual incident' with a teen. See Kyle Swenson, "A Pastor Admitted a Past 'Sexual Incident' with a Teen. His Congregation Gave Him a Standing Ovation," *Washington Post*, January 10, 2018. That said, and in my view, a pastor's physical attractiveness, however defined, is not *necessarily* correlated to his eroticization. At any rate, I accept Daloz's crucial insight that "societal determinants, such as living and working conditions, diet and access to care services and cosmetics, are likely to have strong effects on physical appearance." See Jean-Pascal Daloz, *The Sociology of Elite Distinction: From Theoretical to Comparative Perspectives* (New York: Palgrave Macmillan, 2010), 88. If to be a pastor is, in many cases, to increase one's chances of acquiring these all-important social determinants, then pastoring is a vicarious means of securing physical attractiveness.

45. In the footsteps of Rudolf Gaudio's striking brief on modern desires in urban Nigeria, the current hunger for deodorants, body fragrances,

and antiperspirants—and the concomitant repulsion elicited by body odor and smelly bodies—become fundamental to "discourses of cleanliness" that "index the intimate aesthetics of embodied social interaction that may not be explicitly erotic, but that are . . . imbricated in the desired identifications that impel the construction of the city, migration to and from it, and its policing." See Rudolf Gaudio, "Modern Desires in Urban Nigeria," *Cultural Anthropology*, July 21, 2015, https://culanth.org/.

46. At this link, for instance, an obviously self-satisfied Chris Okotie checks off the names of the designers of his jacket, trousers, shirt, and wristwatch respectively: https://www.youtube.com/watch?v=ieGjq0CMy1k. For more on conspicuous consumption in Africa, especially what the authors describe as "the familiar wirings of power and inequality along the lines of class, race, gender, status, religion and generation," see Deborah Posel and Ilana van Wyk, "Thinking with Veblen: Case Studies from Africa's Past and Present," in *Conspicuous Consumption in Africa*, edited by Deborah Posel and Ilana van Wyk, 1–24 (Johannesburg: Wits University Press, 2019), quotes on 4.

47. Jean-Pascal Daloz, *The Sociology of Elite Distinction*, 61.

48. Ibid., 64. Italics added.

49. See Olivier Driessens, "The Celebritization of Society and Culture: Understanding the Structural Dynamics of Celebrity Culture," *International Journal of Cultural Studies* 16, no. 6 (2013): 641–57.

50. Ibid., 652.

51. See Nikolas Rose, *Powers of Freedom: Reframing Political Thought* (Cambridge: Cambridge University Press, 1999), 3.

52. Mbembe, *On the Postcolony*, 66.

53. See Audre Lorde, "The Uses of the Erotic: The Erotic as Power," in *Sister Outsider: Essays and Speeches* (Berkeley, CA: Crossing Press, 1984), 87.

54. Ibid., 91.

55. Ibid.

FOUR.   When Women Rebel

1. See Ahmed's *What's the Use: On the Uses of Use* (Durham, NC: Duke University Press, 2019). Her work, to use her own words, "follows a rather queer and idiosyncratic path" and is "inspired by scholars working on questions of race, colonialism, gender, sexuality, and disability who write from or about "bodies out of place," "misfits," or "troublemakers" (19). I have no interest in race, colonialism, or disability (at least not in this book), but I am very much attracted to the idea of certain women operating or being perceived as "misfits" and "troublemakers."

2. Here: https://www.youtube.com/watch?v=jvKRJETbIRg.

3. "Do you know who you are talking to?" can mean one of two things. First, Oyedepo could have been referring to his social standing and overall prestige in Nigerian society as a well-known "Man of God," a hugely successful individual and founder-owner-chancellor of a private university, Covenant University, Ota, Ogun State. At the same time, he could have been referring to his putative spiritual prowess in taming demons. The two are not mutually exclusive. There is a third possibility, which is that the streak of auto-reverence and self-monumentalization in Oyedepo may have temporarily risen to the surface. For instance, in 2018 he boasted to his congregation, "I don't share any booty from any government. I have a clear conscience. I am dangerously wealthy. I am rich, what I want, comes. That's what they call wealth." See "I Am Dangerously Wealthy, Says Oyedepo," *Cable* (Abuja), December 6, 2018, https://www.thecable.ng/. Oyedepo's self-glorification (we find the same trait in Pastor Tunde Bakare) calls up the literature on the clergy and narcissistic personality disorder. Two insights from this literature are directly relevant to this study. The first is that the ministerial profession apparently holds an attraction for "individuals with Narcissistic Personality Disorder as a means of supply for their psychological needs," with an embrace of spirituality further intensifying their narcissism. Second, and more troublingly, is the insight that "narcissistic envy apprehends God as a rival to be diminished. This presents a natural tension for the narcissist pastor in that his or her drive for power and adulation runs counter to Christian personality." See R. Glenn Ball and Darrell Puls, "Frequency of Narcissistic Personality Disorder in Pastors: A Preliminary Analysis," paper presented to the American Association of Christian Counselors, Nashville, TN, September 26, 2015. Citations from pages 9 and 2, respectively. We do not know enough about either Oyedepo or Bakare to determine whether they have narcissistic personality disorder, but the inclusion of the possibility in any speculation on their psychological profiles is quite intriguing. At the very least, the insight that pastoring holds an attraction for individuals of a certain mental or behavioral disposition adds an intriguing dimension to our understanding of the social appeal of pastoring in Nigeria today.

4. It is not clear whether Mr. Igbinedion had the woman's imprimatur to file the suit, and it is not impossible that he elected to call her "Ms. Justice" as a way of protecting her identity and saving her from possible social ostracism. As already argued, her anonymity, illustrated by the fact that the media did not deem her important enough to look up her name and biography, is significant in itself. At any rate, the case was thrown out of court on technical grounds, among which was, interestingly enough, the anonymity of the person on behalf of whom it had been filed. The trial judge, Mobolaji

Ojo, had asked: "Who is Miss Justice, how old is she, what is her standing in life, what are her particulars?" Mr. Igbinedion has appealed the dismissal. See Ben Ezeamalu, "Exorcism Slap: Defeated Lawyer Heads to Appeal Court against Bishop Oyedepo," *Premium Times*, September 8, 2012.

5. See, for example, Jonathan Iorkighir, "Gender and the Challenge of Witchcraft," in *Living with Dignity: African Perspectives on Gender Equality*, edited by Elna Mouton, Gertrude Kapuma, Len Hansen, and Thomas Togom, 97–124 (Stellenbosch: Ecumenical Foundation for Southern Africa, 2015).

6. For a critical analysis of this phenomenon, see Rosalind I. J. Hackett, "Discourses of Demonization and Beyond," *Diogenes* 50, no. 3 (2003): 61–75. Cf. Elias Bongmba, *African Witchcraft and Otherness: A Philosophical and Theological Critique of Intersubjective Relations* (Albany: State University of New York Press, 2001). For an analysis of what Bongmba describes as "Pentecostal witchcraft," see Sasha Newell, "Pentecostal Witchcraft: Neoliberal Possession and Demonic Discourse in Ivoirian Pentecostal Churches," *Journal of Religion in Africa* 37 (2007): 461–90.

7. Ebenezer Obadare, *Humor, Silence, and Civil Society in Nigeria* (New York: University of Rochester Press, 2016).

8. Or defiance, since I am writing in America in the summer of 2020.

9. James C. Scott, *Domination and the Arts of Resistance: Hidden Transcripts* (New Haven, CT: Yale University Press, 1990), 227.

10. See Ebenezer Obadare, "Sexual Struggles and Democracy Dividends," in *Contesting the Nigerian State: Civil Society and the Contradictions of Self-Organization*, edited by Mojubaolu Olufunke Okome, 199–215 (New York: Palgrave Macmillan, 2013).

11. The video is available here: https://www.youtube.com/watch?v=HMUWnmW5jPY.

12. Entreaties are common as an informal mechanism for conflict resolution in Nigeria and make an appearance in at least three of the four cases analyzed in this chapter. While they can help to defuse a potentially sticky situation, they can also be frustrating to the extent that, by definition, they sidestep, sometimes to the point of muddling, important points of law. As a matter of fact, and as we see in the cases under consideration here, they can be powerful cultural rituals aimed at reining in dissidence and the reinforcement of the status quo, particularly in relation to gender.

13. See, for instance, Harold Garfinkel, "Conditions of Successful Degradation Ceremonies," *American Journal of Sociology* 61, no. 5 (1956): 420–24. Cf. Robert J. Antonio, "The Processual Dimension of Degradation Ceremonies: The Chicago Conspiracy Trial; Success or Failure?," *British Journal of Sociology* 23, no. 3 (1972): 287–97.

14. For details of the accusations and counter-accusations, see Juliet Ebirim, "Apostle Suleman vs Stephanie Otobo," *Vanguard* (Lagos), February 4, 2018.

15. The video of Ms. Otobo tendering an apology to Pastor Suleman is available here: https://www.youtube.com/watch?v=6CvJ2DUZN38.

16. See "Why I Begged Apostle Suleman—Stephanie Otobo's Mother," *Premium Times*, April 1, 2017, https://www.premiumtimesng.com/. Italics added.

17. See "Stephanie Otobo Retracts Her Claims, Says She Was Paid to Defame Apostle Suleman," *Sahara Reporters*, January 27, 2018, saharareporters.com/. Granted, the tone of this particular statement may suggest that the pastor and his closest aides in the church hierarchy had a hand in the drafting of the statement, but it is fair to say that the sentiments it expresses are widely shared among the congregation.

18. There are other grounds for comparing Ms. Otobo and Ms. Olunloyo, one of which is their marital status (single) at the time of their respective encounters, which could have made them susceptible to indictment in advance of any evidence by the Nigerian public. Interestingly, Ms. Otobo's major complaint was that she had been led to believe that Pastor Suleman himself was single, hence available for marriage. However, although they share the same marital status, both Ms. Otobo and Ms. Olunloyo could not be more different in terms of social class. While, as we have seen, Ms. Otobo comes from a humble background (her mother, Mrs. Bukky Otobo, is a retailer at Okirighwve market, Sapele), Ms. Olunloyo has a more lofty pedigree as the daughter of Dr. Victor Omololu Olunloyo, a mathematician with a PhD from St. Andrews University, UK; commissioner (minister) for economic development for the Western Region during the First Republic; and one-time governor of Oyo State during the Second Republic. Of the three women discussed so far, "Ms. Justice" occupies the lowest rung of the social hierarchy.

19. See https://twitter.com/KemiOlunloyo/status/1259083889273905153.

20. See https://ikengachronicles.com/im-more-intelligent-than-einstein-kemi-olunloyo/.

21. See Akinwale Akinyoade, "Head CNN Africa, Stephanie Busari Faults Kemi Olunloyo's 'CNN Former Employee' Claim," *Guardian* (Lagos), July 22, 2019.

22. See https://www.facebook.com/KemiOlunloyo/posts/2420250664729395?comment_id=2420437978043997.

23. See "'Forgive My Daughter's Behaviour'—Former Oyo Governor, Olunloyo, Begs Pastor Adeboye," *This Day*, July 17, 2016, https://www.thisdaylive.com/.

24. The video is available at https://www.youtube.com/watch?v=gsXdNCmsM6M.

25. The video is at https://www.youtube.com/watch?v=tNUssxgAiPU. Speaking of apologies, it seems as if Ms. Olunloyo has offered a lot of them at different times over the years. In a June 15, 2020, video she apologized to all her fans on social media for any offense she might have caused. The video of that apology is available at https://www.instagram.com/tv/CBd3o0dJElM/?utm_source=ig_embed.

26. See Jamilah Nasir, "FLASHBACK: How COZA Member Accused Fatoyinbo of Sexual Abuse in 2013," *Cable* (Abuja), June 29 2019, https://www.thecable.ng/.

27. See Stephen Charles Kenechukwu, "Stella Damasus: How COZA Pastor Raped My Friend of 15 Years," *Cable*, June 29, 2019, available at https://www.thecable.ng/.

28. Adejumo Kabir, "Another Alleged Victim of COZA Pastor, Biodun Fatoyinbo, Shares Experience," *Premium Times*, July 4, 2019.

29. See Jayne Augoye, "Rape Scandal: COZA Pastor Biodun Fatoyinbo Bows to Pressure, 'Steps Down,'" *Premium Times* (Abuja), July 1, 2019.

30. "COZA: CAN Speaks on Rape Allegation against Fatoyinbo," *Premium Times*, June 29, 2019, https://www.premiumtimesng.com/.

31. See Jethro Ibike, "PFN President, Omobude Speaks on Fatoyinbo's Rape Saga," *PM News Nigeria*, July 2, 2019.

32. Jayne Augoye, "COZA Rape Scandal: Why I Shunned PFN Panel—Fatoyinbo," *Premium Times* (Abuja), August 23, 2019.

33. A copy of his letter of resignation is available at https://www.nairaland.com/5335804/verified-coza-board-member-resigns.

34. See "Not Even as an Unbeliever Will My Husband Rape Someone, Says Pastor Fatoyinbo's Wife," *Vanguard*, June 30, 2019.

35. See https://www.mountainoffire.org/about/dr-daniel-and-sis-shade-olukoya. Italics added.

36. See Victor Agadjanian, "Women's Religious Authority in a Sub-Saharan Setting: Dialectics of Empowerment and Dependency," *Gender & Society* 29, no. 6 (2015): 982–1008, quote on 997.

37. See Kazeem Ugbodaga, "I Didn't Sign Counter Petition, Busola Dakolo Speaks on UK *Guardian*'s Report," *PM News Nigeria*, August 7, 2019, https://www.pmnewsnigeria.com/2019/08/07/i-didnt-sign-counter-petition-busola-dakolo-speaks-on-uk-guardians-report/.

38. Available at https://www.instagram.com/p/CBBb7x4BG0N/?utm_source=ig_embed.

39. See "Fatoyinbo Received Rapturous Welcome from COZA Members Despite Rape Allegation," *PM News Nigeria*, June 30, 2019, https://www.pmnewsnigeria.com/2019/06/30/embattled-fatoyinbo-receives-rapturous-welcome-from-coza-members-despite-rape-allegation/.

40. Ibid.

41. Abimbola Adelakun, "My Adventure in COZA," *Punch* (Lagos), July 25, 2019.

42. See Abimbola Adelakun, "What Does Mrs Fatoyinbo Know?," *Punch* (Lagos), July 4, 2019.

43. Adelakun, "My Adventure in COZA."

44. See Carl Schmitt, *The Concept of the Political* (Chicago: University of Chicago Press, 1995).

Conclusion

1. See Michael Chambers, "Jesus of Oyingbo," *New Society*, April 9, 1964.

2. Ibid., 13.

3. Ibid.

4. Ibid.

5. See Rijk van Dijk, "After Pentecostalism? Exploring Intellectualism, Secularization and Guiding Sentiments in Africa," in *Multiple Secularities beyond the West: Religion and Modernity in the Global Age*, edited by Marian Burchardt, Monika Wohlrab-Sahr, and Matthias Middell, 215–40 (Boston: De Gruyter, 2015), quote on 216.

6. See Matthews A. Ojo, "Religion and Sexuality: Individuality, Choice and Sexual Rights in Nigerian Christianity," working paper, Understanding Human Sexuality Seminar Series 4, Africa Regional Sexuality Resource Centre, Lagos, 2005, 1.

7. Chambers, "Jesus of Oyingbo," 13.

8. Ibid.

9. Ibid., 15.

10. See Lorraine Daston, "Marvelous Facts and Miraculous Evidence in Early Modern Europe," *Critical Inquiry* 18, no. 1 (1991): 93–124, quote on 95.

11. See Robert H. Jackson and Carl G. Rosberg, *Personal Rule in Black Africa: Prince, Autocrat, Prophet, Tyrant* (Berkeley: University of California Press, 1982), 12.

12. Maurizio Lazzarato, "Pastoral Power: Beyond Public and Private," *Open! Platform for Art, Culture & the Public Domain*, April 23, 2010, 3. Italics added.

13. Jeffrey Herbst, *States and Power in Africa: Comparative Lessons in Authority and Control* (Princeton, NJ: Princeton University Press, 2000), 12.

14. See Olufemi Taiwo, "Of Citizens and Citizenship," in *Constitutionalism and Society in Africa*, edited by Okon Akiba, 55–78 (Aldershot, England: Ashgate, 2004), citations from 56 and 65, respectively.

15. See Eghosa Osaghae, "Colonialism and Civil Society in Africa: The Perspective of Ekeh's Two Publics," *Voluntas: International Journal of Voluntary and Nonprofit Organizations* 17 (2006): 233–45, quote on 233.

16. See Tejumola Olaniyan, "Introduction," in *State and Culture in Postcolonial Africa: Enchantings*, edited by Tejumola Olaniyan (Bloomington: Indiana University Press, 2017), 11.

17. See Wendy Willems and Ebenezer Obadare, "Introduction: African Resistance in an Age of Fractured Sovereignty," in *Civic Agency in Africa: Arts of Resistance in the 21st Century*, edited by Ebenezer Obadare and Wendy Willems (Rochester, NY: James Currey, 2014), 124.

18. See Ebenezer Obadare, "Spectacles of Piety: Prayer and the Politics of Mass Arousal in Democratic Nigeria," in *Crowds: Ethnographic Encounters*, edited by Megan Steffen, 51–61 (New York: Bloomsbury Academic, 2020). The ideas of "affective proximity" and "momentary neural binding" are from Ash Amin and Nigel Thrift, *The Arts of the Political: New Openings for the Left* (Durham, NC: Duke University Press, 2013).

19. See Achille Mbembe, interview with Christian Holler, *Mute*, March 17, 2007, available at https://www.metamute.org/editorial/articles/africa-motion-interview-post-colonialism-theoretician-achille-mbembe#. Italics added.

20. Ramon Sarró, "Writing as Rupture: On Prophetic Invention in Central Africa," in *Ruptures: Anthropologies of Discontinuity in Times of Turmoil*, edited by Martin Holbraad, Bruce Kapferer, and Julia F. Sauma (London: UCL Press, 2019), 140–56, quote on 140.

21. See, for instance, Amy Gutmann and Dennis Thompson, *Democracy and Disagreement* (Cambridge, MA: Harvard University Press, 1997); Diana C. Mutz, *Hearing the Other Side: Deliberative versus Participatory Democracy* (Cambridge: Cambridge University Press, 2006). For a reflection on the politics of disagreement in Nigeria, see Ebenezer Obadare, "Sexual Struggles and Democracy Dividends," in *Contesting the Nigerian State: Civil Society and the Contradictions of Self-Organization*, edited by Mojubaolu Olufunke Okome, 199–215 (New York: Palgrave Macmillan, 2013).

BIBLIOGRAPHY

Abbah, Theophilus. "Vultures of Steel: Ajaokuta Where Corruption Is the System." *Daily Trust* (Abuja), July 9, 2019.

Abdulraheem, Tajudeen, and Adebayo Olukoshi. "The Left in Nigerian Politics and the Struggle for Socialism: 1945–1985." *Review of African Political Economy* 37 (1986): 64–80.

Ade-Ajayi, J. F. "Towards an African Academic Community." In *Creating the African University: Emerging Issues in the 1970s*, edited by T. M. Yesufu, 49–64. Ibadan: Oxford University Press, 1972.

Adebanwi, Wale. "The Clergy, Culture, and Political Conflicts in Nigeria." *African Studies Review* 53, no. 3 (2010): 121–42.

———. "Elites and the Enlightenment: Reflections on the Question of Progress in Contemporary Nigeria." Metropolitan Club 60th Anniversary Lecture, Lagos, Nigeria, October 15, 2019.

———. "Introduction: Media Intellectual and the Social Conscience." In *Public Intellectuals, the Public Sphere & the Public Spirit*, edited by Wale Adebanwi, 1–27. Ibadan: Ibadan University Press, 2014.

———. "What Are Friends For? The Fatality of Affinity in the Postcolony." Unpublished manuscript, 2013.

Adebanwi, Wale, and Ebenezer Obadare. "Paper Games: Consulary and Ersatz Lives in Urban Lagos." In *Everyday State and Democracy in Africa: Ethnographic Encounters*, edited by Wale Adebanwi. Athens, OH: Ohio University Press, 2022.

Adebulu, Taiwo. "Magu Probe: We Mistakenly Transferred N573m to Prophet Omale, Says FCMB." *Cable*, August 10, 2020. https://www.thecable.ng/.

Adéẹ̀kọ́, Adéléke. *Arts of Being Yorùbá: Divination, Allegory, Tragedy, Proverb, Panegyric*. Bloomington: Indiana University Press, 2017.

Adejumobi, Said. "Knowledge for Sale? The Politics of University Education Reform in Africa, with a Nigerian Example." In *Manoeuvring in an Environment of Uncertainty: Structural Change and Social Action in Sub-Saharan Africa*, edited by Boel Berner and Per Trulsson, 179–206. Aldershot, England: Ashgate, 2000.

Adejunmobi, Moradewun. "Standup Comedy and the Ethics of Popular Performance in Nigeria." In *Popular Culture in Africa: The Episteme of the Everyday*, edited by Stephanie Newell and Onookome Okome, 175–94. New York: Routledge, 2014.

Adekanye, J. Bayo. "Military Occupation and Social Stratification." Inaugural Lecture, University of Ibadan, Ibadan, 1993.

Adelakun, Abimbola. "My Adventure in COZA." *Punch* (Lagos), July 25, 2019.

———. "What Does Mrs Fatoyinbo Know?" *Punch* (Lagos), July 4, 2019.

Adelakun, Abimbola Adunni. "Godmentality: Pentecostalism as Performance in Nigeria." PhD dissertation, University of Texas at Austin, 2017.

———. "Pastocracy: Performing Pentecostal Politics in Nigeria." In *Africa's Big Men: Predatory State-Society Relations in Africa*, edited by Kenneth Kalu, Olajumoke Yacob-Haliso, and Toyin Falola, 161–76. New York: Routledge, 2018.

Adeogun, A. A. "The Law and the Institutionalization of Labour Protest in Nigeria." *Indian Journal of Industrial Relations* 16, no. 1 (1980): 1–23.

Adeoti, Gbemisola. "Narrating the Green Gods: The (Auto)Biographies of Nigerian Military Rulers." In *Intellectuals and African Development: Pretension and Resistance in African Politics*, edited by Bjorn Beckman and Gbemisola Adeoti, 49–64. London: Zed, 2006.

Adesokan, Akinwumi. "'Jesus Christ, Executive Producer': Pentecostal Parapolitics in Nollywood Films." In *State and Culture in Postcolonial Africa: Enchantings*, edited by Tejumola Olaniyan, 191–206. Bloomington: Indiana University Press, 2017.

Adogame, Afeosemime U., ed. *Who Is Afraid of the Holy Ghost? Pentecostalism and Globalization in Africa and Beyond*. Trenton, NJ: Africa World Press, 2011.

"Africa Local Intellectuals." Special issue. *Africa* 87, no. 1 (2017).

Agadjanian, Victor. "Women's Religious Authority in a Sub-Saharan Setting: Dialectics of Empowerment and Dependency." *Gender & Society* 29, no. 6 (2015): 982–1008.

Agbenson, Victorson. *Moment of Truth: The Compelling Story of Pastor Tunde Bakare*. Ibadan: Safari Books, 2014.

Ahmed, Sara. *What's the Use? On the Uses of Use*. Durham, NC: Duke University Press, 2019.

Akinkuotu, Eniola. "Feminists Tackle Adeboye over Wife's Birthday Message." *Punch* (Lagos), July 15, 2020.

Akinyoade, Akinwale. "Head CNN Africa, Stephanie Busari Faults Kemi Olunloyo's 'CNN Former Employee' Claim." *Guardian* (Lagos), July 22, 2019.

Alatas, Syed Hussein. *Intellectuals in Developing Societies*. London: Franc Cass, 1977.

Amakiri, A. A. *The Left in Nigerian Politics*. Lagos: Amkra Books, 1997.

Amin, Ash, and Nigel Thrift. *The Arts of the Political: New Openings for the Left*. Durham, NC: Duke University Press, 2013.

Amuta, Chidi. "Off Your Marx (Dead End of Marxism)." *Daily Times* (Lagos), September 16, 1991.

Amuta, Chidi, and Biodun Jeyifo. *Theory of African Literature: Implications for Practical Criticism*. London: Zed Books, 2017.

Amuwo, Adekunle. "Between Intellectual Responsibility and Political Commodification of Knowledge: Nigeria's Academic Political Scientists under the Babangida Military Junta, 1985–1993." *African Studies Review* 45, no. 2 (2002): 93–121.

———. "The Discourse of the Political Elites on Higher Education in Nigeria." In *The Dilemma of Post-Colonial Universities*, edited by Yann Lebeau and Mobolaji Ogunsanya (Ibadan: IFRA-Nigeria, 2000).

Anderson, David M., and Douglas H. Johnson, eds. *Revealing Prophets: Prophecy in Eastern African History*. Athens: Ohio University Press, 1995.

"Anita Finalises Divorce from Pastor Chris Oyakhilome." *Vanguard*, February 19, 2016. https://www.vanguardngr.com/2016/02/anita-finalises-divorce-from-pastor-chris-oyakhilome/.

Anti-Homosexuality Act (2014). https://www.refworld.org/pdfid/530crbc64/pdf/.

Antonio, Robert J. "The Processual Dimension of Degradation Ceremonies: The Chicago Conspiracy Trial; Success or Failure?" *British Journal of Sociology* 23, no. 3 (1972): 287–97.

Apter, Andrew H. *The Pan-African Nation: Oil and the Spectacle of Culture in Nigeria*. Chicago: University of Chicago Press, 2005.

Aribisala, Femi. "Article of Faith: Daddy G.O." *Premium Times*, May 11, 2014. https://www.premiumtimesng.com.

———. "Money Laundering in the Churches." *Vanguard*. October 7, 2012. https://www.vanguardngr.com/2012/10/money-laundering-in-the-churches/.

———. "Pastors Are the Real Robbers of God." *Vanguard*, November 19, 2017. https://www.vanguardngr.com/2017/11/pastors-real-robbers-god/.

———. "There Is No Coronavirus in Nigeria." *Vanguard*, April 3, 2020. https://www.vanguardngr.com/2020/04/there-is-no-coronavirus-in-nigeria/.

Asamoah-Gyadu, J. Kwabena. *Contemporary Pentecostal Christianity: Interpretations from an African Context*. Eugene, OR: Wipf and Stock, 2013.

Atteh, Samuel O. "The Crisis in Higher Education in Africa." *Issue: A Journal of Opinion* 24, no. 1 (1996): 36–42.

Augoye, Jayne. "COZA Rape Scandal: Why I Shunned PFN Panel—Fatoyinbo." *Premium Times* (Abuja), August 23, 2019.

———. "Rape Scandal: COZA Pastor Biodun Fatoyinbo Bows to Pressure, 'Steps Down.'" *Premium Times* (Abuja), July 1, 2019.

———. "TB Joshua: Wizard Called Emmanuel Has Been Consumed—Chris Okotie." *Premium Times* (Nigeria), June 8, 2021. https://www.premiumtimesng.com/.

Austin, Dennis. "Universities and the Academic Gold Standard in Nigeria." *Minerva* 18, no. 2 (1980): 201–42.

Ayandele, E. A. *The Educated Elite in the Nigerian Society*. Ibadan: Ibadan University Press, 1979.

Bakare, Tunde. "The Nigeria of My Dreams." Speech, Lagos, November 16, 2014. http://tundebakare.com.

Ball, R. Glenn, and Darrell Puls. "Frequency of Narcissistic Personality Disorder in Pastors: A Preliminary Analysis." Paper presented to the American Association of Christian Counselors, Nashville, TN, September 26, 2015.

Balogun, Oluwakemi M. "Cultural and Cosmopolitan: Idealized Femininity and Embodied Nationalism in Nigerian Beauty Pageants." *Gender & Society* 26, no. 3 (2012): 357–81.

Bangura, Yusuf. "Intellectuals, Economic Reform and Social Change: Constraints and Opportunities in the Formation of a Nigerian Technocracy." *Development and Change* 25, no. 2 (1994): 261–305.

Bataille, Georges. *Erotism: Death and Sensuality*. San Francisco: City Lights Books, 1986.

Baum, Robert M. *West Africa's Women of God: Alinesitoué and the Diola Prophetic Tradition*. Bloomington: Indiana University Press, 2016.

Beckman, Bjorn, and Attahiru Jega. "Scholars and Democratic Politics in Nigeria." *Review of African Political Economy* 22, no. 64 (1995): 167–81.

BellaNaija.com. "Pastor Enoch Adeboye of the Redeemed Christian Church of God on CNN's African Voices This Weekend—Read the Interview Transcripts." *BellaNaija* (blog), February 10, 2011. https://www.bellanaija.com.

"Biodun Jeyifo: Reflections of a Radical Literary Critic, Theorist, Unionist and Columnist." *PM News Nigeria*, February 6, 2016. https://pmnews nigeria.com/2016/02/06/biodun-jeyifo-reflections-of-a-radical-literary-critic-theorist-unionist-and-columnist/.

Bongmba, Elias. *African Witchcraft and Otherness: A Philosophical and Theological Critique of Intersubjective Relations*. Albany: State University of New York Press, 2001.

Burgess, Richard. *Nigerian Pentecostalism and Development: Spirit, Power, and Transformation*. Routledge Research in Religion and Development. New York: Routledge, 2020.

Butticci, Annalisa. *African Pentecostals in Catholic Europe: The Politics of Presence in the Twenty-first Century*. Cambridge, MA: Harvard University Press, 2016.

———. *Na God: Aesthetics of African Charismatic Power*. Padua: Dipartimento de Filosofa, Sociologia, Pedagogia e Psicologia Applicata, Universita Degli Studi Di, 2013.

Cazarin, Rafael, and Marian Burchardt. "Learning How to Feel: Emotional Repertoires of Nigerian and Congolese Pentecostal Pastors in the Diaspora." In *Affective Trajectories: Religion and Emotion in African CityScapes*, edited by Hansjörg Dilger, Astrid Bochow, Marian Burchardt, and Matthew Wilhelm-Solomon, 160–84. Durham, NC: Duke University Press, 2020.

Chabal, Patrick, and Jean-Pascal Daloz. *Africa Works: Disorder as Political Instrument*. Oxford: James Currey, 1999.

Chambers, Michael. "Jesus of Oyingbo," *New Society*, April 9, 1964.

Channing, William Ellery. "On the Elevation of the Laboring Classes." In *The Harvard Classics: Essays English and American*, edited by Charles W. Eliot, 321–80. Norwalk, CT: Easton Press, 1994.

Chiedozie, Ihuoma. "Confusion as 'Prayer Warriors' Compete with Medical Doctors for Patients." *Punch* (Lagos), June 22, 2019. https://punchng.com.

Chua, Amy, and Jed Rubenfeld. *The Triple Package: How Three Unlikely Traits Explain the Rise and Fall of Cultural Groups in America*. New York: Penguin Books, 2014.

Clark, J. P. "When Soyinka, Achebe and I Pleaded with IBB to Spare Vatsa's Life." *NEWS* (Lagos), September 3, 2016. https://www.thenewsnigeria.com.

Coleman, James S. *Nigeria: Background to Nationalism*. Benin City: Broburg & Wilstrom, 1986.

Coleman, Simon. "'Right Now!': Historiopraxy and the Embodiment of Charismatic Temporalities." *Ethnos* 76, no. 4 (2011): 426–47.

Comaroff, Jean, and John L. Comaroff, eds. *Law and Disorder in the Postcolony*. Chicago: University of Chicago Press, 2006.

Comaroff, John L., and Jean Comaroff, eds. *The Politics of Custom: Chiefship, Capital, and the State in Contemporary Africa*. Chicago: University of Chicago Press, 2018.
"Corruption: Oyedepo Blows Hot over Millions Stolen by Church Officials." *Vanguard*, January 12, 2020. https://www.vanguardngr.com/2020/01/churchs-treasury-oyedepo-blows-hot-over-millions-stolen-by-church-officials/.
Coser, Lewis A. *Men of Ideas: A Sociologist's View*. New York: Free Press, 1997.
"COZA: CAN Speaks on Rape Allegation against Fatoyinbo." *Premium Times*, June 29, 2019. https://www.premiumtimesng.com/.
Currid-Halkett, Elizabeth. *The Sum of Small Things: A Theory of the Aspirational Class*. Princeton, NJ: Princeton University Press, 2017.
Daloz, Jean-Pascal. "Elite (Un)conspicuousness: Theoretical Reflections on Ostentation vs. Understatement." *Historical Social Research* 37, no. 1 (2012): 209–22.
———. "Political Elites and Conspicuous Modesty: Norway, Sweden, Finland in Comparative Perspective." *Comparative Social Research* 23 (2006): 171–210.
———. *The Sociology of Elite Distinction: From Theoretical to Comparative Perspectives*. New York: Palgrave Macmillan, 2010.
Daniels, Bisi. "Pastor Adeboye at 76—How He Made Osinbajo Believe in Supernatural." *Premium Times*, March 4, 2018.
Daston, Lorraine. "Marvelous Facts and Miraculous Evidence in Early Modern Europe." *Critical Inquiry* 18, no. 1 (1991): 93–124.
Deacon, Gregory, George Gona, Hassan Mwakimako, and Justin Willis. "Preaching Politics: Islam and Christianity on the Kenya Coast." *Journal of Contemporary African Studies* 35, no. 2 (2017): 148–67.
"Dele Momodu Visits Evelyn, TB Joshua's Wife." *MAD News*, June 13, 2021. https://mirrorafricandiaspora.com/dele-momodu-visits-evelyn-tb-joshuas-wife.
Dijk, Richard A. van. "Young Puritan Preachers in Post-independence Malawi." *Africa* 62, no. 2 (1992): 159–81.
Dijk, Rijk van. "After Pentecostalism? Exploring Intellectualism, Secularization and Guiding Sentiments in Africa." In *Multiple Secularities beyond the West: Religion and Modernity in the Global Age*, edited by Marian Burchardt, Monika Wohlrab-Sahr, and Matthias Middell, 215–40. Boston: De Gruyter, 2015.
"Dolapo Awosika, John Fashanu and Prophet Kasali Controversy: The True Story." *Elites Nigeria*, November 14, 2018. https://www.theelitesng.com/dolapo-awosika-john-fashanu-and-prophet-kasali-controversy-the-true-story/.

Doornbos, Martin. "Church & State in Eastern Africa: Some Unresolved Questions." In *Religion & Politics in East Africa: The Period since Independence*, edited by Holger Bernt Hansen and Michael Twaddle, 260–70. London: James Currey, 1995.

Driessens, Olivier. "The Celebritization of Society and Culture: Understanding the Structural Dynamics of Celebrity Culture." *International Journal of Cultural Studies* 16, no. 6 (2013): 641–57.

Dumo, Eric. "A 'King' Sentenced to Death on His Birthday." *Punch* (Lagos), February 27, 2016.

Ebirim, Juliet. "Apostle Suleman vs Stephanie Otobo." *Vanguard* (Lagos), February 4, 2018. https://www.vanguardngr.com/2018/02/apostle-suleman-vs-stephanie-otobo/.

Echeruo, Michael J. C. *Victorian Lagos: Aspects of Nineteenth Century Lagos Life*. New York: Macmillan, 1977.

"EFCC to Arrest Catholic Priests over Atuche's N45 Million Tithe." *Premium Times*, October 3, 2012. https://www.premiumtimesng.com/.

Eicher, Carl K. "African Universities: Overcoming Intellectual Dependency." In *Creating the African University: Emerging Issues in the 1970s*, edited by T. M. Yesufu, 27–34. Ibadan: Oxford University Press, 1972.

Ekeh, Peter P. "Colonialism and the Two Publics in Africa: A Theoretical Statement." *Comparative Studies in Society and History* 17, no. 1 (1975): 91–112.

Elaigwu, J. Isawa. "Nigerian Federalism under Civilian and Military Regimes." *Publius: The Journal of Federalism* 18, no. 1 (1988): 173–88.

Elischer, Sebastian. "Burkina Faso: State and Religious Authority in Turbulent Times." In *Faith in Balance: Regulating Religious Affairs in Africa*, edited by Haim Malka, 111–36. Lanham, MD: Rowman and Littlefield, 2020.

Ellis, Stephen. "The Okija Shrine: Death and Life in Nigerian Politics." *Journal of African History* 49, no. 3 (2008): 445–66.

———. *This Present Darkness: A History of Nigerian Organized Crime*. New York: Oxford University Press, 2016.

Ellis, Stephen, and Gerrie ter Haar. "Religion and Politics in Africa." *Afrika Zamani* 5, no. 6 (1997): 221–46.

Engelke, Matthew, and Birgit Meyer. "Mediating Tradition: Pentecostal Pastors, African Priests, and Chiefs in Ghanaian Popular Films." In *Christianity and Social Change in Africa: Essays in Honor of J.D.Y. Peel*, edited by J.D.Y. Peel and Toyin Falola, 275–306. Durham, NC: Carolina Academic Press, 2005.

Eyoboka, Sam. "Adeboye at 60: 'The Secrets of My Success.'" *Vanguard*, March 2, 2002.

Ezeamalu, Ben. "Exorcism Slap: Defeated Lawyer Heads to Appeal Court against Bishop Oyedepo." *Premium Times*, September 8, 2012. https://www.premiumtimesng.com/.

Falasca-Zamponi, Simonetta. *Fascist Spectacle: The Aesthetics of Power in Mussolini's Italy*. Berkeley: University of California Press, 2000.

Fatoyinbo, Biodun (@biodunfatoyinbo). "'PSALM 20: 6—Now Know I That the LORD Saveth His Anointed." Instagram post, June 4, 2020. https://www.instagram.com/p/CBBb7x4BG0N/.

"Fatoyinbo Receives Rapturous Welcome from COZA Members Despite Rape Allegation." *PM News Nigeria*, June 30, 2019. https://pmnewsnigeria.com/2019/06/30/embattled-fatoyinbo-receives-rapturous-welcome-from-coza-members-despite-rape-allegation/.

Feierman, Steven. *Peasant Intellectuals: Anthropology and History in Tanzania*. Madison: University of Wisconsin Press, 1990.

Fesenmyer, Leslie. "Pentecostal Pastorhood as Calling and Career: Migration, Religion, and Masculinity between Kenya and the United Kingdom." *Journal of the Royal Anthropological Institute* 24, no. 4 (2018): 749–66.

Festinger, Leon, Henry W. Riecken, and Stanley Schachter. *When Prophecy Fails: A Social and Psychological Study of a Modern Group That Predicted the Destruction of the World*. New York: Harper, 1990.

"'Forgive My Daughter's Behaviour'—Former Oyo Governor, Olunloyo, Begs Pastor Adeboye." *This Day*, July 17, 2016. https://www.thisdaylive.com.

Gaffey, Conor. "Nigeria's T. B. Joshua Explains Unfulfilled U.S. Election Prophecy." *Newsweek*, November 14, 2016.

Garfinkel, Harold. "Conditions of Successful Degradation Ceremonies." *American Journal of Sociology* 61, no. 5 (1956): 420–24.

Garnham, Nicholas. *Emancipation, the Media, and Modernity: Arguments about the Media and Social Theory*. New York: Oxford University Press, 2000.

Gaudio, Rudolf. "Modern Desires in Urban Nigeria." *Cultural Anthropology*, July 21, 2015. https://culanth.org.

Gboah TV. "Shocking! Kemi Olunloyo Apologizes to Iyabo Ojo, Says Am Really Sorry I Put You through Hell." YouTube video, 1:31, August 3, 2019. https://youtu.be/tNUssxgAiPU.

Gerth, Hans H., and C. Wright Mills, eds. *From Max Weber: Essays in Sociology*. London: Routledge, 1991.

GH Gossip (@ghgossipdotcom). "'I'm Sorry If I Offended My Fans on Social Media'—Kemi Olunloyo." Instagram video, June 15, 2020. https://www.instagram.com/tv/CBd3o0dJElM/.

Goode, William J. *The Celebration of Heroes: Prestige as a Social Control System*. Berkeley: University of California Press, 1979.

Gurri, Martin. *The Revolt of the Public and the Crisis of Authority in the New Millennium*. San Francisco: Stripe Press, 2018.

Gutmann, Amy, and Dennis Thompson. *Democracy and Disagreement*. Cambridge, MA: Harvard University Press, 1997.

Guyer, Jane I. "Preface." In *Money Struggles & City Life: Devaluation in Ibadan and Other Urban Centers in Southern Nigeria, 1986–1996*, edited by Jane I. Guyer, LaRay Denzer, and Adigun Agbaje, ix–xv. Ibadan: BookBuilders, 2003.

Guyer, Jane I., LaRay Denzer, and Adigun Agbaje. "Introduction: The Nigerian Popular Economy—Strategies Toward a Study." In *Money Struggles & City Life: Devaluation in Ibadan and Other Urban Centers in Southern Nigeria 1986–1996*, edited by Jane I. Guyer, LaRay Denzer, and Adigun Agbaje, xvii–xlv. Ibadan: BookBuilders, 2003.

Hackett, Rosalind I. J. "Discourses of Demonization and Beyond." *Diogenes* 50, no. 3 (2003): 61–75.

Hackman, Melissa. *Desire Work: Ex-Gay and Pentecostal Masculinity in South Africa*. Durham, NC: Duke University Press, 2018.

Haynes, Jonathan. *Nollywood: The Creation of Nigerian Film Genres*. Chicago: University of Chicago Press, 2016.

Herbst, Jeffrey. *States and Power in Africa: Comparative Lessons in Authority and Control*. Princeton, NJ: Princeton University Press, 2000.

———. *States and Power in Africa: Comparative Lessons in Authority and Control*. Princeton, NJ: Princeton University Press, 2014.

Heyck, Thomas W. "From Men of Letters to Intellectuals: The Transformation of Intellectual Life in Nineteenth-Century England." *Journal of British Studies* 20, no. 1 (1980): 158–83.

———. *The Transformation of Intellectual Life in Victorian England*. London: Croom Helm, 1982.

Hofstadter, Richard. *The Age of Reform: From Bryan to F.D.R.* New York: Vintage Books, 1955.

Höller, Christian, and Achille Mbembe. "Africa in Motion: An Interview with the Post-Colonialism Theoretician Achille Mbembe." *Mute*, March 17, 2007. https://www.metamute.org.

"Holy Trap! Dirty Portrait of Dolapo Awosika and Prophet Kasali." *This Day* (Lagos), November 18, 2018. https://www.thisdaylive.com/.

Hopkins, D. N. "The Construction of the Black Male Body: Eroticism and Religion." In *Loving the Body: Black Religious Studies and the Erotic*, edited by D. N. Hopkins and A. B. Pinn, 178–98. New York: Palgrave Macmillan, 2004.

"I Am Dangerously Wealthy, Says Oyedepo." *Cable* (Abuja), December 6, 2018. https://www.thecable.ng/.
Ibekwe, Nicholas. "COZA Abuja Senior Pastor in Sex Scandal." *Premium Times* (Abuja), August 25, 2013. https://www.premiumtimesng.com/.
———. "Synagogue Building Collapse: Why I Exposed T. B. Joshua for Bribing Journalists." *Premium Times*, September 23, 2014. https://www.premiumtimesng.com/.
Ibike, Jethro. "PFN President, Omobude Speaks on Fatoyinbo's Rape Saga." *PM News Nigeria*, July 2, 2019.
Ibrahim, Jibrin. "Political Scientists and the Subversion of Democracy in Nigeria." In *The State and Democracy in Africa*, edited by Georges Nzongola-Ntalaja and Margaret C. Lee, 114–24. Trenton, NJ: Africa World Press, 1998.
Ibrahim, Murtala. "Sensational Piety: Practices of Mediation in Christ Embassy and NASFAT." PhD thesis, Utrecht University, Utrecht, 2017.
Ifowodo, Ogaga. "The Communist as Teacher—the Example of Biodun Jeyifo." *Premium Times*, February 18, 2016. https://www.premiumtimesng.com/.
Ike, Chukwuemeka. *The Naked Gods*. London: Harvill, 1970.
Ilesanmi, Simeon O. *Religious Pluralism and the Nigerian State*. Athens: Ohio University Center for International Studies, 1997.
Inyang, Ifreke. "How Adeboye Saved Me from Death in Plane Crash." *Daily Post* (Nigeria), October 21, 2017. https://dailypost.ng/.
Iorkighir, Jonathan. "Gender and the Challenge of Witchcraft." In *Living with Dignity: African Perspectives on Gender Equality*, edited by Elna Mouton, Gertrude Kapuma, Len Hansen, and Thomas Togom, 97–124. Stellenbosch: Ecumenical Foundation for Southern Africa, 2015.
Jackson, Robert H., and Carl G. Rosberg. *Personal Rule in Black Africa: Prince, Autocrat, Prophet, Tyrant*. Berkeley: University of California Press, 1982.
Jarvis, Chris. "The Rise and Fall of the Pyramid Schemes in Albania." *IMF Staff Papers* 47, no. 1 (2000): 1–29.
Jega, Attahiru. "Nigerian Universities and Academic Staff under Military Rule." *Review of African Political Economy* 22, no. 64 (1995): 251–56.
John, Elnathan. *Be(com)ing Nigerian: A Guide*. London: Cassava Republic Press, 2019.
Kabir, Adejumo. "Another Alleged Victim of COZA Pastor, Biodun Fatoyinbo, Shares Experience." *Premium Times*, July 4, 2019. https://www.premiumtimesng.com/.
Kaldor, Mary. *Global Civil Society: An Answer to War*. London: Polity, 2004.

Kalu, Ogbu. *African Pentecostalism: An Introduction*. New York: Oxford University Press, 2008.

Katsaura, Obvious. "Theo-Urbanism: Pastoral Power and Pentecostals in Johannesburg." *Culture and Religion: An Interdisciplinary Journal* 18, no. 3 (2017): 232–62.

Kellerman, Barbara. "Leadership—It's a *System*, Not a Person!" *Daedalus, the Journal of the American Academy of Arts & Sciences* 145, no. 3 (2016): 83–94.

Kenechukwu, Stephen Charles. "Stella Damasus: How COZA Pastor Raped My Friend of 15 Years." *Cable*, June 29, 2019. https://www.thecable.ng/.

Kingston, Kato Gogo. "Concealment of Illegally Obtained Assets in Nigeria: Revisiting the Role of the Churches in Money Laundering." *African Journal of International and Comparative Law* 28, no. 1 (2020): 106–21.

Kirk-Greene, A.H.M. "His Eternity, His Eccentricity, or His Exemplarity? A Further Contribution to the Study of H. E. the African Head of State." *African Affairs* 90, no. 359 (1991): 163–87.

Klaver, Miranda. "Pentecostal Pastorpreneurs and the Global Circulation of Authoritative Aesthetic Styles." *Culture and Religion* 16, no. 2 (2015): 146–59.

Knights, Ben. *The Idea of the Clerisy in the Nineteenth Century*. New York: Cambridge University Press, 1978.

Kohnert, Dirk. "Trump's Tariff Impact on Africa and the Ambiguous Role of African Agency." *Review of African Political Economy* 45, no. 157 (2018): 451–66.

Korkus, Stella Dimoko. "Stephanie Otobo Confesses and Apologises to Apostle Suleman." YouTube video, 3:18, January 27, 2018. https://youtu.be/6CvJ2DUZN38.

Larkin, Brian. *Signal and Noise: Media, Infrastructure, and Urban Culture in Nigeria*. Durham, NC: Duke University Press, 2008.

Latona, Olayinka. "OLIVER TWIST! Redeemed Pastor Who Has Six PhD Degrees Wants More." *Vanguard* (Lagos), July 7, 2019. https://www.vanguardngr.com/2019/07/oliver-twist-redeemed-pastor-who-has-six-phd-degrees-wants-more/.

Lauterbach, Karen. "Becoming a Pastor: Youth and Social Aspirations in Ghana." *Young: Nordic Journal of Youth Research* 18, no. 3 (2010): 259–78.

Lazzarato, Maurizio. "Pastoral Power: Beyond Public and Private." *Open! Platform for Art, Culture & the Public Domain*, April 23, 2010.

Lebeau, Yann, and Mobolaji Ogunsanya, eds. *The Dilemma of Post-Colonial Universities*. Ibadan: IFRA-Nigeria, 2000.

Lende, Gina. "The Rise of Pentecostal Power: Exploring the Politics of Pentecostal Growth in Nigeria and Guatemala." PhD dissertation, Norwegian School of Theology, Oslo, 2015.

LeVan, A. Carl. *Dictators and Democracy in African Development: The Political Economy of Good Governance in Nigeria.* New York: Cambridge University Press, 2015.

Lindhardt, Martin. "Men of God: Neo-Pentecostalism and Masculinities in Urban Tanzania." *Religion* 45, no. 2 (2015): 252–72.

Lorde, Audre. "The Uses of the Erotic: The Erotic as Power." In *Sister Outsider: Essays and Speeches.* Berkeley, CA: Crossing Press, 1984.

Lovejoy, Paul E., and Jan S. Hogendorn. *Slow Death for Slavery: The Course of Abolition in Northern Nigeria, 1897–1936.* New York: Cambridge University Press, 1993.

Luckham, Robin. *The Nigerian Military: A Sociological Analysis of Authority and Revolt.* Cambridge: Cambridge University Press, 1971.

Lukau, Pastor Alph. "Pastor Alph Lukau Official and Ceremonial Grand Entrance at Alleluia Ministries International." YouTube video, 2:16, November 12, 2018. https://youtu.be/gUoHk1gOwzw.

Magubane, Bernard. "Crisis in African Sociology." *East African Journal* 5, no. 12 (1968): 21–40.

Makovicky, Nicolette. "Me, Inc.? Untangling Neoliberalism, Personhood, and Postsocialism." In *Neoliberalism, Personhood, and Postsocialism: Enterprising Selves in Changing Economies*, edited by Nicolette Makovicky, 1–16. Surrey, England: Ashgate, 2014.

Mamdani, Mahmood. "The African University." *London Review of Books* 40, no. 4 (2018): 29–32.

Marshall, Ruth. *Political Spiritualities: The Pentecostal Revolution in Nigeria.* Chicago: University of Chicago Press, 2009.

"Martin Ssempa, Anti-Gay Ugandan Pastor, Shows Church Gay Porn Videos." *HuffPost*, May 25, 2011. https://www.huffingtonpost.com/2010/02/18/martin-ssempa-anti-gay-ug_n_467157.html.

Mayer, Adam. *Naija Marxisms: Revolutionary Thought in Nigeria.* London: Pluto Press, 2016.

Mazrui, Ali A. "The Lumpen Proletariat and the Lumpen Militariat: African Soldiers as a New Political Class." *Political Studies* 21, no. 1 (1973): 1–12.

Mbembe, Achille. *On the Postcolony.* Berkeley: University of California Press, 2001.

Mbembe, Achille, and Janet Roitman. "Figures of the Subject in Times of Crisis." *Public Culture* 7 (1995): 323–52.

McCauley, John F. "Africa's New Big Man Rule? Pentecostalism and Patronage in Ghana." *African Affairs* 112, no. 446 (2013): 1–21.

Melton, J. Gordon. "Spiritualization and Reaffirmation: What Really Happens When Prophecy Fails." *American Studies* 26, no. 2 (1985): 17–29.

Meyer, Birgit. *Mediation and the Genesis of Presence: Towards a Material Approach to Religion*. Utrecht: Universiteit Utrecht, 2012.

———. "Religious Sensations: Why Media, Aesthetics, and Power Matter in the Study of Contemporary Religion." In *Religion: Beyond a Concept*, edited by Hent de Vries, 704–23. New York: Fordham University Press, 2008.

Mhando, Nandera Ernest, Loreen Maseno, Kupakwashe Mtata, and Mathew Senga. "Modes of Legitimation by Female Pentecostal-Charismatic Preachers in East Africa: A Comparative Study in Kenya and Tanzania." *Journal of Contemporary African Studies* 36, no. 3 (2018): 319–33.

Miescher, Stephan F. *Making Men in Ghana*. Bloomington: Indiana University Press, 2005.

"The Mission of the RCCG." In *The Redeemed Christian Church of God in Prophecy: The Story of the Explosion and a Call to Service*, edited by Tony Ojoibukun, 65–66. Laurel, MD: Honeycombs Publishers.

Mojeed, Musikilu. "Why Some Nigerian Pastors Hated T. B. Joshua—Fani-Kayode." *Premium Times*, June 8, 2021. https://www.premiumtimesng.com/.

Mountain of Fire and Miracles Ministries. "About MFM." n.d.

Mutz, Diana C. *Hearing the Other Side: Deliberative versus Participatory Democracy*. Cambridge: Cambridge University Press, 2006.

Nagesh, Ashitha. "Bishop Claims to Make Men's Penises Larger by Massaging Them with His Hands." *Metro* (London), December 6, 2016. http://metro.co.uk/2016/12/06/bishop-claims-to-make-mens-penises-larger-by-massaging-them-with-his-hands-6304158/.

Namubiru, Lydia, and Khatondi Soita Wepukhulu. "Exclusive: US Christian Right Pours More Than $50m into Africa." *Open Democracy*, October 29, 2020. https://www.opendemocracy.net/en/5050/africa-us-christian-right-50m/.

Nasir, Jamilah. "FLASHBACK: How COZA Member Accused Fatoyinbo of Sexual Abuse in 2013." *Cable* (Abuja), June 29, 2019. https://www.thecable.ng/.

Nasiru, Jemilat. "I Am Dangerously Wealthy, Says Oyedepo." *Cable*, December 6, 2018. https://www.thecable.ng/.

Newell, Sasha. "Pentecostal Witchcraft: Neoliberal Possession and Demonic Discourse in Ivoirian Pentecostal Churches." *Journal of Religion in Africa* 37, no. 4 (2007): 461–90.

Nichols, Thomas M. *The Death of Expertise: The Campaign against Established Knowledge and Why It Matters*. New York: Oxford University Press, 2017.

"Nigerian Preacher TB Joshua Deletes Prophecy of Clinton Win." *BBC News*, November 9, 2016. https://www.bbc.com/news/world-africa-37924086.

Nlebem, Anthony. "Pastor Adeboye Leads Prayer Walk against Killings and Insecurity in Nigeria." *Business Day*, February 2, 2020.

"Not Even as an Unbeliever Will My Husband Rape Someone, Says Pastor Fatoyinbo's Wife." *Vanguard*, June 30, 2019.

Nsehe, Mfonobong. "Wealthy Nigerians, Pastors Spend $225 Million on Private Jets." *Forbes*, May 17, 2011. https://www.forbes.com/.

Nwankwo, Arthur Agwuncha. *African Dictators: The Logic of Tyranny and Lessons from History*. Enugu, Nigeria: Fourth Dimension Publishing, 1990.

Obadare, Ebenezer. "Brain versus Brawn in Nigerian Universities." *CODESRIA Bulletin* 1 (1997): 6–9.

———. *Humor, Silence, and Civil Society in Nigeria*. Rochester, NY: University of Rochester Press, 2016.

———. "The Muslim Response to the Pentecostal Surge in Nigeria: Prayer and the Rise of Charismatic Islam." *Journal of Religious and Political Practice* 2, no. 1 (2016): 75–91.

———. "On the Theologico-Theatrical: Explaining the Convergence of Pentecostalism and Popular Culture in Nigeria." *Africa at LSE* (blog), August 1, 2018. https://blogs.lse.ac.uk/africaatlse/2018/08/01/on-the-theologico-theatrical-explaining-the-convergence-of-pentecostalism-and-popular-culture-in-nigeria/.

———. "On the Theologico-Theatrical: Popular Culture and the Economic Imperative in Nigerian Pentecostalism." *Africa: Journal of the International African Institute* 92, no. 1 (2022): 93–111.

———. *Pentecostal Republic: Religion and the Struggle for State Power in Nigeria*. African Arguments. London: Zed, 2018.

———. "Revalorizing the Political: Towards a New Intellectual Agenda for African Civil Society Discourse." *Journal of Civil Society* 7, no. 4 (2011): 427–42.

———. "Sex, Citizenship and the State in Nigeria: Islam, Christianity and Emergent Struggles over Intimacy." *Review of African Political Economy* 42, no. 143 (2015): 62–76.

———. "Sexual Struggles and Democracy Dividends." In *Contesting the Nigerian State: Civil Society and the Contradictions of Self-Organization*, edited by Mojubaolu Olufunke Okome, 199–215. New York: Palgrave Macmillan, 2013.

———. "Spectacles of Piety: Prayer and the Politics of Mass Arousal in Democratic Nigeria." In *Crowds: Ethnographic Encounters*, edited by Megan Steffen, 51–61. New York: Bloomsbury Academic, 2020.

———. "State of Travesty: Jokes and the Logic of Socio-Cultural Improvisation in Africa." *Critical African Studies* 2, no. 4 (2010): 92–112.

———. "The Uses of Ridicule: Humour, 'Infrapolitics' and Civil Society in Nigeria." *African Affairs* 108, no. 431 (2009): 241–61.

Obadare, Ebenezer, and Wendy Willems, eds. *Civic Agency in Africa: Arts of Resistance in the 21st Century*. Rochester, NY: James Currey, 2014.

Ochonu, Moses E. "Introduction: Toward African Entrepreneurship and Business History." In *Entrepreneurship in Africa: A Historical Approach*, edited by Moses E. Ochonu, 1–28. Bloomington: Indiana University Press, 2018.

———. "Vice-Chancellors and Trends of Embarrassing 'Accomplishments.'" *EduCeleb*, April 5, 2021. https://educeleb.com/vice-chancellors-and-trends-of-embarrassing-accomplishments/.

Odunuga-Samuel, Biodun. "He Touched Me: How I Got Victory over Cancer through Adeboye's Voice on Radio." *Sunday Tribune* (Ibadan), June 21, 2019.

Ogbonna, Anthony. "RCCG Warns Pastors, Members against Participating in MMM, Other Ponzi Schemes." *Vanguard* (Lagos), January 24, 2017. https://www.vanguardngr.com/2017/01/rccg-warns-pastors-members-participating-mmm-ponzi-schemes/.

Ogugbuaja, Charles, and Dom Ekpunobi. "25-Year-Old School Leaver Commits Suicide in Imo." *Guardian* (Lagos), July 23, 2017.

Ogundele, Kamarudeen, and Bayo Akinloye. "Adeboye Commends Fayose's Boldness, Prays for Him." *Punch* (Lagos), December 25, 2016. https://punchng.com.

Ogunjimi, Opeoluwani. "Chris Okotie's Crashed Marriage: Ex-Wife Opens Up." *Vanguard*, July 6, 2012. https://www.vanguardngr.com/2012/07/chris-okoties-crashed-marriage-ex-wife-opens/.

Ogunsanwo, Gbolabo. "The Man They Love to Call 'Daddy.'" *Guardian* (Lagos), March 17, 2002.

Ojediran, Bisi, Isaac Achor, and Ohi Alegbe, eds. *How I Was Called: Testimonies of Ministers of God*. Lagos: Booksplus Nigeria, 2003.

Ojo, Matthews A. *The End-Time Army: Charismatic Movements in Modern Nigeria*. Trenton, NJ: Africa World Press, 2006.

———. "Religion and Sexuality: Individuality, Choice and Sexual Rights in Nigerian Christianity." Working paper, Understanding Human Sexuality Seminar Series 4, Africa Regional Sexuality Resource Centre, Lagos, 2005.

Ojoibukun, Anthony. *The Redeemed Christian Church of God in Prophecy: A History of the Explosion and a Call to Divine Service*. Laurel, MD: Honeycombs Publishers, 2010.

Ojomoyela, Rotimi. "Drama as Fayose-Led Ekiti PDP Camp Takes Secret Oath." *Vanguard*, July 21, 2020. https://www.vanguardngr.com/2020/07/video-drama-as-fayose-led-ekiti-pdp-camp-takes-secret-oath/.

Okanlawon, Taiwo. "Don't Marry Man Who Has No Job—Pastor Adeboye." *PM News Nigeria*, February 19, 2020. https://www.pmnewsnigeria.com/2020/02/19/dont-marry-man-who-has-no-job-adeboye/.

Okonkwo, Rudolf Ogoo. "This Obasanjo Sef & Other Unreplied Letters." *Sahara Reporters* (New York), December 18, 2013.

Okoro, Judex. "UNICAL Professors Declare for APC over Vice Chancellorship Contest." *Sun* (Lagos), June 24, 2020.

Olagunju, Tunji, and Sam Oyovbaire, eds. *Portrait of a New Nigeria: Selected Speeches of IBB*, vol. 1. London: Precision Press, 1989.

Olaniyan, Tejumola, ed. *State and Culture in Postcolonial Africa: Enchantings*. Bloomington: Indiana University Press, 2017.

Olowoopejo, Monsuru. "Synagogue: NANS Protest in Lagos, Demands Halt in Coroner Inquest." *Vanguard*, February 25, 2015. https://www.vanguardngr.com/2015/02/synagogue-nans-protest-in-lagos-demands-halt-in-coroner-inquest/.

Olubummo, Adegoke. "What Does It All Add Up To?" Valedictory Lecture Delivered at the Send-Off Function Organized by the Faculty of Science, University of Ibadan, Ibadan, July 17, 1985. Akure: Afrografika.

Olukoshi, Adebayo O., ed. *The Politics of Structural Adjustment in Nigeria*. London: James Currey, 1993.

Omojuwa, J. J. Twitter post, October 19, 2019, 10:44 a.m. https://twitter.com/Omojuwa/status/1185582592512483328.

Omololu-Olunloyo, Kemi. "CAREER HISTORY: Today #RxKemi30 September 8th 2019 Marks 30 Years I Became a PHARMACIST." Facebook post, September 8, 2019. https://www.facebook.com/KemiOlunloyo/posts/2420250664729395\.

———. Twitter Post, May 9, 2020, 6:32 a.m. https://twitter.com/KemiOlunloyo/status/1259083889273905153.

Onanuga, Adebayo. "Flashy Pastor Chris Okotie at Grace\Karis Award 2013." YouTube video, 1:06, December 10, 2013. https://youtu.be/ieGjq0CMy1k.

Onehi, Victoria. "FG to Spend $1.45bn on Ajaokuta Steel, Iron Ore Coy." *Daily Trust* (Abuja), July 7, 2020.

O'Neill, Kevin Lewis. "I Want More of You: The Politics of Christian Eroticism in Postwar Guatemala." *Comparative Studies in Society and History* 52, no. 1 (2010): 131–56.

Onoge, O. "Revolutionary Imperatives in African Sociology." In *African Social Studies: A Radical Reader*, edited by C. W. Gutkind and Peter Waterman, 32–43. New York: Monthly Review Press, 1977.

Onoja, Adoyi. "The Pentecostal Churches: The Politics of Spiritual Deregulation since the 1980s." In *Religion in Politics: Secularism and National Integration in Modern Nigeria*, edited by Julius O. Adekunle, 263–73. Trenton, NJ: Africa World Press, 2009.

Onuoha, Browne. "Publishing Postcolonial Africa: Nigeria and Ekeh's Two Publics a Generation After." *Social Dynamics* 40, no. 2 (2014): 322–37.

Onyegbula, Esther. "Fake Pastor in Police Net over Alleged N10m Fraud." *Vanguard*, February 11, 2015. https://www.vanguardngr.com/2015/02/fake-pastor-police-net-alleged-n10m-fraud/.

Osaghae, Eghosa. "Colonialism and Civil Society in Africa: The Perspective of Ekeh's Two Publics." *Voluntas: International Journal of Voluntary and Nonprofit Organizations* 17 (2006): 233–45.

Osha, Sanya. *African Postcolonial Modernity: Informal Subjectivities and the Democratic Consensus*. New York: Palgrave Macmillan, 2014.

———. "Violence and Decay within the Nigerian University System: Notes from Ladoke Akintola University of Technology, Ogbomoso." In *The Dilemma of Post-Colonial Universities*, edited by Yann Lebeau and Mobolaji Ogunsanya (Ibadan: IFRA, 2000).

Oshorun, A. O. *Pastor E. A. Adeboye: A Man of Life of Submission and Service to God: The General Overseer of the Redeemed Christian Church of God*. Ibadan: Ethical Financial & Investments Consultants, 2014.

Osinulu, Adedamola. "The Road to Redemption: Performing Pentecostal Citizenship in Lagos." In *The Arts of Citizenship in African Cities: Infrastructures and Spaces of Belonging*, edited by Mamadou Diouf and Rosalind Fredericks, 115–35. New York: Palgrave Macmillan, 2014.

Owete, Festus, and Idris Ibrahim. "Why I Begged Apostle Suleman—Stephanie Otobo's Mother." *Premium Times*, April 1, 2017. https://www.premiumtimesng.com.

Owolabi, Femi. "EXTRA: Army Organises Spiritual Warfare against Boko Haram." *Cable* (Abuja), September 30, 2019. https://www.thecable.ng/.

Paglia, Camille. *Sexual Personae: Art and Decadence from Nefertiti to Emily Dickinson*. New York: Vintage Books, 1991.

"Pandemic Won't Disappear Completely, Says Adeboye." *This Day*, May 25, 2020. https://www.thisdaylive.com/.

Patterson, Amy S., and Tracy Kuperus. "Mobilizing the Faithful: Organizational Autonomy, Visionary Pastors, and Citizenship in South Africa and Zambia." *African Affairs* 115, no. 459 (2016): 318–41.

Peel, J.D.Y. "The Pastor and the *Babalawo*: The Interaction of Religions in Nineteenth-Century Yorubaland." *Africa* 60, no. 3 (1990): 338–69.

———. "Syncretism and Religious Change." *Comparative Studies in Society and History* 10, no. 2 (1968): 121–41.

Piot, Charles. *Nostalgia for the Future: West Africa after the Cold War*. Chicago: University of Chicago Press, 2010.

Poloma, Margaret M., and Matthew T. Lee. "Prophecy, Empowerment, and Godly Love: The Spirit Factor in the Growth of Pentecostalism." In *Spirit and Power: The Growth and Global Impact of Pentecostalism*, edited by Donald E. Miller, Kimon H. Sargeant, and Richard Flory. Oxford: Oxford University Press, 2013.

Posel, Deborah, and Ilana van Wyk. "Thinking with Veblen: Case Studies from Africa's Past and Present." In *Conspicuous Consumption in Africa*, edited by Deborah Posel and Ilana van Wyk, 1–24. Johannesburg: Wits University Press, 2019.

Pype, Katrien. "Of Fools and False Pastors: Tricksters in Kinshasa's Television Fiction." *Visual Anthropology* 23, no. 2 (2010): 115–35.

Ray, Benjamin C. "Aladura Christianity: A Yoruba Religion." *Journal of Religion in Africa* 23, no. 3 (1993): 266–91.

Raz, Joseph. "Introduction." In *Authority*, edited by Joseph Raz, 1–19. New York: New York University Press, 1990.

Reno, William. "The Politics of Public Intellectuals under Abacha and After." In *Vision and Policy in Nigerian Economics: The Legacy of Pius Okigbo*, edited by Jane I. Guyer and LaRay Denzer, 129–47. Ibadan: Ibadan University Press, 2005.

Reynolds, Paul D. "Sociology and Entrepreneurship: Concepts and Contributions." *Entrepreneurship Theory and Practice* 16, no. 2 (1992): 47–70.

Ronu, Yoruba. "KasaliGate." *Yoruba Voice of Reason* (blog), November 21, 2018. https://yorubavoiceofreason.wordpress.com/.

Rose, Nikolas. *Powers of Freedom: Reframing Political Thought*. Cambridge: Cambridge University Press, 1999.

Ruef, Martin, and Lucien Karpik. *The Entrepreneurial Group: Social Identities, Relations, and Collective Action*. Princeton, NJ: Princeton University Press, 2010.

Sackey, Emmanuel. "Election Prophecies and Political Stability in Ghana." In *Christian Citizens and the Moral Regeneration of the African State*, edited by Barbara Bompani and Caroline Valois, 49–62. New York: Routledge, 2019.

SaharaTV. "Bishop Oyedepo Brags about Slapping a Girl." YouTube video, 6:06, January 18, 2012. https://youtu.be/HMUWnmW5jPY.

———. "Nigerian Pastor Oyedepo Assaults Teenager in Church." YouTube video, 3:45, n.d. https://youtu.be/jvKRjETbIRg.

Said, Edward W. *Representations of the Intellectual*. New York: Vintage Books, 1996.

Sampson, Isaac Terwase. "Religion and the Nigerian State: Situating the de Facto and de Jure Frontiers of State-Religion Relations and Its Implications for National Security." *Oxford Journal of Law and Religion* 3, no. 2 (2014): 311–39.

Sanghani, Radhika. "Bra and Knickers? Sorry, Not in My Church." *Telegraph* (London), March 4, 2014. http://www.telegraph.co.uk/women/womens-life/10675818/Bra-and-knickers-sorry-not-in-my-church.html.

Sarró, Ramon. "Writing as Rupture: On Prophetic Invention in Central Africa." In *Ruptures: Anthropologies of Discontinuity in Times of Turmoil*, edited by Martin Holbraad, Bruce Kapferer, and Julia F. Sauma, 140–56. London: UCL Press, 2019.

Sawada, Nozomi. "The Educated Elite and Associational Life in Early Lagos Newspapers: In Search of Unity for the Progress of Society." PhD thesis, University of Birmingham, England, July 2011.

Schmitt, Carl. *The Concept of the Political*. Chicago: University of Chicago Press, 1995.

Scott, James C. *Domination and the Arts of Resistance: Hidden Transcripts*. New Haven, CT: Yale University Press, 1990.

Sennett, Richard. *Authority*. New York: Knopf, 1980.

Shils, Edward. *Selected Papers of Edward Shils: The Calling of Sociology and Other Essays on the Pursuit of Learning*. Chicago: University of Chicago Press, 1980.

Shipley, Jesse Weaver. "Comedians, Pastors, and the Miraculous Agency of Charisma in Ghana." *Cultural Anthropology* 24, no. 3 (2009): 523–52.

Sklar, Richard L. "Beyond Capitalism and Socialism in Africa." *Journal of Modern African Studies* 26, no. 1 (1988): 1–21.

Smith, Ben. "Praying for Rain." *Politico*, April 4, 2011. https://www.politico.com.

Smith, Daniel Jordan. *A Culture of Corruption: Everyday Deception and Popular Discontent in Nigeria*. Princeton, NJ: Princeton University Press, 2008.

———. *To Be a Man Is Not a One-Day Job: Masculinity, Money, and Intimacy in Nigeria*. Chicago: University of Chicago Press, 2017.

Soyinka, Wole. *The Open Sore of a Continent: A Personal Narrative of the Nigerian Crisis*. Oxford: Oxford University Press, 1996.

———. *You Must Set Forth at Dawn: Memoirs*. Ibadan: Bookcraft, 2006.

Spronk, Rachel. *Ambiguous Pleasures: Sexuality and Middle Class Self-Perceptions in Nairobi*. New York: Berghahn, 2015.

"Stephanie Otobo Battles Apostle Suleman, Discloses Account, Payments Details." *Vanguard* (Lagos), April 9, 2017. https://www.vanguardngr.com/2017/04/stephanie-otobo-battles-apostle-suleman-discloses-account-pay ments-details/.

"Stephanie Otobo Retracts Her Claims, Says She Was Paid to Defame Apostle Suleman." *Sahara Reporters*, January 27, 2018. http://saharareporters.com/.

Swenson, Kyle. "A Pastor Admitted a Past 'Sexual Incident' with a Teen. His Congregation Gave Him a Standing Ovation." *Washington Post*, January 10, 2018.

"Synagogue: NANS Protest in Lagos, Demands Halt in Coroner Inquest." *Vanguard*, February 25, 2015.

Taiwo, Olufemi. *Africa Must Be Modern: A Manifesto*. Bloomington: Indiana University Press, 2014.

———. "Colonialism and Its Aftermath: The Crisis of Knowledge Production." *Callaloo* 16, no. 4 (1993): 891–908.

———. *How Colonialism Preempted Modernity in Africa*. Bloomington: Indiana University Press, 2010.

———. "Of Citizens and Citizenship." In *Constitutionalism and Society in Africa*, edited by Okon Akiba, 55–78. Aldershot, England: Ashgate, 2004.

Taylor, Charles. *A Secular Age*. Cambridge, MA: Belknap Press, 2007. https://www.theelites.ng.com/.

Thornton, Patricia H. "The Sociology of Entrepreneurship." *Annual Review of Sociology* 25, no. 1 (1999): 19–46.

Thrift, Nigel, and Ash Amin. *Arts of the Political: New Openings for the Left*. Durham, NC: Duke University Press, 2013.

Titiloyeblog. "Verified COZA Board Member Resigns." *Nairaland Forum*, August 1, 2019. https://www.fairaland.com.

Trovalla, Eric, and Ulrika Trovalla. "Infrastructure as a Divination Tool: Whispers from the Grids in a Nigerian City." *City* 19, nos. 2–3 (2015): 332–43.

Trovalla, Ulrika Andersson. *Medicine for Uncertain Futures: A Nigerian City in the Wake of a Crisis*. Uppsala, Sweden: Uppsala Universitet, 2011.

Trovalla, Ulrika, and Eric Trovalla. "Infrastructure Turned Suprastructure: Unpredictable Materialities and Visions of a Nigerian Nation." *Journal of Material Culture* 20, no. 1 (2015): 43–57.

Tunde Bakare. "Videos," n.d. http://tundebakare.com/videos/.

Twitchell, James B. *Shopping for God: How Christianity Went from in Your Heart to in Your Face*. New York: Simon & Schuster, 2007.

Udenwe, Obinna. *Holy Sex: A Church Erotica*. Chicago: Brittle Paper, 2016.

Ugbodaga, Kazeem. "I Didn't Sign Counter Petition, Busola Dakolo Speaks on UK *Guardian*'s Report." *PM News Nigeria*, August 7, 2019. https://www.pmnewsnigeria.com/2019/08/07/i-didnt-sign-counter-petition-busola-dakolo-speaks-on-uk-guardians-report/.

Ukah, Asonzeh F.-K. *A New Paradigm of Pentecostal Power: A Study of the Redeemed Christian Church of God in Nigeria*. Trenton, NJ: Africa World Press, 2008.

———. "'Those Who Trade with God Never Lose': The Economics of Pentecostal Activism in Nigeria." In *Christianity and Social Change in Africa: Essays in Honor of J.D.Y. Peel*, edited by Toyin Falola, 253–74. Durham, NC: Carolina Academic Press, 2005.

Umukoro, Arukaino. "I Don't Believe My Father Plotted a Coup, He Told Me He Didn't—Mamman Vatsa's Son." *Punch* (Lagos), January 8, 2017. https://punchng.com.

van Klinken, Adriaan, and Martin Zebracki. "Porn in Church: Moral Geographies of Homosexuality in Uganda." *Porn Studies* 3, no. 1 (2016): 89–92.

Vatsa, Mamman Jiya. *Nupe Dance Poems*. Athenaeum Books (UK), 1978.

———. *The Poetry of Abuja: Nigeria's Capital*. Lagos: Cross Continent Press, 1983.

———. *Reach for the Skies*. Lagos: Cross Continent Press, 1985.

———. *Reflections on Warminster*. Outposts Publications (UK), 1975.

Vaughan, Olufemi. *Religion and the Making of Nigeria*. Durham, NC: Duke University Press, 2016.

Vincent, Joan. *African Elite: The Big Men of a Small Town*. New York: Columbia University Press, 1971.

Wariboko, Nimi. "Governance as Trauma in Nigeria: Turning Evangelicalism into Pentecostal Incredible." Unpublished manuscript, 2019.

———. *Nigerian Pentecostalism*. Rochester, NY: University of Rochester Press, 2014.

———. *Nigerian Pentecostalism*. Illustrated edition. Rochester, NY: University of Rochester Press, 2014.

———. "West African Pentecostalism: A Survey of Everyday Theology." In *Global Renewal Christianity: Spirit-Empowered Movements Past, Present, and Future*, vol. 3, edited by Vinson Synan, Amos Yong, and Kwabena Asamoah-Gyadu, 1–18. Lake Mary, FL: Charisma House Book Group, 2014.

"Watch Bakare's Video Declaring Himself Nigeria's Next President—PM News." *PM News Nigeria*, 2019. https://pmnewsnigeria.com/2019/09/23/watch-bakares-video-declaring-himself-nigerias-next-president/.

"Why I Begged Apostle Suleman—Stephanie Otobo's Mother." *Premium Times*, April 1, 2017. https://www.premiumtimesng.com/.

Willems, Wendy, and Ebenezer Obadare. "Introduction: African Resistance in an Age of Fractured Sovereignty." In *Civic Agency in Africa: Arts of Resistance in the 21st Century*, edited by Ebenezer Obadare and Wendy Willems. Rochester, NY: James Currey, 2014.

Williams, Adebayo. "Intellectuals and the Crisis of Democratization in Nigeria: Towards a Theory of Postcolonial Anomie." *Theory and Society* 27, no. 2 (1998): 287–307.

Williams, Gavin. *State and Society in Nigeria*, 2nd edition. Lagos: Malthouse Press, 2019.

Yazdi, Majid. "Patterns of Clerical Political Behavior in Postwar Iran, 1941–53." *Middle Eastern Studies* 26, no. 3 (1990): 281–307.

Yesufu, T. M. "Introduction." In *Creating the African University: Emerging Issues in the 1970s*, edited by T. M. Yesufu. Ibadan: Oxford University Press, 1972.

Zachernuk, Philip Serge. *Colonial Subjects: An African Intelligentsia and Atlantic Ideas*. Charlottesville, VA: University Press of Virginia, 2000.

Zimpapers Digital. "TB Joshua Predicts Hillary Clinton as Winner of US Election." YouTube video, 7:14, November 12, 2016. https://youtu.be/7DkSP-7e4bU.

Znamenski, Andrei. *Socialism as a Secular Creed: A Modern Global History*. Lanham, MD: Rowman and Littlefield, 2021.

INDEX

Abacha, Sani, 39, 42
Aboaba, Doyin, 45
Aborisade, Femi, 46
Abuja High Court, 112
Academic Staff Union of Universities (ASUU), 36–38, 41, 44, 46; slogans, 41; strike, 36, 38
Achebe, Chinua, 25–26
Adamu, Haroun, 45
Ade-Ajayi, Jacob, 31, 33
Adebanwi, Wale, 12
Adebayo, Adeyinka, 35, 36
Adeboye, Enoch (Daddy G.O.), 2, 8, 50–51, 70–71, 77, 115, 143n15, 144n17, 150n46; anointing, power of, 50, 138n92; brand of politics, 59; calling, 67; masculinity of, 10, 155–56n38; relationship with God, 50, 60; reverence accorded to, 51, 137–38n92, 139n94; sixtieth birthday, 50; style, 61, 73; visit to Ajaokuta Steel Complex, 57–64; visit to Ibrahim Idris, 57–58
Adeboye, Foluke (Mummy G.O.), 143n15
Adéèkó, Adéléke, 11
Adejumo, Funke, 15–16
Adejunmobi, Moradewun, 15, 127n28
Adekanye, Bayo, 27, 29, 35–36
Adelakun, Abimbola, 113, 114
Adetoro, Joseph Eyitayo, 32, 36
Adeyemi, Sam, 68
Africa/African: cosmological principle, 61; personal rule, tradition of, 117–18; sexual dimension of citizenship in, 87–88; sexuality, 87–88; traditional religion, 153n7; traditional ruler, 10
Agada, Lawrence, 147n21
Agadjanian, Victor, 112
Agape Christian Ministries, Inc., 16
Agbaje, Adigun, 48
Ahmadu Bello University (ABU), 42
Ahmed, Sara, 98
Ajaokuta Steel Company Limited (ASCL), 58–59, 70, 142n6
Ajaokuta Steel Complex, 57–64
Ake, Claude, 40, 45
Akerdolu, "Arakunrin" Rotimi, 131n12
Akin-John, Francis Bola, 49
Aladura, 153n7
Alatas, Hussein, 5

Alimadu Bello University, Zaire, 132n17
All Progressives Congress (APC), 55
Alleluia Ministries, 139n94
Ambrose Alli University (AAU), 42
Amuta, Chidi, 43–45
Anti-Homosexuality Act, 84
Anunobi-Ekwu, Aucharia, 127n28
Aregbesola, Ogbeni Rauf, 131n12
Aribisala, Femi, 8, 61, 145–46n18; "calling," 66–67
Armed Forces Ruling Council (AFRC), 25, 129n10
Asamoah-Gyadu, Kwabena, 89
Aso Rock, 40; visitations to, 10, 58
Association of Nigerian Authors (ANA), 24
Atuche, Francis, 147n21
authority: concept of, 8–11; everyday performance of, in Nigeria, 5–6; "Man of God," 4, 26; "Man of Letters," 4, 26; masculinity and, 10; moment of consent to, 9; pastoral, 6–7, 9, 27, 63; pastoral authority in Nigeria, nature of, 9–10, 23–55, 95; pre-modern forms of, 10; public construction of, 69; secular, 5–6; spiritual, 11; state, 9; surrender of, 27–28; traditional, 10–11
Ayandele, Emmanuel, 29–31, 37
Awe, Bolanle, 45
Awosika, Dolapo, 81–83, 152n2
Azuzu, Ernest, 127n28

Baba Alaseyori, 81
Babangida, Ibrahim, 23–26, 31, 39, 46, 129n10; academic retainers, 41; charm offensive, 39–40; profile of, 40

Babangida's Transition Program (BTP), 40
Bakare, Tunde, 8, 61–62, 71, 146n18, 150n42, 158n3; prophesy, 77, 78, 144–45n17; "State of the Union" broadcasts, 145n17; style, 73
Banda, Joyce, 139n100
Bangura, Yusuf, 35, 37–38, 42
Banigbe, Obafemi, 111
Bank PHB, 147n21
Bataille, Georges, 87–88
Baum, Robert, 75
Beckman, Bjorn, 36–37
Bekederemo, John Pepper Clark, 25–26
Benson, Liz, 127n28
Berlin Wall, 43
Bible City Church, 149n33
Boko Haram, 59
Bolaji, S. Labanji, 45
Bourdieu, Pierre, 28
Bridge Network, The, 8
Brigade of Guard Headquarters, 24
British colonialism, 29–31, 34
Buhari, Muhammadu, 39, 129n10, 144n17
Busari, Stephanie, 107
Butticci, Annalisa, 89

calling, 62–63, 79; definition, 66–69; suggestive circumstances from birth, 68–69
capitalism, free-market, 43–44
Catholic Church, 12, 147n21
Centre for Advanced Social Science (CASS), 40
Centre for Democratic Studies (CDS), 40
Chabal, Patrick, 10
Chambers, Gani Fawehinmi, 73
Chambers, Michael, 115–17
Channing, William Ellery, 5

Chestmore (Rev.), 68
Chigozie, 110n103
Chinweizu, 45
Christ Embassy, 86, 93, 138n92, 147n21
Christ the King primary school, 67
Christian Association of Nigeria (CAN), 73, 111
Christian Praying Assembly, 52
#ChurchToo, 110
Clark, J. P., 25
CNN, 70, 107, 142n9
Cold War, 43
Coleman, James, 29
Coleman, Simon, 60
Coleridge, Samuel Taylor, 4
Comaroff, Jean, 8
Comaroff, John, 8
Commonwealth of Zion Assembly (COZA), 92, 109, 111, 113, 155n38
Coronavirus, 77–78, 146n18
Coser, Lewis, 5
Covenant University, 158n3

Daily Times, 43; "Off Your Marx (Dead End of Marxism)," 43–44
Dakolo, Busola, 109–13
Dakolo, Timi, 109
Daloz, Jean-Pascal, 10, 28, 93, 131n12
Damasus, Stella, 110
Dare, Olatunji, 45
Daston, Lorraine, 117
Days of Prayer for Rain, 149–50n41
Daystar Christian Ministry, 68
death: denial of, 1–3; divine intervention in, 3; mourning, normal structures of, 3
Decree No. 23, 36
degradation ceremonies, 102, 104, 108, 112–14

Democratic Socialist Movement, 46, 47
Denzer, LaRay, 48
development decade, 37
Divine Hand of God Prophetic Ministry, 62
divine libido, 92
Dodan Barracks, 25, 26
Driessens, Olivier, 93

Economic and Financial Crimes Commission (EFCC), 62
Economic Freedom Fighters, 73, 139n100
Einstein, Albert, 107
Ekeh, Peter, 148n21
Ekiti State, 59
Ellis, Stephen, 53, 57, 61, 76
El-Rufai, Nasir, 62, 145n18
emancipatory ideologies, 46
"Erotic as Power, The" (Lorde), 95
eroticism, 88; economy, 83–86; pastor as an erotic subject, 16, 83, 79–96, 121
Ezeugo, Chukwuemeka (Pastor King), 52

Facebook, 107
Faculty of Education, 41
Fashanu, John, 82
Fashina, Dipo, 46
Fashola, Babatunde, 51
fatidic politics, 72–78
Fatoyinbo, Biodun "Gucci Pastor," 92–93, 109–12, 155n38; appearance and wardrobe, 92–93, 109, 138n92; leave of absence, 110–11
Fatoyinbo, Modele, 111–13
Fayose, Ayo, 59, 151n56
Federal Capital Territory (FCT), 24; High Court, 112

Federal Polytechnic, Ado–Ekiti, 68
Federalist Society, 151n56
Fesenmyer, Leslie, 53
Festinger, Leon, 78
Foucault, Michel, 94, 118
Fountain of Life Church, 86
"419," 53, 140n106
Fubara, Alatuwo Elkanah, 107
Fulani herdsmen, 59, 62

Gaudio, Rudolf, 156n45
Giwa, Dele, 45
Gomwalk, Umaru, 42
"governance by franchise," 8
Gowon, Yakubu, 32, 36
Guardian, The, 46, 47
Guyer, Jane, 41–42, 48

Haar, Gerrie Ter, 57, 61
Haruna, Mohammed, 45
Healing Wings, 8
Heathrow International Airport, 50
Herbst, Jeffrey, 118
Heyck, Thomas, 4
Hickman, Melissa, 84
"hidden transcripts," 101
Highpoint Church, 156n44
homosexuality, 84–85, 102
Household Church of God International Ministries, 73, 86

Ibiyeomie, David, 106–9
Ibiyeomie, Peace, 106, 108, 111
Ibrahim, Jibrin, 39, 41
Ibrahim, Murtala, 138–39n92
Idiagbon, Tunde, 129n10
Idols West Africa, 109
Idris, Ibrahim, 57–58
Igbinedion, Robert, 100, 158–59n4
Igbinedion University, 130n12
Ighodalo, Ituah, 146n18
Ike, Chukwuemeka, 37

Instagram, 110, 150n46
intellectual(s)/intellectual class, 4–5, 24, 27, 29–31, 34; class envy, 35–36; coping strategies, 41–42; cultivation of, 25–26; cultural influence of, 31; definition of, 5, 125n9; de–professionalization of, 42; expectations of, 29, 31–35, 129n11; fall of, 23, 28, 41–47; global left, 44; idea of, 5; "professional," 5; public, 45; relationship with military class, 35, 38, 42; religious identity of, 31; reputation of, 28, 54–55; restoration, 5; *Saro* (Western-educated), 30; self-centeredness of, 29–30; side jobs, 41–42, 135n66; social standing of, 26, 28, 47; tension with majority population, 31; trust of, 7
International Church Growth Ministry, 49
International God's Way Church (IGWC), 90
International Monetary Fund (IMF), 137n86
Ise l'oogun ishe (Odunjo), parody of, 13–15
Islam, 59, 63, 70, 144n17
Isokun, M. I., 42
Iyare, Air, 45

Jackson, Michael, 93
Jackson, Robert, 118
Jega, Attahiru, 36–37
Jesus of Oyingbo, 115–16
Jeyifo, Biodun, 45, 136n73
Jibo, Mvendaga, 45
John, Elnathan, 12
Joint Admissions and Matriculations Board (JAMB), 133n43
Jonah, Samson, 111
Jonathan, Goodluck, 51

Joshua, Temitope Balogun "T. B.", 8, 51; criminal negligence, 51–52, 73; death, 52, 73, 150n46; economic status of congregation, 52; personal limitations, 73–74; prophesy regarding Coronavirus, 77–78; prophesy regarding U.S. election, 72–74; social connections, 73–74, 139–140n100

Kaldor, Mary, 46
Kanayo, Kanayo O., 127n28
Karpik, Lucien, 64
Kasali, Moses Muyideen, 81–83, 152n2
Keyamo, Festus, 103, 105
Klaver, Miranda, 65
Kogbara, Donu, 45
Kogi State, 57–58
Kohnert, Dirk, 142n6
Koldsweat, Larry, 127n28
Kontagora, Mamman, 42
Kwara State University, 73

Lagos State High Court, 52
Lagos State University Teaching Hospital (LASUTH), 1
Latter Rain Assembly Church, 8, 144n17
Lauterbach, Karen, 11, 53
"lawyer" anecdote, 1–3; attempts at resurrecting, 2; wife, 1–2
Lazzarato, Maurizio, 118
Lee, Matthew, 75
LeVan, Carl, 39
liberal democracy, 6, 94
Lindhardt, Martin, 91
Living Faith Church, 146n18
Living Faith Tabernacle, 99
Lorde, Audrey, 95
Lord's Propeller Redemption Church, 90

Lugard House, Lokoja, 58
Lukau, Alph, 139n94

Macebuh, Stanley, 45
Madojemu, Francis, 8, 146n18
Madunagu, Edwin, 45–46
Magu, Ibrahim, 62
Makovicky, Nicollete, 53
Malema, Julius, 73, 139n100
Mama, Amina, 46
"Man of God," 58, 83; authority of, 4, 26; enthronement of, 9; instrumentality of, 3; standing up to, 99–109
"Man of Letters": authority of, 4, 26–27; "homeless," 45
Marxism-Socialism, 37, 43–44, 46–47, 136n71; downfall of, 45–46
masculinity, 91–94
Mass Mobilization for Self-Reliance, Social Justice, and Economic Recovery (MAMSER), 40
Mayer, Adam, 46–47
Mbadinuju, Chinwoke, 151n56
Mbembe, Achille, 88, 92, 95, 120, 135n66
"Me, Inc.," 53
#MeToo movement, 110
Meyer, Birgit, 88–89
military rule, 6, 27, 34–35, 47; collapse of, 6; relationship with intellectual class, 35, 38, 42; resistance to, 6
Mills, John Atta, 139n100
"MMM" (Mavrodi Mundial Moneybox), 53–54, 140–41n106, 141n1
mode of knowledge production (MOKP), 34
Mountain of Fire and Miracles Ministries (MFM), 70, 112, 120

Mountain of Mercy, 81
"Ms. Justice," 99–102, 105, 160n18
Murtala Muhammed International Airport, 66–67

Naked Gods, The (Ike), 37
narcissistic personality disorder, 158n3
National Association of Nigerian Students (NANS), 38
National Association of University Teachers (NAUIT), 36
National Electoral Commission (NEC), 40
National Rifle Association, 151n56
National Steel Council Decree, 58
National Universities Commission (NUC), 133n43
Ndiomu, Charles, 24
Nematandani, Kirten, 73
Ngige, Chris, 151n56
Nigeria: 1960s, 37; 1970s, 34; 1980s, 4; British, 30; character of state, 7–8; class miscegenation, 81–82; clerical power in, social origins of, 23–55; crime and society in, 53; crisis of state, 48; concurrent list, 36; democracy, subversion of, 41, 121–22; development decade, 37; economic angst, 49; erotic economy, 83–86; everyday performance of authority in, 5–6; exclusive list, 36; First Republic, 160n18; Fourth Republic, 12, 16, 28, 55, 58, 63, 69, 70, 77; independence, 28, 29, 31, 36, 132n17; middle class, 47; military rule, 6, 27, 34–35, 47; moral economy, 12, 74; national development, 29, 33; nationalist movement, 29; pastoral authority in, nature of, 10, 23–55, 95; political subjectivity, 87; postcolonial, 34–35, 45, 58; postmilitary, 95; presidential election, 2015, 10, 51; prestige economy, 28, 130n12; secular authority, 5–6; Second Republic, 24, 160n18; social status, 12, 52; theological universe, 61; trade unions, 38, 46, 134n52; trust in the state, 48
Nigeria Labor Congress (NLC), 38, 46
Nigerian Army, 142–43n11
Nigerian Economic Society, 39
Nigerian Medical Association (NMA), 1
Nigerian National Order of Merit Award Winner's Lecture, 25
Nigerian Political Science Association, 39
Nigerian Tribune, 83
Njohi (Reverend Pastor), 90
Nkrumah, Kwame, 118
Nnaegbo, Chibuzor, 147n21
Nobel Prize for Literature, 25
Nollywood, 107, 110, 127n28
non-governmental organizations (NGOs), 42
Nyerere, Julius, 118

oath-taking, 151n56
Obafemi Awolowo University, 41, 43, 139n94
Obasanjo, Olusegun, 54, 77–78
Obinim, Daniel Kwadwo, 90
Ochonu, Moses, 64
Ode Omu, Osun State, 44
Odesola, Funsho, 130n12
Odukoya, Nomthi Rosemary Simangele, 154n15
Odukoya, Taiwo, 86, 154n15

Odumosu, Emmanuel (Olufunmi-layo), 115–16; calling, 116–17; power over congregation, 116–17
Odunjo, J. F., 13
Ofeimun, Odia, 45
Ogan, Amma, 45
Ogun State High Court, 100–2
Ogundipe-Leslie, Molara, 45–46
Ogunlana, Gbade, 149n33; calling, 67–68
Ogunsanwo, Gbolabo, 45
oil industry, nationalization of, 46
Ojo, Iyabo, 107–8
Ojo, Matthews, 116
Ojo, Mobolaji, 158–59n4
Okolie, Chris, 45
Okotie, Kris, 73, 86, 138n92, 150n46, 157n46
Okotie, Stephanie, 86
Okoye, Ifeoma, 46
Olagunju, Tunji, 40
Olaniyan, Tejumola, 118
Oloyede, Caleb, 67
Olubummo, Adegoke, 135n66
Olukoya, D. K., 70, 112, 120
Olukoya, Shade, 112
Olunloyo, Kemi, 105–9, 113, 160n18, 161n25
Olunloyo, Victor Omololu, 160n18
Omale, Emmanuel, 62
Omega Fire Ministries Worldwide, 85, 102
Omojuwa, Japhet, 130n12
O'Neill, Kevin, 89
online diploma mills, 130n12
Orji, Zack, 127n28
Osaghae, Eghosa, 118, 130n12
Osinulu, Adedamola, 50, 91–92, 137n92
Osoba, Segun, 45
Osundare, Niyi, 45
Otobo, Bukky, 104–5, 160n18

Otobo, Stephanie, 85, 93, 102–6, 113, 160n18
Oyakhilome, Anita, 86
Oyakhilome, Chris, 86, 93, 138n92, 147n21
Oyebola, Areoye, 45
Oyedepo, David, 99–102, 146n18, 147n21; stye, 73; YouTube video, 99–102, 158n3
Oyedepo, Faith Abiola, 146n18
Oyovbaire, Sam, 40

Paglia, Camille, 87
Paito Wa (Gbade Ogunlana), 8
pastorpreneurs, 65
#PastorStepDown, 110
Patience, Ebiye, 107
Peel, J. D. Y., 11
Pentecostal Christianity/Pentecostalism, 2, 8, 55; African context of, 4; community, 61; culture, 4; domesticity, 91; ecstatic properties of, 88–89; foundation tenets, 60; "high church," 89; Latin American, 89; Nigerian, 4, 7, 90; politics, 61; theory of causality, 34, 60–61; power of, 28; praxeology, 60–61; prayer in the context of, 63, 70–72; sensual aspect of, 91; sexual restraint and, 84–85; as a social force, 84; West African, 89; worldview, 48; worship service, 89
Pentecostal Fellowship of Nigeria (PFN), 73
Pentecostal pastors: altar, importance of, 91–92, 112–14; anointing, 11, 113; appearance, importance of, 17, 92–93; authority, nature of, 10, 23–55, 95; authority, public construction of, 69; authority of, 6–7, 9,

27, 63; body of, 86–87, 89, 138n92; commerce of, 121; definition of, 75; emergence as a person of consequence, 15, 43–49, 55; as an erotic subject, 16, 83, 79–96, 121; ethical indulgence of, 11; "fake," 12; female, 15–16; "genuine," 12; influence of, 3, 7–8; lumpen wing, 73; origins of social power in, 23–55; as political entrepreneur, 57–79; political obedience to, 94–96; popular culture's perception of, 127n28; prayer, 63, 70–72; prophesy and, 75–76, 95; reason for becoming, 11–15, 18, 49–54; sex scandals, 85, 96–114; social prestige/power of, 11, 26, 27, 47; "sowing a seed," 138–39n92, 147n21; United Kingdom, 53; wives of, 10, 111–12; youth, 53, 77

Pentecostal Republic, 3, 26, 63, 94

"people power," 6

Perry, Rick, 149–50n41

Piot, Charles, 53

Political Bureau, 40, 46

political entrepreneurship, 64–66

Poloma, Margaret, 75

popular economy, 48

prayer, 9, 79; politics and, 70–72; power of, 60; public, 71; social control through, 9–10; spiritual economy and, 63; versus protest, 71

Prayer Walk against Insecurity in Nigeria, 59

Premium Times, 104–5, 145–46n18

Presidential Advisory Council, 40

prophesy, 9, 48, 63, 73–74, 95, 121, 151n57; definition of, 75–76; emissary, 75; exemplary, 75; social control through, 9–10, 77–78; spiritual authenticity of the prophet, 63; substance of, 75; technology of rule, 74; as a weapon, 75–76

protest versus prayer, 71

Punch, 3, 83, 113

Purefoy, Christian, 142n9

Quigley, Joan Ceciel, 76

Raz, Joseph, 10

Reagan, Nancy, 76

Reagan, Ronald, 76

Redeemed Christian Church of God (RCCG), 2, 8, 10, 50, 54, 59, 67; altar, importance of, 91–92; mission statement, 60; Redemption Camp, 2, 59, 142n7, 147n21

"Religion and Politics in Africa" (Ellis and Haar), 57

Reynolds, Paul, 64–65

Riecken, Henry, 78

Rivers State University of Science and Technology, Port Harcourt (RSUST), 108

Roitman, Janet, 135n66

Rosberg, Carl, 118

Rose, Nikolas, 94

Ruef, Martin, 64

rule by prodigy, 117–22; democratic consequences of, 121; main objective of, 120

Salvation Ministries, Port Harcourt, 107

Sampson, Terwase, 7

Sarró, Ramon, 121

Savage, Andy, 156n44

#SayNoToRape, 110

Schachter, Stanley, 78

Schmitt, Carl, 114
Scott, James, 75, 101
Segun Omotosho Ebenezer, 112
sexuality: African, 86–87; demonic properties of, 87; Pentecostalism and, 79–86, 121; religion and, 87, 88–89
Shagari, Shehu, 24, 39
Sheraton Hotel, Lagos, 147n21
Shils, Edward, 45
Sklar, Richard, 45–46
Smith, Daniel Jordan, 53, 58
Snapchat, 103
social power, transfer of, 26–27, 55
"social scientist" anecdote, 2; wife, 2
Socialist Party of Nigeria, 46
Solarin, Tai, 45
Solanke, Folake, 45
Sony BMG Music Entertainment, 109
South African Football Association (Safa), 73
Southern Kaduna, 62
Soyinka, Wole, 24–26, 45, 129n10
Spiritual Warfare Seminar, 142–43n11
Spronk, Rachel, 86
Ssempa, Martin, 84–85
St. Andrews University, 160n18
St. Augustine Catholic Church, 147n21
St. Monica Catholic Church, 147n21
Structural Adjustment Program (SAP), 48, 137n86
Suleman, Johnson, 85, 93, 102–6, 160n18
Suleman, Lizzy Johnson, 106, 111
Sunmonu, Hassan, 46
Super Eagles, 72
Synagogue, Church of All Nations (SCOAN), 8, 51, 72

Taiwo, Olufemi, 30–31, 34, 118
Tar, Usman A., 46
Taylor, Charles, 60
Theory of African Literature Implications for Practical Criticism (Amuta), 43
This Day, 46, 47, 81–82
Trump, Donald J., 74
Tsvangirai, Morgan, 139–40n100
Tukur, Mahmud, 45
Twitchell, James, 65
Twitter, 107

Ugandan Interfaith Rain Coalition Against Homosexuality, 84
Ukah, Asonzeh, 137n92
United Kingdom, 53
United States, 47
Universal College of Regeneration, 116
universities, 19, 26, 27–29; 1970s, 34; 1980s, 37, 38; Africanized curriculum, 33–34, 37; autonomy, 33; changes in cultural and social characteristics of, 37; crisis of, 34–35, 39; first generation, 31; funding, 33; government and, 39–43; Marxism-Socialism, 37, 43–44; military rules of, 42–43; mode of knowledge production (MOKP), 34; opinion of, 32–33; policy, 32; relevance of, 33; strike, 36, 38; tension between society and, 33, 34, 37; as training schools for technocrats, 34; vice chancellor, choosing, 54–55
University of Benin, 132n17
University of Calabar (UNICAL), 55
University of Ibadan, 36, 67

University of Ife, 43, 132n17
University of Lagos, 67, 132n17
University of Nigeria, Nsukka, 132n17
University of Nigeria (UNN), 42
University of Texas at Austin, 113
University of the Sciences in Philadelphia, 107
Unlimited Liability Company (Soyinka), 24
Usman, Yusufu Bala, 45
Uzoh, Ann, 52

van Dijk, Rijk, 116
Vatsa, Haruna, 24
Vatsa, Mamman Jiya, 23–28; execution of, 23, 129n10; friendship with General Babangida, 24, 129n10; military tribunal, 24; popularity of, 23–24
Veblen, Thorstein, 5
Victorian England, 30

Walter, Ese, 110
War on Indiscipline, 39

Wariboko, Nimi, 89–90, 139n92
Weber, Max, 62, 69, 75, 87–88
"White Garment" churches, 153n7
Williams, Adebayo, 45
Winners Chapel, 147n21
witches/witchcraft, 99–102, 159n6
women, 16; disruptive power of, 16, 96–114, 153n5; feminist socialists, 46; pastors, 16; "useless," 16, 97–99, 157n1
World Bank, 137n86

"Yahoo Yahoo," 53, 140n106
Yar'Adua, Umaru Musa, 26
Yazdi, Majid, 61
Yesufu, T. M., 32
Yoruba, 90, 116, 149n33; poetry, 13–14; spirituality, 11
YouTube, 99–102, 108, 161n25

Znamenski, Andrei, 45
zombification, 120

EBENEZER OBADARE

is Douglas Dillon Senior Fellow for Africa Studies at the Council on Foreign Relations (CFR) and a fellow at the University of South Africa's Research Institute for Theology and Religion. Before joining CFR, he was professor of sociology at the University of Kansas, Lawrence.
He is the author of *Pentecostal Republic: Religion and the Struggle for State Power in Nigeria*.

Jacob K. Olupona

is professor of African religious traditions
at Harvard Divinity School and professor of
African and African American studies at Harvard University.

www.ingramcontent.com/pod-product-compliance
Lightning Source LLC
Chambersburg PA
CBHW050442050825
30595CB00021B/340